St. Pius Tenth Church

5 Barbara Street
South Yarmouth, MA 02664
(508) 398-2248

Our Lady of the Highway Chapel

St. Pius X Church (inside)

The year 2004 marks the 100th Anniversary of the Diocese of Fall River by Pope Pius X. This current year also marks the 50th Anniversary of the Canonization of St. Pius X on August 21st, 1954 and the establishment of St. Pius X Parish Community, by Bishop James L. Connolly. During those 50 years, dedicated priests, deacons and lay men and women have worked to make our parish a community that truly follows the motto of St. Pius X "to restore all things to Christ."

St. Pius X had a great love for children. The facade of our church depicts him surrounded by children and it has always been one of our parishes priorities to provide a vibrant Religious Education Program for our children. The children's Mass on Sunday is a joy. Our summer Bible school is packed. Our Religious Directors and Catechists are qualified, dedicated and creative. It is also a particular delight that in this our fiftieth year, we will open our new parish school.

Anniversaries are a time to stop and look at where we have come from, where we are, and where we are headed. We are grateful for our past, it's gift of faith and the ministry lived out by so many priests, deacons, religious and parishioners of this community. The parish is now a vibrant one serving not only our own parishioners but reaching out to our neighbors with the charity and compassion of Jesus Christ. We are grateful to all those who minister in over 30 different parish organizations.

We hope and rely on God's gracious goodness to provide for the future of our parish and hope that those who follow us will continue to live the motto of St. Pius X "to restore all things to Christ."

In a special way may these few words unite all of us in the faith and love of Jesus Christ and His Church. May we continue to work together so that Jesus Christ will be found and faithfully followed by all who come to this community of faith, love and service.

St. Pius X Parish Life Center

Architectural sketch of St. Pius X Parish School

Bearing Fruit By Streams of Waters

A History of The Diocese of Fall River

Barry W. Wall

PIUS PP. X.

Ad perpetuam rei memoriam Supremi Apostolatus officium [illegible]
[illegible]
[illegible] plebis utilitatem cedant. [illegible] Venerabilis Frater Matthaeus Harkins Episcopus Providentien-
sis in Statibus Foederatis Americae Septentrionalis [illegible] postulavit a Sancta Sede, ut ad incrementum re-
ligionis et ad maius bonum animarum nova Dioecesis erigeretur per divisionem Dioecesis commissae sibi,
cumque Venerabilis Frater Archiepiscopus Bostoniensis et Episcopi Comprovinciales ejusdem petitionem unani-
mi consensu commendaverint: Nos, collatis consiliis cum VV. FF. NN. S. R. E. Cardd. negotiis Propagan-
dae Fidei praepositis, [illegible] suffragio Venerabilis Fratris Diomedis Falconio Delegati Apostolici in
praefata Regione, oblatis precibus annuendum existimavimus. Quae cum ita sint, omnes et singulos quibus
Nostrae hae Litterae favent peculiari benevolentia complectentes et a quibusvis excommunicationis et in-
terdicti aliisque ecclesiasticis sententiis, censuris et poenis, si quas forte incurrerint, huius tantum rei gratia absolven-
[illegible]
Apostolicae Nostrae potestatis plenitudine, perpetuumque in modum e Dioecesi Providentien-
sium partem distrahimus, quae sita est in Statu vulgo Massachusetts appellato, atque e ea novam Dioece-
sim constituimus cum episcopali residentia in civitate Fall River, a qua ipsa nomen [illegible] habe-
bit, et cum Cathedratico pro sua mensa Episcopali [illegible] Episcopo imponendo. Decernentes has Lit-
teras firmas, validas et efficaces existere et fore, suosque plenarios et integros effectus sortiri et obtinere, illisque
ad quos spectat et spectare poterit in omnibus et per omnia plenissime suffragari, sicque in praemissis per quos-
cumque Judices ordinarios et delegatos judicari et definiri debere, atque irritum et inane si secus super his a
quoquam quavis auctoritate scienter vel ignoranter contigerit attentari. Non obstantibus contrariis quibuscumque. Datum
Romae apud S. Petrum sub annulo Piscatoris die XII Martii MDCCCCIV Pontificatus Nostri Anno [illegible]

PIUS X. PONT. MAX.

Aloys. Card. Macchi

Acknowledgements:

Gratitude is extended to Archbishop Sean O'Malley, OFM, Cap. for initiating this work and to Bishop George W. Coleman for his participation in the project from its inception. Others who have been most helpful include the staff of the Bishop's Office, *The Anchor*, the Communications Office, the Catholic Education Department and Holy Rosary Parish in Fall River, the Diocesan Archives of Boston and Providence, as well as the parish priests who have generously loaned photographs. The author has relied on the writings of Fall River historian, Philip T. Sylvia, Jr., on *The History of the Archdiocese of Boston* by Robert H. Lord, John E. Sexton and Edward T. Harrington, *Catholicism in Rhode Island and the Diocese of Providence* by Robert W. Hayman and the works of many dedicated parish historians for which he is most grateful.

PUBLISHER:
Editions du Signe
B.P. 94 - 67038 Strasbourg - France

PUBLISHING DIRECTOR:
Christian Riehl

DIRECTOR OF PUBLICATION:
Joëlle Bernhard

PUBLISHING ASSISTANT:
Marc de Jong

DESIGN AND LAYOUT:
Juliette Roussel

PHOTOENGRAVING
Editions du signe - 104703

ISBN 2 - 7468 - 1253 - 3
Printed in China by Sun Fung Offset Binding Co. Ltd

Table of Contents

Part One

The Setting: Colonial Massachusetts

Part Two

The Foundation: A Church Beyond Boston

Part Three

The Expanding Structure: Under Divine and Earthly Providence

Part Four

The New Diocesan Church: Fall River Now Sister to Crete and Ephesus

Part Five

Appendix

Foreword

My Dear Sisters and Brothers in Christ,

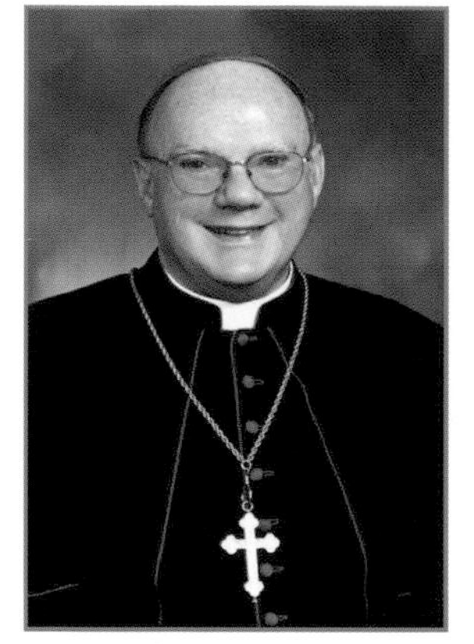

As we celebrate the one hundredth anniversary of the Diocese of Fall River, I am very pleased to offer you this pictorial history of our local church.

The story of the church in southeastern Massachusetts began long before the founding of our diocese. The first Catholics came in the early nineteenth century attracted by opportunities for work afforded by the growing whaling, textile, and glass blowing industries. To provide for the spiritual needs of the pioneer Catholics, the Bishops of Boston established nine parishes and fifteen churches from North Easton to Nantucket. After 1872 under the pastoral care of the Bishops of Providence, parishes were multiplied, the first communities of religious men and women arrived, and schools and charitable institutions were founded.

Throughout the twentieth century undaunted by depression and war and encouraged by prosperity and the renewal inspired by the Second Vatican Council, the Catholic faithful of the Diocese of Fall River continued to grow. In recent decades we have welcomed people from Latin America and Asia who have joined our various ethnic groups and the many descendants of earlier immigrants from Europe and Canada.

In the pages that follow the story of the bishops, priests, deacons, religious, and lay people who have played a role in building up our community of faith is carefully told. I am sincerely grateful to Father Barry W. Wall, our diocesan archivist, and to all who assisted him in preparing this work.

May it awaken in all of us an appreciation for the sacrifices of the past and a desire to do our part in advancing the kingdom of God in the twenty-first century.

Devotedly in Christ,

+George W. Coleman

Bishop of Fall River

DOMINI SUMUS

Introduction

In the sermon preached at the Mass commemorating the Golden Jubilee of the Diocese of Fall River fifty years ago, Bishop William O. Brady reminded all of us assembled on that beautiful June morning, "...the building up of the church in this Diocese was not the work of the priests alone, nor of the bishops alone, nor alone of both together. It was the work of the people of God who brought to it the culture of various places, the traditions of various peoples, the melodies of various tongues and the customs of various lands. The people of God in the Diocese of Fall River make up a Pentecostal list."

It is an ever growing list including the Irish, English, Portuguese, French Canadians, Italians, Polish, Cape Verdians, Brazilians, Spanish-speaking people from Central and South America, the Caribbean and Mexico, also Koreans, Filipinos, Vietnamese, and others from Asia, and we should acknowledge the contribution of our Eastern Rite brothers and sisters of Lebanese, Syrian, Egyptian and Ukrainian origin.

The scope of this work permits only an overview of our Diocesan Community, and the growth of the Catholic Church in southeastern Massachusetts. This underlines the importance of preserving local history within each parish community. The inspiring and often colorful stories of the men and women of faith who have built up our local church need to be told and remembered. A sampling might include the grandson of a Portuguese whaling captain, Dr. Francis M. Rogers, a native of St. John the Baptist Parish in New Bedford, late professor of Romance languages and Dean of the Graduate School of Arts and Sciences at Harvard University, and perhaps the Fall River grocer, Alphonse N. Bourget, who left his native Quebec as a young man in 1869 to join the military volunteers defending the Papal States and fifty years later was honored for his service by Pope Benedict XV with knighthood in the Order of Pius IX, and also Mrs. Christopher Brady, a public school teacher and a native of Sandwich, who as young Josephine Swansey learned her catechism there from Father Thomas F. Clinton and, in turn, taught the truths of the faith to the children of Corpus Christi Parish with only brief interruptions for seventy years.

To all who have gone before us in faith, to all who are the living stones in the spiritual temple, which is the Church of Fall River, this work is gratefully dedicated.

Barry W. Wall

Part One

The Setting: Colonial Massachusetts

The Diocese of Fall River was brought into being by the brief of Pope Pius X, "Supremi Apostolatus Officium," dated March 12, 1904. By this act 1,194 square miles in southeastern Massachusetts were separated from the Diocese of Providence and became a new local church. The territory comprises the counties of Bristol, Barnstable, easily recognizable on any map, as Cape Cod, the island counties of Nantucket and Dukes, the latter, embracing Martha's Vineyard and the Elizabeth Islands, and to connect Bristol and Barnstable Counties the towns of Mattapoisett, Marion and Wareham in Plymouth County.

1. Explorers, Puritans and Acadians

In this stronghold of the Pilgrims, Catholic life did not begin to flourish until the early nineteenth century, however a dozen years before the Mayflower dropped anchor off the present Provincetown, the cross of Christ was planted on Cape Cod by a Catholic, Samuel deChamplain, whom Samuel Eliot Morrison describes as a man "loyal to his king, his wife and his church." Champlain, a member of the expedition of Sieur de Monts, was a cartographer who had a royal commission from the King of France to survey the New England coast. He sailed along our coast in the fall of 1606 as far as Cape Cod. In mid-October the party landed at Stage Harbor in Chatham. The natives seemed friendly at first but on October 15, they attacked and killed five men who had remained ashore to enjoy the hot biscuits they had baked in an oven built on the beach. The French buried their dead beneath a cross they had previously erected. During a committal service a contemporary reports the natives danced and howled afar off. After the French returned to their ship the Indians reappeared, desecrated the graves and tore down the cross. When the tide permitted, the French came ashore again, reinterred the dead, and set up the cross before they departed. This was the first celebration of Catholic burial rites, although without the presence of a priest. The chaplain of the expedition, Father Nicholas Aubry, perished in the severe winter of 1605. Champlain called the land he reached Cap Blanc. The name Cape Cod originated with Bartholomew Gosnold, the Englishman who explored Buzzards Bay in the spring of 1602. He discovered the mouth of the Acushnet River and stayed for a month on Cuttyhunk, the westernmost of the Elizabeth Islands. Today they make up the town of Gosnold, the smallest political entity in the diocese.

At the opposite side of the diocese there is more mysterious and equally interesting evidence of the presence of Catholic explorers. Near the Taunton River, north of Fall River, in the town of Berkley there is a glacial boulder called Dighton Rock. It is covered with ancient carvings whose origin has been much debated. The intricate inscription has been attributed to Native American peoples, Vikings, even ancient Phoenicians. A fourth interpretation gained strength in the twentieth century. It attributes some of the carvings to Miguel Corte Real, a Portuguese explorer. Together with the date of 1511 and the Portuguese coat-of-arms, the inscription is interpreted to read "Miguel Corte Real, by the will of God, here chief of the Indians." Miguel was the son of Joao Vaz Corte Real of the island of Terceira. In the year 1500-1501 he and his brother, Gaspar, each commanding a ship, sailed to Greenland, Labrador and the New England coast. The ships became separated and Gaspar's ship was never seen again. Miguel returned in 1502 to search for his brother, and in one of the ironies of history he too

Samuel De Champlain Monument at Stage Harbor in Chatham

Dighton Rock before it was removed from the water.
(Charles Hathaway Photo)

disappeared. Other evidence suggests the presence of Corte Real in the area. Roger Williams noted in 1643 light-skinned members of the Wampanoag tribe who also had Portuguese words in their vocabulary. In nearby Newport there is a mysterious and locally famous stone tower which some judge to be of Portuguese origin. Does all this prove that shipwrecked Portuguese explorers and mariners lived in southern New England and that Dighton Rock and its inscription is in the tradition of the stone markers set up by the Portuguese? The debate is ongoing.

The first Europeans to set up a permanent colony in Massachusetts were the English religious dissenters known to history as the Pilgrims. They arrived at the tip of Cape Cod in November of 1620, and here they drew up the Mayflower Compact to regulate their affairs when they established themselves on land, which had not been officially granted to them since they had drifted off course. The same month the term New England was first used in an English land grant. The same document stated that no Roman Catholic who had not taken the oath of Royal Supremacy acknowledging the King as the head of the Church would be permitted in the territory. The Irish were a particular object of hostility because of their religion and because of the political and military clashes between the English and the Irish in the sixteenth and seventeenth centuries. The French, too, were seen as a special threat since at the very time that the English colonist were establishing themselves in Massachusetts, the French were setting up trading posts at Quebec, Montreal, and in northern Maine, New Hampshire, and New York. Catholic missionaries were intent upon preaching the Gospel to Native Americans, and the English feared they would become allies of the French. This fear was at least partly responsible for an act passed by the Massachusetts General Court in 1647 banning the presence of any priest in the colony. The punishment for the first offense was banishment, for the second offense death. In spite of the hostile atmosphere, Catholics were present in the colony of Massachusetts. There were in Boston Irish and Scottish servants and undoubtedly some had been Catholic in the old country. In 1687 a French refugee reported he discovered eight or ten Papists, both French and Irish, including a surgeon and his family. Portuguese names can be found at this period also. The next year Ann Glover was accused of witchcraft and put to death. It was alleged she could recite the Lord's Prayer in Latin, English, and Irish. She died forgiving her enemies and proclaiming her Catholic faith. The Irish population increased significantly between 1730 and 1740 and some were Catholic. There is indication of a number of French in Boston who were involved in trade with the West Indies. Unable to worship without a priest, none of these were conspicuous because of their religion.

Of all the Catholics to come to Massachusetts in the colonial period, none were more unfortunate than the Acadians. The Acadian settlers of Nova Scotia lived between two empires. As they struggled to maintain neutrality, they often became pawns in the conflict between the French and English. Their presence set a concrete limit to English expansion. A decision to deport the entire population was implemented beginning in September 1755. Acadian men, women and children were forced on to ships and dispersed among the American colonies. The condition of the first arrivals in Boston was so desperate as to arouse the sympathy of public officials who provided them with immediate relief. Legislation was enacted to provide basic necessities, but the deported people who had owned homes, farms, livestock and tools were now paupers, and most painful of all, were deprived of exercise of their Catholic faith. They were parceled out to the towns in the various counties of the province including Barnstable, Bristol, and Dukes. Very likely they were the first Catholic residents in these communities. The Dartmouth town meeting on October 16, 1756, voted that the selectmen should take care of the French sent to the town and place them according to their best discretion and the least expense to the town. Old Dartmouth then still included the present Acushnet, Dartmouth, Fairhaven, New Bedford and Westport. A few months before, Sandwich received a contingent of ninety-nine Acadians in the most difficult circumstances. They were part of a larger group that had set out from Georgia attempting to return to their beloved homeland. They arrived on the shore of Buzzards Bay on July 20 in seven makeshift two masted boats hoping to have them transported across to Cape Cod Bay. Unable to accomplish this, they were eventually settled in Boston. Where it was possible, the Arcadians were accustomed to gather on Sunday. They chanted parts of the Mass, listened to the Epistle and Gospel, and joined in prayer. Their leader, one of "les anciens" was delegated in 1761 by the Vicar General of the Bishop of Quebec in Halifax to receive the consent of couples residing in New England who wished to celebrate the sacrament of Matrimony. In doing so, Father Pierre Maillard wrote movingly to Louis Robichaud in Cambridge "every Sunday not only do I carefully keep you in mind and think of you as united with us in the Holy Sacrifice of the Mass, but I also make express mention of it to all in the congregation. Do you on your side, do the same for us in your common prayers..."

The Falmouth Shore of Buzzard's Bay: A timeless scene which could have been viewed by the exiled Acadians

After the Treaty of Paris ending the French and Indian War in 1763, some hoped to keep the industrious Acadians here even if it meant providing a Catholic priest, but that was not permitted, and the Acadians left Massachusetts. If any stayed behind they lost their identity through intermarriage and the complete inability to practice their faith. So it was with their brothers and sisters in the faith who came before them. The immigrants clung to their faith as best they could, but with no priests to celebrate Mass and the sacraments even occasionally, children and grandchildren would seek spiritual comfort and perhaps social acceptance in Protestant Churches.

Traditional anti-Catholic hostility intensified when the Quebec Act was passed in the summer of 1774, finally guaranteeing the freedom of religion for the Catholics of Canada promised in the Treaty of Paris. In spite the anti-Catholic feeling with which Massachusetts entered the American Revolution, before the end of the war freedom of worship had been constitutionally granted to Catholics. The Congress had quickly come to realize the importance of support and aid from the Catholics of Canada, and a document justifying freedom of religion as a right for Catholics in Canada was adopted. Cosmopolitan Philadelphia had had its effect on the Massachusetts delegates also. They discovered a diversity of religious tradition among the delegates; they saw the toleration afforded Catholics in Pennsylvania and they met Catholic Patriots. John Adams was impressed with the education and wealth of Charles Carroll who would be the only Catholic and last surviving signer of the Declaration of Independence.

Mosaic of the Holy Cross at Our Lady of LaSalette Shrine, Attleboro

Freedom of religion finally came for the Catholics of Massachusetts when the final version of a new state constitution was adopted in June 1780 and went into effect on the last Wednesday of October. A Bill of Rights provided freedom of conscience for all religions, but the document whose draft was almost entirely written by John Adams was amended to specify that anyone owing allegiance to any foreign power was disqualified from holding public office. In the common estimation this applied to Catholics; nonetheless the world had changed for Catholics in Massachusetts.

John E. Sexton writing in the first volume of the *History of the Archdiocese of Boston* succinctly captures the significance of what had taken place. "Thus freedom of worship came to the Catholics in Massachusetts... It replaced both charter and British Constitution in this state. It replaced the essential exclusiveness of the whole colonial tradition of Massachusetts. It was, in fine, one of the most important, and at the same time, unexpected, results of the Revolution."

2. New England's First Catholic Parish

In spite of their good fortune now to be free to worship publicly, Catholics could not do so until they had a priest. Between 1788 and 1792, three priests served the small Catholic congregation in Boston, of which it has been said the Irish were more numerous, but the French were more important. They were Claude Florent Bouchard who styled himself Abbe de la Poterie (1788-1789), Louis Rousselet (1789-1791), and John Thayer (1791-1792). The Abbe de la Poterie, a former chaplain with the French fleet, celebrated the first public Mass in Boston on November 2, 1788, in a chapel on School Street formerly owned by French Protestants. Unfortunately Father de la Poterie and his successor, Father Rousselet, had to be dismissed. Both were guilty of transgressions in France. The Abbe was later reconciled and returned to ministry in France. Father Rousselet went to the island of Guadeloupe where in 1794 in the midst of the French revolution he and many others were imprisoned and sentenced to death. He died heroically. Admitting his sins and who he was, he urged all to contrition and in this extraordinary situation imparted absolution, and then led his fellow prisoners to the guillotine singing the psalm *Laudate Dominum.*

Father Francis A. Matignon

Father Thayer was born in Boston in 1758. A Yale graduate, he served as a chaplain in the Revolutionary War. At the age of 25 he entered the Catholic Church in Rome, and in 1787 after preparing at the Sulpician Seminary, he was ordained a priest in Paris. Father Thayer returned to Boston in January 1790. He was a worthy priest, but his ministry in Boston turned our to be a great disappointment. Serving for a short time with Father Rousselet, the congregation became divided along ethnic lines. To restore unity, the recently consecrated Bishop of Baltimore, John Carroll, visited Boston in May and early June of 1791, having asked Father Rousselet to resign. The next year Father Thayer willingly accepted another assignment realizing the merits of his successor, Francis Anthony Matignon.

Father Matignon arrived in Boston on August 20, 1792. He was thirty-eight years old. A Doctor of Theology from the Sorbonne, he was forced by the French Revolution to flee to England and then offered himself for missionary work in America. Father Matignon sought help among his former confreres, and a young priest also forced to leave his country responded. Jean Lefebvre de Cheverus, son of a prominent family in the town of Mayenne, was ordained a priest of the Diocese of Le Mans on December 18, 1790, in Paris, just before the outbreak of the Revolution. He arrived in Boston on October 3, 1796. Together these two learned, humble, and zealous priests sanctified the faithful and edified Puritan Boston by preaching and living the Gospel. At the beginning of the nineteenth century, there were about a thousand Catholics in Boston. In 1808 the Diocese of Baltimore, which embraced the whole United States, was divided. John Carroll was named Metropolitan Archbishop and the Dioceses of Boston, New York, Philadelphia, and Bardstown, Kentucky, were created. John Cheverus was consecrated first Bishop of Boston in Baltimore on November 1, 1810. His diocese took in the six New England States.

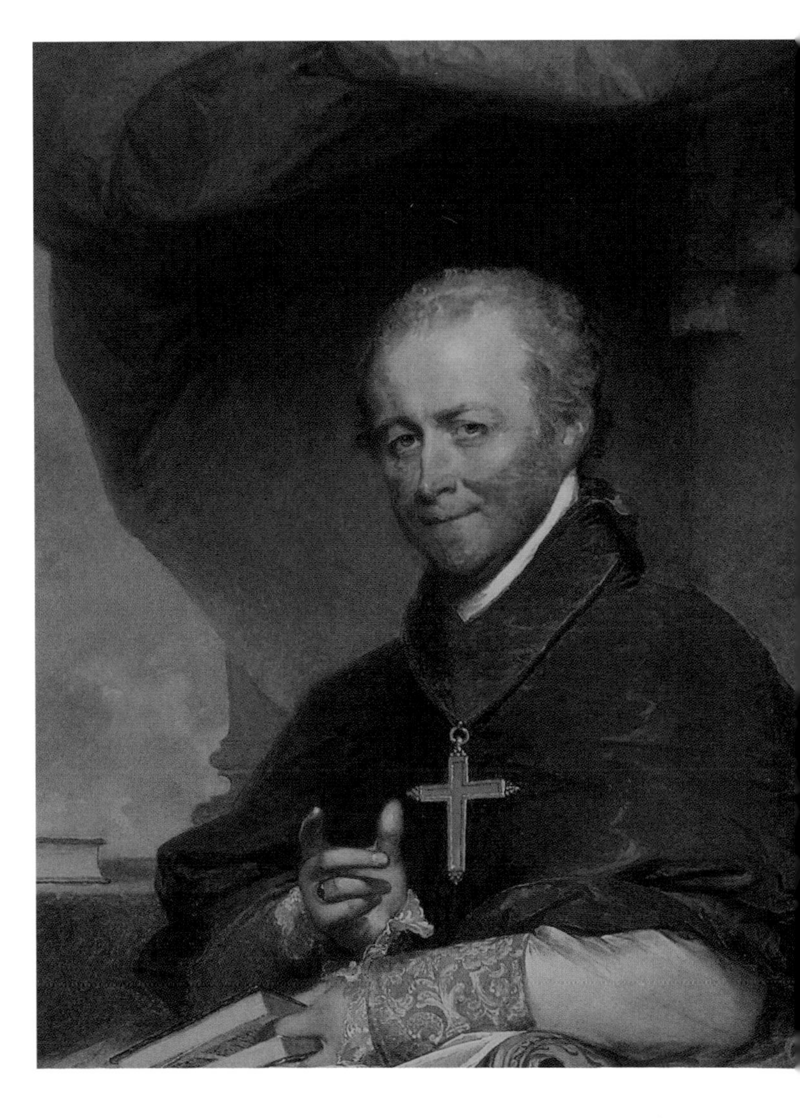

Bishop John Lefebvre de Cheverus
(Courtesy of the Museum of Fine Arts, Boston)

Part Two

The Foundation: A Church South of Boston

When Father Matignon first arrived it was necessary for him to devote his attention to the needs of the church in Boston. It was not until after the arrival of Father Cheverus that the priests began to care for missions south of Boston

1. Iron, Yarn, and Whale Oil

1793

Daûby — Die vigesimâ octavâ Julii baptisatus est Alexander Carolus filius Alexandri Dauby+ et Annae Switains, P.P. Ludovicus Carolus Dumaine et Charlotte Elizabeth du Pavillon, lesquelles ont signé avec nous.

+Ancien officier au service du Roy demeurant à Mansfield

A. Daûby   Cherot Dumaine   Cherot Cherot Dupavillon
Matignon

Record of the baptism of Charles Alexander Dauby of Mansfield, July 28, 1793

The earliest settlements on Cape Cod and in Bristol County were made by people from the Plymouth Colony. Bog iron was soon discovered in the Two Mile River in Raynham, and Henry Howe describes its significance in the development of the Taunton River Valley in a fascinating little book, *Salt Rivers of the Massachusetts Shore.* Enterprising Tauntonians began the smelting of iron in 1656. Demand for tools, latches, nails, kettles, and household utensils caused forges and iron works to be built at Whittenton, Norton, Easton, and East Freetown. At Wareham a nail making machine was invented and a new industry sprang up. When the Jefferson embargo and the War of 1812 brought foreign trade to a standstill and the demand for goods manufactured at home soared, the men of the Taunton River valley were prepared to respond. For generations they had been using waterpower to fashion their tools and utensils. Now they would direct their skills and resources in a new direction. Power driven yarn spinning mills came into being throughout the region, at Easton, Taunton, and at Attleboro, originally part of the expanded Rehoboth Purchase, settled in 1643. Fall River's first cotton mill was a small operation established by Joseph Durfee in 1811 near the present Globe Corners, then part of Tiverton, Rhode Island. Its modest supply of power came from a stream that flowed from Cook Pond into the Bay. Other mills followed closer to the center of the village along the Quequechan River. The power loom was introduced in 1817. In 1803, the village of Fallriver spelled as one word voted to separate from the town of Freetown settled from Plymouth in 1656. The name of the new town didn't please everyone, and it was voted the next year to change the name to Troy and the town was known by that name until 1834 when the name Fall River was resumed.

While Father Matignon and Bishop Cheverus ministered to Catholics at Newport, Providence, and at Portsmouth where a rich seam of coal discovered 1809 brought Irish laborers, there is no evidence of their visiting any community within the present Diocese of Fall River. However, there is definite evidence of the presence of a Catholic family in the town of Mansfield in 1793. Father Matignon has recorded that on July 28 he baptized in Boston, Alexander Charles Dauby, son of Alexander Dauby and Anne Switains, and he noted in French that the child's father was a former officer in the service of the King now living in Mansfield.

To the east, Dr. Howe writes, the villages of the township of Old Dartmouth had developed a Buzzard's Bay civilization of their own around the tidal rivers of the Bay, the Acushnet, the Paskamansett, and the Westport. Like their neighbors along the Taunton River, they set up water wheels on dammed streams, which provided power for the gristmill, the sawmill, and the iron foundry, but from the settlement made on the west bank of the Acushnet River in 1711, Joseph Russell in 1755 introduced whaling along the nearby coast. Various craftsmen were attracted, and iron and copper works, and candle factories were established. Bedford village prospered, and although

The nail factory in Wareham is typical of early 19th century mills

burned by the British in 1778, it recovered when independence came; together with the village of Fairhaven on the east bank of the river, it was incorporated as the town of New Bedford in 1787 with a population of more than 3,000 people. By 1803 there were fifty-nine vessels belonging to the port. After the War of 1812, a shrewd decision was made to specialize in whaling. Population and prosperity continued to grow. The combined population of New Bedford and Fairhaven, which had become a separate town in 1812, reached almost 6,700 by 1820.

2. Churches at New Bedford, Sandwich, Taunton, and Fall River

It should not be surprising that we find the first evidence of a Catholic community in the thriving town of New Bedford. Civil records under the date of May 17, 1806, contain the marriage intentions of James Magrath and Sally Golliver. Beside each name is the notation *Irish.* This doesn't necessarily indicate they were Catholic, nor does their subsequent civil marriage on June 10, 1806, indicate they were not. James Magrath is listed in the 1810 Federal Census, as is Peter Connor (O'Connor), a known Catholic. He and his wife, Eleanor had four children at the time. Father Philip Lariscy, an energetic Irish Augustinian Friar who was accepted into the diocese by Bishop Cheverus in 1818, visited New Bedford early in 1821. From March 14 to March 20, Father Lariscy baptized ten children of various ages. The family names of parents and sponsors were Connor, Ryan, Heth, Brothers, Hurly, Galahan, and Brian. On March 19, 1821, Edward and Lydia Wing for the sum of $80 conveyed a forty-rod parcel of land to John Cheverus. On this land a small frame church was built by a local carpenter, Dudley Davenport, at a cost of $800. On July 20, the weekly newspaper, *The Mercury* announced "that the Roman Catholic Church erected in this town by the influence and exertion of the Reverend Philip Lariscy of Boston will be dedicated to the worship of God on Sunday (July 29) by the Rt. Rev. Bishop Cheverus of Boston" but a week later the same paper reported "we have been requested to announce that the dedication of the Roman Catholic Church in this town will not take place on Sunday next as was intended in consequence of the indisposition of Bishop Cheverus." The deferral of the dedication of the church is undoubtedly connected with the unexpected departure of Father Lariscy from the Boston Diocese. In April Bishop Cheverus had received Father William Taylor into the Diocese, and now with an additional priest in Boston, he decided to take a much needed vacation. Leaving Father Lariscy in charge, the Bishop traveled to Baltimore and Montreal. When the Bishop returned, he found the relationship between Fathers Lariscy and Taylor strained to the breaking point. It should have been foreseen. Although both were Irish, they were completely different in temperament and background, one a boisterous Irish speaking friar, the other an urbane convert from the Anglican Church. Furthermore, Father Taylor had come from New York where, in a dispute between some leading laymen and the Bishop, he had been on the side opposed to the Bishop and a priest friend of Father Lariscy. Bishop Cheverus found it necessary to make a choice, and he chose to let the very difficult Father Lariscy go, but mindful of his past service, he gave him a gift of a hundred dollars and allowed a collection to be taken up from the congregation. Father Lariscy went to the Diocese of New York where he served on Staten Island and along the Hudson. He eventually made his way to Philadelphia where he joined the members of his Order at St. Augustine's Church. He died in 1824 and is buried there. Bishop Cheverus did come to New Bedford and on October 28, 1821, dedicated Father Lariscy's church, later called St. Mary's. It was the fourth Catholic Church in Massachusetts, preceded by Holy Cross Cathedral, St. Augustine's Chapel in South Boston and St. Mary's in Salem. *The New Bedford Mercury* of November 2, reported "the audience was so numerous many... were unable to gain admittance." Given the scarcity of priests, the new church must have been little used during the next several years. We know Father Taylor visited the town in April of 1823 and that he preached at the Congregational Church. Father James Fitton describes in fascinating detail a journey to New Bedford, after his ordination in December 1827. A message concerning a sick call arrived after the mail stage had left so he set out in a hired conveyance. He reached New Bedford after a journey of several hours, at four o'clock in the morning to find the stricken man had died yearning for the sacraments but with contrition in his heart.

Father James Fitton

The interior of New Bedford's second church with the altar from the original church.

Meanwhile Bishop Cheverus had returned to France where he became successively Bishop of Montauban and Archbishop of Bordeaux and a Cardinal. He was succeeded in Boston by Benedict J. Fenwick, S.J. in 1825. Bishop Fenwick was a native of Maryland, a huge man of about three hundred pounds, who had served in difficult pastoral assignments in New York and Charleston and as President of Georgetown College. The challenge before him was to organize the Church in the six New England States. A challenge he met successfully with zeal, prudence, and unfailing good humor.

Father Robert D. Woodley

The most pressing need was for priests, and the Bishop looked beyond the diocese for priests who would be willing to serve in New England. One of the first to come to Boston was Robert D. Woodley, a Virginian who had graduated from Georgetown in 1825, the last year Benedict Fenwick was president. Father Woodley prepared for the priesthood under Bishop John England of Charleston and came to Boston in January 1828. The Bishop sent him to the southern missions with his residence at Providence. In early February Father Woodley visited Taunton, the shire town of Bristol County since 1746 when the town of Bristol became part of Rhode Island. A military center during the colonial era Taunton developed anti-British and patriotic sympathies early in the pre-Revolutionary period. In October of 1774 Taunton patriots raised the famous Liberty and Union flag over Taunton Green.

The first cotton mill was established in 1806, and in 1823 the Taunton Manufacturing Company was formed, including mills for the rolling of copper and iron, as well as the manufacture of wool and cotton cloth. An important part of this operation was the Taunton Print Works, the first in the country for the printing of calico cloth. It was here that many pioneer Catholics were employed. Father Woodley found a congregation of about eighty Catholics on February 10, 1828, when he celebrated the first Sunday Mass in Taunton. During the visit he baptized the infant son of James and Catherine Farrel and three children of James and Rhonda Lannigan, ages 2, 3 and 6. He also witnessed the marriage of Patrick and Sarah Delany. Father Woodley continued to visit Taunton every two months officiating in a rented schoolhouse. Before the end of the month, Father Woodley visited New Bedford for the first time, where on February 28, 1828, he baptized six children; three of them younger siblings of children baptized by Father Lariscy seven years before. Father Woodley reported to the Bishop that he intended to visit New Bedford "once in two months." and he set about rehabilitating Father Lariscy's little church. Collections for plastering and other repairs were taken up, and with help from members of the Protestant community, Father Woodley was able to open the newly refurbished church with a celebration on New Years Day 1830. In the spring of 1828 Father Woodley made his first visit to Fall River where on May 19 he officiated at the marriage of James Finney, a native of Ireland, and Miss Ardelia Jane Pollock. The witnesses were Patrick Kennedy and Peter and Jemima McLarin. The Catholics of Fall River numbered about twenty. Patrick and Helen Kennedy and their five children are believed to have been the first Catholic family in the town. The tradition is that it was in their home, with their kitchen table as the altar, that the first Mass in Fall River was offered. It would seem most likely that this took place during the first visit of Father Woodley on May 18, 1828, which was a Sunday. Other nearby places to receive the ministration of Father Woodley, in addition to Newport, were Wareham where he visited on more than one occasion to celebrate baptisms and a marriage and also Norton where he baptized in April of 1829, but the needs of the faithful continued to draw him to more distant points too. He traveled to Quincy and Dorchester, into Worcester, and as far as New London, New Haven, and Hartford. The usual transportation was the stagecoach, which traveled six or seven miles an hour. In Providence the American born Father Woodley found it hard to relate to his Irish parishioners, and tensions were heightened by economic pressures. In December of 1830 Father Woodley was transferred to the Cathedral in Boston. There he made a decision surely with the wise counsel of Bishop Fenwick, to return to Georgetown where he entered the Society of Jesus; he continued to serve the church faithfully in Maryland until his death at Port Tobacco on October 26, 1857. Robert D. Woodley's dedicated ministry is a bright page in the early history of the church in southern New England. The missions he served are now located in six dioceses.

Sandwich

While Father Woodley was establishing Catholic communities at New Bedford, Taunton, and Fall River, the fourth of the pioneer Catholic congregations was developing at Sandwich on Cape Cod. The town was established in 1639 from Plymouth, and Captain Myles Standish laid out its boundaries. In 1825 Deming Jarvis began the manufacture of glass which was to become world famous. Workers were recruited from among the Irish employees of the New England Glass Company in East Cambridge. Soon this small group of Catholics, who missed the proximity of a priest to provide Mass and the sacraments and a place to worship, was petitioning Bishop Fenwick for a church. In September 1829 the Bishop sent Father William Tyler, a newly ordained priest and the future first Bishop of Hartford, to visit the Sandwich community. Father Tyler accepted the hospitality of John Doyle and in Mr. Doyle's parlor celebrated the first Mass in Sandwich. The Bishop himself came in June of 1830. He found a congregation of seventy Catholics, baptized three infants, and received one adult into the church. With a view to building a church, the Bishop gave approval for the purchase of a lot of land, which cost one hundred twenty-five dollars. The Bishop had ordered the frame for a church to be made in Boston, and it was floated down by water to Sandwich. Father Tyler was dispatched again to supervise the construction of the church and to prepare for the dedication of the church, which was scheduled for September 19, 1830. The day was bright and clear. The Catholics of Sandwich were joined by a delegation from Wareham; some had walked the eighteen miles to take part in this joyful celebration but anticipation turned to apprehension. The Bishop, Father Virgil Barber, S.J., Father Tyler's cousin, and some members of the Holy Cross Cathedral choir had set out on Saturday morning from Boston on the packet, *Henry Clay,* intending to be in Sandwich by nightfall. Headwinds and heavy seas prolonged the voyage. After waiting long past the hour at which the ceremony was to begin. Father Tyler, resigned that there would be no dedication that day, prepared to celebrate Mass and as the familiar tale has been handed down, just as he descended the altar steps to begin the Prayers at the Foot of the Altar, the bedraggled party arrived. The Bishop asked for a half-hour delay while all repaired to John Doyle's house where they had sufficient time to collect themselves before forming the procession. The dedication of the church under the title of St. Peter proceeded to the satisfaction of all. On October 2, 1830, Bishop Fenwick appointed a newly ordained Irishmen, Peter Connolly, pastor of Sandwich and also to succeed Father Woodley in New Bedford. From this base Father Connolly conducted a roving apostolate that took him as far as Quincy, Easton, Foxboro, and Walpole; no wonder the people of Sandwich complained to the Bishop in that they seldom saw him.

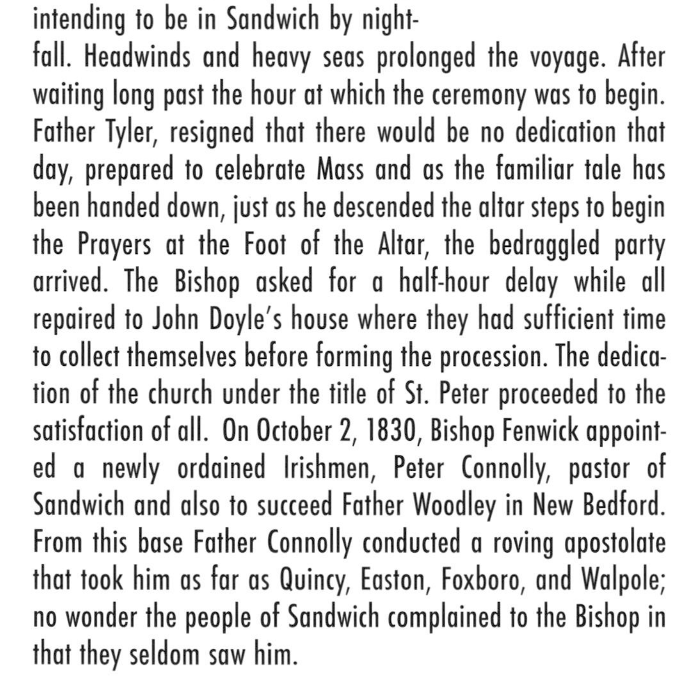
William Tyler, pastor in Sandwich in 1830 and later Bishop of Hartford

The Sandwich-New Bedford-Mission

The progress of the Church in the 1830's was unpredictable. When the times were good there was an increase in the Catholic population because there was work for Irish immigrants. Increasing numbers often produced tension among factions and between parishioners and clergy who were often young and inexperienced. This caused a constant shifting of priests by the concerned Bishop in pursuit of peace and progress. In the fall of 1832 Bishop Fenwick saw the need to make some pastoral changes affecting the Sandwich, New Bedford and Wareham mission. The Bishop again visited Sandwich. On Sunday, November 4, 1832, he celebrated early Mass at St. Peter's Church and later in the morning preached and confirmed twelve people at the High Mass. He tells us in his journal that the Catholics of Sandwich numbered no more than seventy and that prejudice against Catholics "runs high" in the town and consequently only a few Protestants were in attendance. On Monday Bishop Fenwick with Father Connolly and Father Patrick Canavan traveled in the stage from Sandwich to Wareham "over a sandy plane as barren as it is possible to conceive it." They visited the nail factory where the Catholics were employed and invited them to meet with the Bishop in the evening at the only place available, the large room in the tavern. Seventy or eighty assembled of which only three or four were married men. The Bishop expressed his hope that one day they would have a church, and he told them what arrangements he was planning to make for their pastoral care. The next day, Tuesday, November 6, the two priests and the Bishop left for New Bedford in the only means of transportation available, an open wagon, and unfortunately it rained. They arrived about one o'clock, and after dinner Father Connolly gave the Bishop a tour of New Bedford and Fairhaven in a hired chaise. It was the Bishop's first visit to New Bedford, and he was favorably impressed with the town, finding it larger than he expected and with potential opportunities for Catholics in the near future. In the evening the Bishop spoke to the people gathered in the church in much the same vein as he

Benedict J. Fenwick, S.J., Bishop of Boston 1825-1844

had done in Wareham. He told them he looked forward to the day when he could assign a priest to live there but for the present he intended to unite New Bedford, Sandwich and Wareham into one mission under the care of Father Canavan, since he had need to transfer Father Connolly to Providence. Concerning the church in New Bedford Bishop Fenwick reported that it was small and the sacristy was still unfinished; he judged the land to be valuable although it was on the outskirts of the town. He went on to say that some rich people living in the vicinity would like to buy the church and remove it because they considered it an eyesore but he concluded, "The Bishop is not in the habit of accommodating such folks when actuated by such a motive." The opportunities the Bishop hoped for unfortunately were not soon in coming. The Bishop recorded on April 9, 1834, that Father Canavan arrived from New Bedford and reported "that there is great distress there among the laboring classes." A month before Father Canavan had written to the Bishop that in his whole district there were only 150 Catholics. He told the Bishop the number of Communions at Sandwich was 14, at Wareham 24, and at New Bedford 43. In the two latter places the majority of the Catholics were unmarried men who came and went, as work was available. Father Canavan's brief pastorate ended, when in July of 1834, he was transferred to Dover, New Hampshire, where he remained the rest of his life. His successors at the Sandwich, and New Bedford churches and the mission at Wareham were Francis Kiernan, 1834-35, John Brady, 1835-37, and Father Kiernan again in 1837. These priests were listed as living in Sandwich but Bishop Fenwick often mentions the priests arriving in Boston from New Bedford where they no doubt stayed at various times. Father Kiernan reported to the Bishop in September of 1837 "that the Catholics had almost all gone off and too few remain to support him." Therefore in October the Bishop directed Father Keirnan to take charge of Waltham, Randolph, and Canton and to visit the people of New Bedford occasionally, however the year end-report for 1837 lists New Bedford, Sandwich and Wareham for the first time in the care of the priest residing in Newport, who at this time was Constantine Lee. A Doctor of Sacred Theology whom the Bishop called "a polished Irish gentleman", Father Lee found it difficult to support himself in difficult economic times and left the Diocese in 1839, going to Canada. James O'Reilly, an Irish priest recently ordained in Baltimore succeeded him. On Sunday, August 15, 1841, Bishop Fenwick administered Confirmation in New Bedford. The Bishop's *Memoranda* again provides us with wonderful details of his visit. He had come the day before "in the cars" as the Bishop always called the train and after celebrating early Mass the Bishop returned to church where at Mass celebrated by Father O'Reilly he confirmed "10 people great and small." He noted the church was crowded and there was no music of any kind. In the afternoon the Bishop preached again to a crowded church with some respectable Protestants in attendance. The Bishop went on to observe that the church was "the same pitiful little building" built by Father Lariscy. This description has been often quoted and never completely. The Bishop wrote that he found the "pitiful little building" with its one aisle, 24 pews and adjoining sacristy "brushed up, newly painted, white-washed and in good repair."

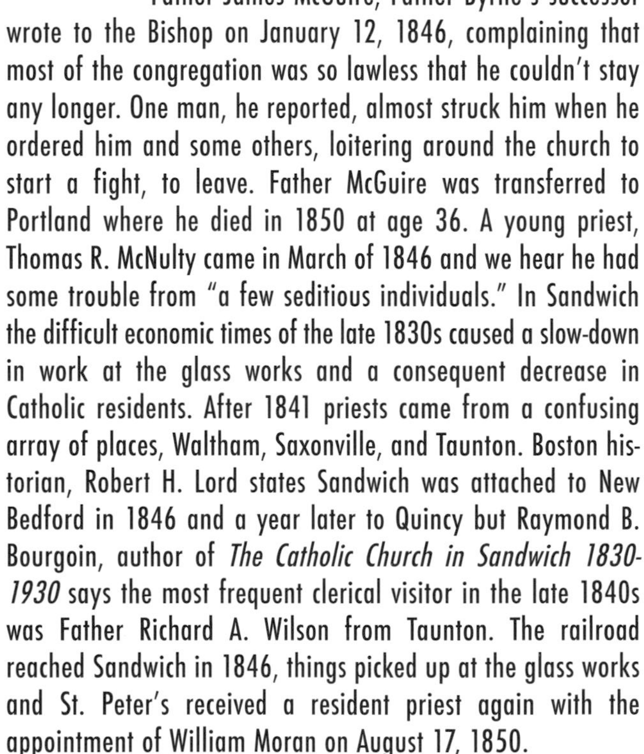

John Brady, Pastor of Sandwich, New Bedford and Wareham 1835-1837

In 1842 the congregation at Newport diminished due to the stoppage of construction work at Fort Adams. The Bishop sent Father O'Reilly to live with Father Murphy in Fall River late in 1843 but he continued to care for Newport and New Bedford until Newport with all Rhode Island and Connecticut became part of the new Diocese of Hartford early in 1844. The restless Father O'Reilly moved to Boston and then in 1854 after serving about a year at St. Joseph's in Providence he went to Ireland and on to Rome for further studies. In 1856 he drowned in a lake at Tivoli. A Swiss Guard recovered his body and he was buried in the Cathedral there. On June 29, 1844, Patrick Byrne who was ordained by Bishop Cherverus succeeded Father O'Reilly in New Bedford becoming the first resident pastor. Father Byrne's pastorate was brief. He died on December 4, 1844. His funeral Mass was celebrated at the Holy Cross Cathedral and he was buried in St. Augustine Cemetery in South Boston. In spite of the fact that in 1843 Bishop Fenwick mentions "some good Catholics there", Father James McGuire, Father Byrne's successor wrote to the Bishop on January 12, 1846, complaining that most of the congregation was so lawless that he couldn't stay any longer. One man, he reported, almost struck him when he ordered him and some others, loitering around the church to start a fight, to leave. Father McGuire was transferred to Portland where he died in 1850 at age 36. A young priest, Thomas R. McNulty came in March of 1846 and we hear he had some trouble from "a few seditious individuals." In Sandwich the difficult economic times of the late 1830s caused a slow-down in work at the glass works and a consequent decrease in Catholic residents. After 1841 priests came from a confusing array of places, Waltham, Saxonville, and Taunton. Boston historian, Robert H. Lord states Sandwich was attached to New Bedford in 1846 and a year later to Quincy but Raymond B. Bourgoin, author of *The Catholic Church in Sandwich 1830-1930* says the most frequent clerical visitor in the late 1840s was Father Richard A. Wilson from Taunton. The railroad reached Sandwich in 1846, things picked up at the glass works and St. Peter's received a resident priest again with the appointment of William Moran on August 17, 1850.

Father James F. Roach leads a procession from St. Mary's Church in Taunton possibly during the Holy Year of 1900

Taunton

On November 3, 1830, Bishop Fenwick sent John Corry, a young Irish priest to assist Father Woodley by taking charge of the Taunton, Fall River and Newport portions of his mission and six weeks later when Father Woodley was transferred to Boston the Providence and Pawtucket congregations became Father Corry's responsibility too. Father Corry who proved to be an energetic and capable leader was ordained by Bishop Fenwick together with Peter Connolly on August 8, 1830. He was born in Belturbet, Co. Cavan, Ireland and prepared for the priesthood at Mt. St. Mary's Seminary at Emmitsburg, Maryland. Father Corry took up residence in Taunton, which the Bishop considered the center of the mission. On June 24, 1831, he purchased a parcel of land, the site of the present St. Mary's Rectory and there built a small gothic church costing $2000. When the Bishop came to Taunton on October 28, 1832 for the dedication of the church, he expressed his admiration for what Father Corry and the congregation of a hundred and fifty people had accomplished. Bishop Fenwick confirmed 42 people there on July 17, 1836. In August of 1837 the Bishop felt that he needed Father Corry in Providence and William Wiley replaced him in Taunton where he found a congregation of 500 people. In January of 1842 the Bishop asked Father Wiley to take charge of the new St. Patrick's Parish in Providence. Shortly thereafter, the talented but inflexible John Corry left the Diocese going first to the new Diocese of Little Rock and then to the Diocese of Albany where he remained until his death in 1863 as pastor of St. John's Parish in Rensselaer. Father Denis Ryan after 25 years in Whitfield, Maine came to Taunton. The parishioners, upset over the transfer of Father Wiley at first refused to accept Father Ryan and he "accepted their outbursts with poor grace," wrote Maydell Murphy, never sacrificing politeness for directness. The ill feeling was brief and so was Father Ryan's tenure. He was replaced by John O'Beirne at the end of 1842. He in turn was succeeded by Richard A. Wilson who came from Augusta, Maine in May of 1846.

Fall River

When Father Peter Connolly was given charge of Providence and Pawtucket in 1832, Father Corry was able to concentrate on Taunton, Fall River and Newport. By 1830 the population of Fall River had grown to 4,100. On February 18, 1835, Father Corry purchased a 38 1/2 rod parcel of land on Spring Street from Peter McLarin for $659.67 and the next year he built a small wooden chapel and placed it under the patronage of Saint John the Baptist, his patron. Bishop Fenwick saw it for the first time on August 21, 1837. Travelling from Newport to Boston by stagecoach, he had an hour's wait in Fall River an he took the opportunity to take a walk and visit the new church. He recorded his approval, writing, "it is 60' by 40' and the whole finished off with pews and a nice belfry which reflects honor on the pastor and the people." There were then about 450 Catholics in the town. It was at this time the Bishop asked Father Corry to move from Taunton to Providence but he continued to care for his Fall River flock with occasional help from Father Wiley in Taunton and Father James O'Reilly in Newport until November 25, 1839, when Father Richard B. Hardey, a friend of the Bishop from Maryland was appointed Fall River's first resident pastor. On November 5, 1838, Bishop Fenwick was with Father Corry in Providence when news was brought that a few nights earlier the new church in Fall River had been vandalized, as the Bishop recorded, "by a party of unprincipled rascals." Windows had been broken and sashes, blinds and shutters smashed. "It was no doubt the work of the ruffians that abound in that village and done in hatred of the Catholic religion" the Bishop wrote.

3. Catholics Become Visible

The 1840s saw the introduction of such inventions, as the sewing machine and the telegraph; but in southeastern Massachusetts it was the development of steam power that would have the greatest impact. The first effect of steam power would be felt in the coming of the railroad; the second was in the replacement of water power with steam power in manufacturing. In 1836 the railroad had reached Taunton and July 1, 1840, amid a great deal of fanfare the first steam locomotive pulled into New Bedford. The journey from Boston could now be made in three hours instead of the eight to ten hours the trip took by stagecoach. In 1845, the railroad was extended from Taunton to Fall River.

In Fall River the mills continued to be organized, one after the other. The first steam powered mill, the Massasoit Steam Mill, began operation in 1846. Work in the construction and in the operation of the mills attracted an increased number of laborers, among them many Irish immigrants. The population of Fall River in 1840 reached 6,738 an increase of 60% in a decade. The Catholic congregation numbered about two thousand when in April of 1840 a young Irish priest, Edward Murphy, began his legendary pastorate of forty-seven years. Father Murphy was born in County Kilkenny, Ireland and after studying in Ireland and at the Catholic University of Louvain in Belgium came to the United States. He was ordained by Bishop Fenwick in Boston on June 16, 1838. His first assignment outside of Boston was at Old Town, Maine as pastor of the Penobscot tribe. The energetic young priest endeared himself to his Native American parishioners by reviving their mission and school. Their regard for their pastor was so great that the local tradition is that on one occasion a delegation Penobscots appeared in Fall River to pay their respects to Father Murphy and beg him to return to them. Within a few months of Father Murphy's arrival the parish was prepared to welcome Bishop Fenwick who on August 30, 1840, dedicated the little church of St. John the Baptist on Spring Street. At the same ceremony sixty-six people were confirmed in Fall River's first Confirmation celebration. As always the congenial Bishop has left us homely details concerning the weather, the attendance and the music. The weather was "excessively warm,...the church was greatly crowded the whole day...and the choir was pretty well conducted...for a country church. The crowded church became a concern for Father Murphy. With the aid of parishioners the church was enlarged and a basement dug. When the Bishop returned the following summer to confirm forty-seven candidates on August 8, 1841, he commented favorably on the improvements and wrote that he had the pleasure of seeing assembled in the new church basement three hundred children, "neat, decently habited and observing the greatest order."

When Bishop Fenwick returned to Fall River to confirm on December 10, 1843, he met with the discontented people who opposed his sending Father O'Reilly to live with Father Murphy. They threatened to reduce pew rents thereby depriving the priests of sufficient income. The Bishop stood firm and warned the people of the consequences of their proposed action. He also tried to convince them of the benefit to them and to their children of having two priests. This was one of the few instances where Bishop Fenwick was confronted with a suggestion of trusteeism.

The late 1840s seemed to be a turning point for the Church in southeastern Massachusetts. The economic depression of the late 1830s was past. New England was becoming a manufacturing center. Increasing numbers of Irish laborers found work in mill and railroad construction and various public works. The four original parishes had achieved a measure of stability, although there were problems ahead for the Taunton congregation. The Church would have a new bishop to guide it through the changing times. Bishop Benedict J. Fenwick, S. J. died on August 11, 1846. Although he had been suffering with heart disease for several months he was able to carry on a limited schedule and socialize with the priests at the Cathedral Rectory until a few days before his death. Old Boston witnessed a religious procession winding through its streets and ten thousand stood in respectful silence as the Bishop's casket was escorted from the Cathedral to the train that would take the body of the beloved bishop to Worcester for burial in the Jesuit cemetery at Holy Cross College. This congenial southern gentleman, never completely at home in the city, by his considerable learning, optimistic outlook and missionary zeal firmly established the church in the six New England States and with great foresight had provided the Diocese with a gifted successor.

Father Edward Murphy, pastor of St. Mary's Church in Fall River 1840-1887

Famine Relief and Temperance

The new Bishop, John Bernard Fitzpatrick, a native of Boston was only 34 years old. He was ordained a priest in Paris in 1840 and named Coadjutor Bishop in 1844. He would guide the Church of Boston in dealing with a multitude of needy immigrants fleeing the Irish famine, the era of the anti-Catholic Know-Nothings and the Civil War. In January of 1847 the first detailed news of the famine in Ireland and of the dreadful suffering of the people reached Boston. Bishop Fitzpatrick wrote an impassioned pastoral letter appealing for aid, which was read in every church in the diocese on Sunday, February 7. The Bishop himself read the letter from the Cathedral pulpit to an utterly silent congregation, which sat stunned by the seriousness of message and the eloquence of its delivery. By June a contribution surpassing $150,000 had been sent to Ireland by the Diocese of Boston. Non-Catholics and civic officials joined Catholics in their relief efforts by organizing public meetings to raise funds for the suffering Irish. Not all who emigrated were destitute. Some had a bit of property or were tradesmen or farmers but in the early years all were subject to the intolerable conditions on the ships and to ship fever. Many arrived in a desperate state of filth and disease. Boston, which usually admitted three or four thousand immigrants a year, received 37,000 in 1847. The care of the increasing numbers of Catholic immigrants became a major concern of Bishop Fitzpatrick's ministry. The impact on southeastern Massachusetts was more gradual than in the larger manufacturing centers of the Commonwealth, however in New Bedford the number of Baptisms increased from 45 in 1845 to 192 in 1855.

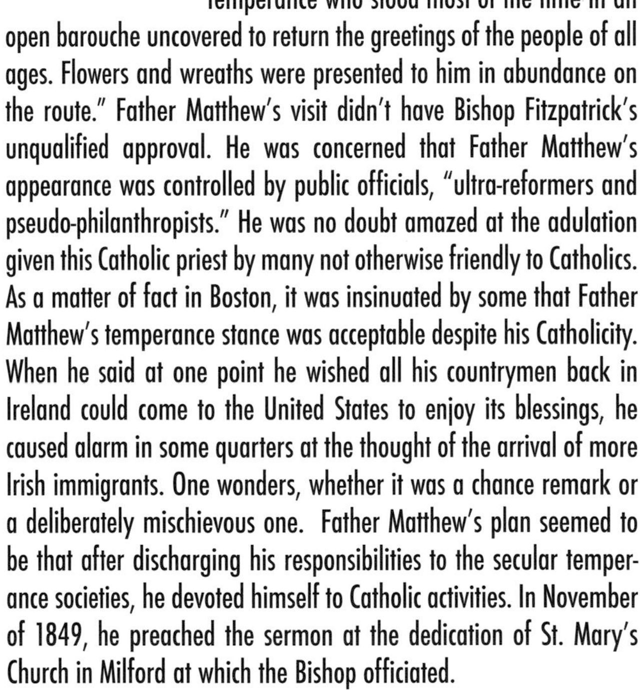

John B. Fitzpatrick, Bishop of Boston 1844-1866

In addition to famine relief another social ill, which brought Protestants and Catholics together was the temperance movement. Popular among Protestants in the 1830s, Catholics showed little interest until Father Theobald Matthew, an Irish Capuchin Friar began a cruscade for total abstinence at Cork in 1838. In the next few years it touched every parish in Ireland. Now Irish Catholics embraced the temperance movement as both a moral issue and a patriotic cause. Bishop Fenwick in 1841 urged the formation of temperance societies, and many of the priests became enthusiastic supporters of the movement, like Father Edward Murphy, who formed the St. John's Temperance and Benevolent Society in Fall River. Protestant journals praised the work of the Catholic clergy and attested to the faithfulness of Catholics who took the pledge in keeping it. Samuel Rodman, a merchant of a leading Quaker family in New Bedford has left an interesting entry in his dairy. On Sunday afternoon, September 6, 1840, he went to the Catholic Church not to attend a temperance meeting but a "doctrinal discourse" which he had seen advertised in the newspaper. He heard a sermon on the Eucharist based on the sixth chapter of John preached by Father James O'Reilly, however he wrote that on the way home he spoke with one of the parishioners concerning the temperance movement and the wonderful work of Father Matthew in Ireland. In the summer and the fall of 1849 Father Matthew visited several places in New England, including Fall River where he was the guest of Dr. Nathan Durfee and New Bedford. Samuel Rodman was on the committee of city fathers that welcomed him to the latter city on September 26. Again his diary provides us with interesting details. He writes that after giving the pledge to 150 people at the Catholic Church early in the morning, Father Matthew and city officials rode in a procession of carriages to a thronged temperance meeting. School children and adults lined the streets "eager to set their eyes on the Apostle of Temperance who stood most of the time in an open barouche uncovered to return the greetings of the people of all ages. Flowers and wreaths were presented to him in abundance on the route." Father Matthew's visit didn't have Bishop Fitzpatrick's unqualified approval. He was concerned that Father Matthew's appearance was controlled by public officials, "ultra-reformers and pseudo-philanthropists." He was no doubt amazed at the adulation given this Catholic priest by many not otherwise friendly to Catholics. As a matter of fact in Boston, it was insinuated by some that Father Matthew's temperance stance was acceptable despite his Catholicity. When he said at one point he wished all his countrymen back in Ireland could come to the United States to enjoy its blessings, he caused alarm in some quarters at the thought of the arrival of more Irish immigrants. One wonders, whether it was a chance remark or a deliberately mischievous one. Father Matthew's plan seemed to be that after discharging his responsibilities to the secular temperance societies, he devoted himself to Catholic activities. In November of 1849, he preached the sermon at the dedication of St. Mary's Church in Milford at which the Bishop officiated.

Know-Nothing, Slavery and Civil War

Politically these years saw the rise of an anti-immigrant and anti-Catholic political party, active nationally and very successful in Massachusetts. Officially known as the American Party it was popularly known as the Know-Nothing party because of its secrecy. The anti-Catholic feeling it stirred up was not really new to Massachusetts Catholics. One manifestation in Fall River, perhaps more bizarre than malicious, was recounted in 1890, forty years after the fact in the daily press. The writer recalls that life could be difficult for the Irish because prejudice was strong among some in the community. The Irish were long suffering but would resist any affront to their religion and traditions. On St. Patrick's Day, they would come out to parade wearing medals and green ribbons and silk ties, "in spite of all efforts of employers to keep them at work and the indignities that the rowdies of the town would heap upon them." On one occasion "the smart alecks" took a simple fellow, bedecked him with green ribbons and pieces of tin to represent medals, hung a string of potatoes around his neck, a codfish on his back and sent him off to the Catholic Church. As the worshipers became aware of the poor man as he stood in their midst, devotion turned to commotion. "Infuriated men and scandalized women sprung from their seats and rushed for the poor idiot and it took all the persuasive powers and brawny muscles of the late Father Murphy, who was officiating at the altar, to prevent the strong men from making jelly of the intruder." The writer says the outrage was so intense that "few dared to risk the results of more experiments of this kind" and concludes with a surprising comment "that was forty years ago and times have changed in Fall River mightily since then. St. Patrick's Day in now a more generally celebrated anniversary than {the} Fourth of July and the French Canadians will soon be running that a close race with St. John's Day." Father Bourgoin writes that twice Father Moran of Sandwich was threatened with violence. Once he was prevented from entering Wareham by a hostile gang and on another occasion when leaving Wareham he was dragged from his carriage. Fortunately at that moment a man with a shotgun appeared, a non-Catholic named Holland, saying he would shoot the first man to lay a hand on the priest.

Lawrence S. McMahon, Civil War Chaplain, Pastor in New Bedford 1865-1879, Bishop of Hartford 1879-1893

Nationally slavery was the burning political issue. In New England the newly arrived Irish immigrants had too many problems of their own than to become involved in the slavery question; furthermore they had no sympathy for the militant abolitionists who denounced the American constitution and supported the Know-Nothings. In general Catholic leaders avoided the subject, not wanting to divide their fragile congregations. Many like Father John Rodden, editor of *The Pilot* were influenced by Pope Gregory XVI who in 1839 condemned the slave trade, but while considering slavery a social evil did not teach that slavery was an evil per se especially in the case of a slave serving a kind master. *The Pilot* considered slavery to be an evil but like many felt nothing could be done about it. Although Bishop Fitzpatrick chose silence concerning a volatile issue he couldn't resolve Professor Thomas O'Connor reminds us that the Bishop placed great confidence in two African-American priests, James A. Healy and his younger brother Alexander Sherwood Healy. He named James the first chancellor of the diocese in 1855.

When the Civil War broke out Bishop and clergy rallied to the support of the Union and President Lincoln. Massachusetts raised two Irish regiments, the 9th and 28th. Fall River men served in both. Three priests from the Diocese served as chaplains including Lawrence S. McMahon later pastor in New Bedford. In 1862 Bishop Fitzpatrick went to Europe, traveling through Italy and France to Belgium where he stayed for some time at the American Legation in Brussels. Although usually described as trip taken to restore the health of the Bishop who had been struggling with the effects of a stroke he suffered in 1855, it now seems likely the Bishop was in Europe to enlist friends for the Union cause in Catholic countries.

The Pioneer Churches Replaced

The first large stone church to be built in the present Diocese of Fall River is appropriately our Cathedral Church. Father Edward Murphy in Fall River bought land adjacent to the original church in 1849 and soon thereafter engaged Patrick C. Keely, the most prominent Catholic Church architect of the day to design a church that would provide for his growing congregation. Plans were submitted for a church in English gothic style constructed of native granite. The cornerstone was laid on August 8, 1852, by Bishop Fitzpatrick who wrote in his journal "the Bishop lays the cornerstone of the Church of the Assumption of the B.V. M. in Fall River. It is to be a large stone church built on the same spot now occupied by the Church of St. John the Baptist". Bishop Fitzpatrick came to Fall River again for the dedication of the church on December 16, 1855. Although in the beginning the church had little interior decoration, after the completion of the beautiful stone spire St. Mary's was perhaps the most graceful gothic church in the Diocese of Boston.

In New Bedford Father McNulty was able to purchase the former Universalist Church in the center of town for $3,000. The church had 70 pews and a deep gallery. Bishop Fitzpatrick after his visit for confirmation on December 1, 1849, wrote the church was well situated and the site was worth half the total price. New Bedford had become a city in 1847 and now had a population of 16,000. Father Lariscy's Church was divided in two and sold. On section survives as part of a dwelling at 65 Forest Street near the original site. Father McNulty was transferred in 1853. He was followed by two young priests, Henry E. S. Henniss, a gifted young priest from Philadelphia, a graduate of Holy Cross College who

St. Mary's Cathedral as it looked in 1855

The second St. Peter's Church in Sandwich about 1865

was ordained for the Diocese of Boston in Montreal in 1852. He was the first American born priest since Father Woodley to serve in New Bedford. Highly regarded by the Bishop, popular with his parishioners and respected by the Protestant community, Father Henniss died at age 37 in 1859. Tuberculosis is often given as the cause but Bishop Fitzpatrick mentions a throat ailment that did not respond to treatment. Father Joseph P. Tallon, assistant to Father Henniss for two years, succeeded him as pastor and he unfortunately died in 1864. Father Henniss purchased land for a future church at County and Hillman Streets and for St. Mary's Cemetery. Between April and June of 1856 he supervised the transfer of 500 bodies from the burying ground adjacent to the original church on Allen Street to the new cemetery. Father Henniss also left two manuscripts referred to as *Notes on the New Bedford Mission* and *Notes on the Nantucket Mission* in which is preserved a brief history of the church in these towns, as well as on Martha's Vineyard. Father Tallon had plans for a brick church, however the Civil War and his untimely death intervened. In January of 1865 Lawrence S. McMahon began his fruitful pastorate in New Bedford, which culminated in his being named Bishop of Hartford in 1879.

In Taunton, Bishop Fitzpatrick instructed Father Wilson to make only minimal repairs to the original St. Mary's Church and to look for land for a new church. This, the pastor did and early in 1849 the building of a new church began as did a period of great strife for the parish. Shoddy workmanship was discovered in the construction of the walls and on December 1, 1849, in a severe windstorm the roof blew off, virtually destroying the building. Since the architect was the Bishop's brother-in-law they both bore the brunt of the parishioners'ire. Things became so unpleasant that Father Wilson gave up his pastorate in February of 1850. The parish was left without a priest for two years. During this time parishioners had to travel to neighboring parishes for Mass and the sacraments, going preferably, if one source can be believed, to Pawtucket because it was outside Bishop Fitzpatrick's jurisdiction. Father Daniel Hearne became the next pastor in the spring of 1852. He had originally come from Ireland to conduct an appeal for a Catholic University in Ireland and when he decided to stay, Bishop Fitzpatrick asked him to go to Taunton. Father Hearne found the people still agitated over the destruction of the church and when it was rebuilt they adamantly refused to accept it, claiming it was unsafe. Since no amount of persuasion on the part of Father Hearne could move them to change their minds, the pastor made plans in 1854 for a new church to be designed by Mr. Keely. Before any progress could be made the controversial church burned down on June 1, 1856, and a temporary structure had to be built adding to the financial burden of the parish. Work proceeded slowly on the new church but apparently not without Father Hearne's close supervision for on one occasion be ascended the tower in a bricklayer's tub and narrowly escaped serious and perhaps fatal injury when a rope broke and the tub landed on a pile of sand. For several years Father Hearne was zealous in caring for Catholics in many surrounding villages as well as in Taunton but ill health forced him to retire on January 1, 1865. He was succeeded by Thomas H. Shahan from St. James Church in Salem. Father Shahan a man of considerable ability, was faced with a debt of $80,000 and a church under construction, which he stopped. He next settled the $20,000 claim of Tobias Boland, the builder of the damaged, rebuilt and rejected church. The suit against the parish technically had the Bishop as defendant in the action brought about by the contractor who was his brother in law. Father Shahan proceeded to reduce the debt and continue with the construction of the church, which was completed in 1868.

In 1851 Father William Moran replaced the original St. Peter's Church in Sandwich, which survives as a hardware store on

Jarvis Street with a brick edifice at a new location on what is now Church Street. The cornerstone of the second St. Peter's Church was laid in 1854. The church was briefly famous for the large globe of ruby glass near the top of the church tower, which could be seen for miles at sea when it caught the rays of the sun. Unfortunately, in a severe storm on January 6, 1857, the steeple fell causing major damage to the roof and walls. This may explain why the church was not dedicated until May 14, 1865, by Bishop McFarland of Hartford. Father Moran was one of the most unforgettable missionary pastors of mid-nineteenth century. He was a large man with a strong personality who was also an accomplished musician. His labors took him from Plymouth to Provincetown tending stations at Wareham, Hyannis, and Harwich and baptizing in almost every town on the Cape. After fourteen years, Father Moran was transferred to Ware in 1864 and was succeeded by Father Peter Bertoldi, who came to the Diocese from Italy in 1861. On August 14, 1865, he bought an abandoned Baptist church for the Catholics of Wareham and placed it under the patronage of St. Patrick. This venerable building survives as the parish center.

4. Island, Cape and Country Churches

As the four original churches were being replaced, new mission churches and chapels were being established during this period in rather rapid succession at North Easton, East Taunton, Provincetown, Nantucket and Attleboro Falls and a bit later at Norton, Harwich and Mansfield. We know that Father Peter Connolly visited North Easton from Sandwich in the summer of 1831 where he encountered anti-Catholic bigotry. In 1840 Father Wiley from Taunton celebrated Mass for fifteen people in North Easton and probably visited there as regularly as he could. In September of 1850 the Ames family, employers of virtually all the Catholic laborers in the town gave a parcel of land on the north side of Pond Street overlooking Shovel Shop Pond for a chapel. Father Thomas Fitzsimmons of Saints Peter and Paul Church in South Boston saw to the construction of small frame church, which Bishop Fitzpatrick dedicated under the title of the Immaculate Conception on August 3, 1851. It was served from Canton and again from South Boston and after January 1853 by Father Aaron L. Roche, O. P. from Bridgewater and in 1856 by Father Thomas B. McNulty from North Bridgewater, now Brockton. In 1857 Father McNulty acquired land in Easton for Immaculate Conception Cemetery. By now the congregation numbered four hundred and Father McNulty purchased land on Main Street for a new and larger church, which was built 1865. In January of 1871 Francis J. Quinn became the first resident pastor of Immaculate Conception Parish.

The first Immaculate Conception Church in North Easton about 1851

The next village to have a church was East Taunton then known as Squabetty. Father Hearne began celebrating Mass in homes there and by 1855 plans were being made for a church to be built on Liberty Street. Most say the church was finished by 1858 and it came to be known as the Church of the Holy Family.

In August of 1852 Bishop Fitzpatrick sent Father Joseph M. Finotti from Holy Cross Cathedral to Provincetown to preach a mission. Father Finotti found about seventy Catholics, most of them Irish. In December of 1853 he purchased a former school building known as Snow's Block and converted it into a chapel with quarters for a visiting priest. Father Finotti a native of Ferarra, Italy served for a time as literary editor of *The Pilot.* He eventually went west for his health and he is well known as the compiler of a catalogue of Catholic books published in the United States before 1821, *Bibliographia Catholica Americana.* One of the priests who came from Boston after Father Finotti was James A. Healy, later Bishop of Portland.

The Island of Nantucket

Thomas Mayhew of Watertown and later of Martha's Vineyard purchased Nantucket from English interests in 1641 and the first white settlers were families from Salisbury who arrived on the island in 1659. They had been Quaker sympathizers in Essex County and were probably looking for a place removed from the restrictions imposed by the Puritan leadership of the Massachusetts Bay Colony. Before the War of Independence, the islanders were making a name for themselves in whaling. Despite serious set backs during the Revolution and again in the War of 1812, Nantucket by the 1843 had nine thousand people and eighty-eight whalers. As the Catholic laborers found employment on the New Bedford waterfront and in the homes of the wealthy, so too in Nantucket. According to Father Henniss the first Catholics, the Blessing and Gallagher families came to the island from New Brunswick or Nova Scotia in 1831. Father Patrick Canavan while serving as pastor of the Sandwich-New Bedford mission celebrated the first Mass in Nantucket in October of 1833. For the next decade information is scarce but Father Henniss in his *Notes* mentions several priests who visited the island from New Bedford during that time, celebrating Mass at he home of Patrick Doyle. When Father Patrick Byrne was appointed pastor of New Bedford in 1844, he was also specifically given charge of the Catholics in Nantucket but it seems the first priest to leave a lasting impression was Father Thomas R. McNulty who made his first visit to Nantucket in 1846 according to Father Henniss. Nantucket at the height of its prosperity had a Catholic community of about 300. The chief benefactors at this time were William Sullivan and his wife Lucy. The Sullivans suffered the tragedy of loosing their three-year old son, Charles in an accident. Mrs. Sullivan was a Nantucket native and a faithful Episcopalian. Sources differ concerning the details but Mrs. Sullivan became devout convert and she and her husband provided generously for the priest who offered Mass in their home. Mrs. Sullivan taught Sunday school classes there also. In 1856 Father Henniss was able to buy a building built by a temperance society a decade earlier, known as Harmony Hall, for $1,800. In the summer of 1857 a permanent altar and tabernacle were set up and another church was established for divine worship. Father Henniss estimated that the island now had two hundred and fifty Catholics, young and old. Priests continued to come to Nantucket from New Bedford until steamship service was interrupted and then the island Catholics came under the care of St. Peter's in Sandwich and after 1868 Holy Trinity in Harwich. Father O'Connor of Harwich purchased land for a Catholic cemetery, which was blessed by Father Bertoldi of Sandwich with the delegation of Bishop Williams on Sunday, July 23, 1871.

Attleboro

As the 1850s drew to a close, a second church was built in northern Bristol County, the predecessor of St. Mary's in North Attleboro. We can speak of North Attleboro as a town only after 1887. It was then that the citizens Attleboro voted by a small majority of 23 votes to divide themselves into two towns. North Attleboro and Attleboro, the latter including the villages of South Attleboro and East Attleboro. Settlers from Weymouth first purchased land in this area in 1643; incorporated as Rehoboth two years later, in 1660 more land was purchased to include the original town of Attleboro which was incorporated in 1694. The first Catholic may have been the unnamed man of French origin who is credited with the beginning of the jewelry industry at his forge in 1780. Whatever the case, John Graham, an Irishman who came to Attleboro in 1826 to learn the jewelry trade was surely a Catholic. Attleboro's first Catholics undoubtedly traveled to St. Mary's Church in Pawtucket, which was dedicated on Christmas Day 1829 by Father Woodley, to attend Mass and receive the sacraments. Among them were possibly some Irish Catholics from the villages of Hebronville and Dodgeville who found employment in the 1840s in the cotton mill owned by the Dodge family. Father Joseph McNamee became pastor in 1847 and in October of the following year is believed to have offered the first Mass in Attleboro in the home of Mrs. Graham. In 1856 Father Philip Gillick, pastor of Greenville, a village in the town of Smithfield, Rhode Island was given charge of Attleboro. Father Gillick supervised the construction of a church on land bought by Father McNamee at Falls Village in 1852, which was dedicated by Bishop Fitzpatrick on June 19, 1859. The Bishop wrote in his journal "the Catholics of Attleboro appear to be an orderly and pious people. Many of them are comfortably off and own property; indeed all seem to have unusual habits of thrift. They are principally from the north of Ireland." In 1858 there were seventy-three baptisms and twenty-five marriages in Attleboro. Perhaps in 1866 Father Gillick moved to Attleboro, which had become larger than Greenville. The arrangement was a curious one.

Holy Trinity Church at Harwich Center about 1866

Father Gillick was a priest of the Diocese of Hartford, which still included the State of Rhode Island and Massachusetts was under the jurisdiction of the Bishop of Boston.

Harwich Center

The story of the church in this particular area of Barnstable County and of the Cape in general has been well told by Harold A. Whelan, SS. CC., author of *Catholicism on Cape Cod: The History of Holy Trinity Parish, West Harwich, Massachusetts* published in 1984. The small band of Catholics in Harwich and Brewster had as their leader Patrick Drum, a native of Killeshandra, Co. Cavan, Ireland who came to Harwich around 1849. On July 12, 1865, Father Bertoldi of Sandwich purchased a parcel of land in Harwich Center from Chester and Susan Snow for $150. In October, a local builder, George T. Swift, began construction of a church, which was dedicated to the Holy Trinity on June 1, 1866. Father Thomas Sheehan was appointed the first resident pastor possibly early in 1868. He was there a very short time when he died on September 8, 1868. Father Lawrence S. McMahon whose curate Father Sheehan had been in New Bedford went to Harwich to celebrate his funeral Mass. The burial took place at Holyhood Cemetery in Brookline. According to his obituary in *The Pilot* Father Sheehan was forty-seven years old and a native of Skibbereen County, Cork. On December 11, 1868, Father Cornelius O'Connor replaced Father Sheehan. In Provincetown Father O'Connor found that the congregation, swelled by Portuguese immigration, had out grown the chapel in Snow's Block, and he began to think of a church. In 1869 he bought land for a cemetery and another parcel for a church. The centennial parish history, *Church of St. Peter, the Apostle: The First Hundred Years,* quotes the *Provincetown Advocate* as reporting there were an estimated five hundred "heads of families" in the town. The report goes on to say "most of these are Portuguese who as a mass have most of the money, they being as a class much more economical than the Irish." Father O'Connor didn't go through with his plans for a church and instead rented Adams Hall where he first celebrated Mass on December 24, 1871. By now, the Diocese of Boston had a new Bishop, John Joseph Williams. Bishop Fitzpatrick had returned home from Europe in September of 1864. He had a slow recovery from a paralytic stroke suffered in May of 1863 but his active days were over. In January of 1866 the Vicar General, John J. Williams was named coadjutor bishop. Before he could be consecrated Bishop Fitzpatrick died on February 13.

John Bernard Fitzpatrick is considered by many to be Boston's most intellectually gifted Bishop. He was beloved by the members of his flock who knew him as Bishop John and respected by others in the community with whom he had a variety of associations as a native of the city and as a graduate of Boston Latin School. This enabled him to work energetically to aid and defend great numbers of Irish immigrants arriving in Boston and to patiently avoid destructive confrontation with the enemies of the church knowing that there were many admirers in the wider community who would outlast the extremists. The loyalty and bravery of the Irish in the Civil War and Bishop Fitzpatrick's support of the Union cause had the good effect of strengthening the Catholic Church in Massachusetts.

There were in 1866 in southeastern Massachusetts, eleven churches and mission chapels with only five resident pastors. Modest progress continued during the six years the area was under the jurisdiction of Bishop Williams. Four Parishes were established and two mission churches built.

Norton and Mansfield

In Norton, Father Shahan of Taunton built a small chapel in 1868 on land donated by Patrick Cosgrove. Norton was one of the stations on Father Woodley's circuit; on April 26, 1829, he baptized Catherine, infant daughter of James and Sarah McCormick. Priests from Taunton visited here over the years and Father Hearne began celebrating Mass on a regular basis in the fall of 1852. In nearby Mansfield, there were now about forty Catholic families. Since it was now no longer possible to gather for Mass in private homes, the Roman Catholic Society of Mansfield was formed in November of 1870 to discuss the needs of the Catholic community and to provide a place for worship and catechetical instruction. Although we know of the presence of the former French officer, Alexander Dauby and his family in 1793, the next Catholics we hear about in Mansfield were Irish laborers who came after 1830 when the building of the Boston and Providence Railroad commenced. The discovery of coal in West Mansfield in 1835, even though the mining operation was of short duration, also drew Irish Catholic immigrants, such as the family of Patrick O'Rourke that came in 1844. The O'Rourke home became the center of Catholic life and the place where the missionary priest would gather the faithful for Holy Mass. Previous to this, however Mass was first offered in the Sullivan home in West Mansfield by Father Patrick Byrne who was sent from Boston by Bishop Fenwick about 1838. After 1836 it would have been possible to travel by train from Mansfield to Taunton to attend Mass and receive the sacraments. When Father Aaron Roche took charge of Immaculate Conception Church in North Easton from Bridgewater in 1853, Mansfield was one of his stations. His successor Father Thomas B. McNulty continued to care for Mansfield from Easton and North Bridgewater. Andrew J. Todesco, author of *Saint Mary's Parish Centennial History 1894-1994* has preserved for us some wonderful local anecdotes of this period. For example he relates that Father Roche, officiating at a wedding in the O'Rourke home, discovering the couple had no ring, borrowed the metal ring from the end of Patrick O'Rourke's stove poker and continued with the ceremony. In May of 1859 Foxboro received a resident pastor, Michael X. Carroll who had care of several surrounding towns including Mansfield. After one attempt to revive the Foxboro parish whose church burned down in 1862, perhaps at the hands of the Know-Nothings, Mansfield and neighboring towns became the responsibility of the zealous Father Gillick of Saint Mary's at Attleboro Falls in 1863. Following the initial meeting of the Roman Catholic Society of Mansfield, plans were set in motion to raise funds and to purchase a piece of land on Church Street. Two men from the society met with the Bishop and told him they could more easily count on the cooperation of non-Catholics if the deed remained with them. The fair-minded Bishop assured of their good will and the vigilance of Father Gillick allowed the society to retain the deed. The first Mass in the new church was celebrated on Christmas Day, 1871.

5. The First National Parishes

When Fall River became a city in 1854, the population was just over 12,000 and by the end of the Civil War it was 17, 525. The increase in population went hand in hand with the increase in the number of jobs in the textile industry. In the post-Civil War years French Canadians poured into the mill towns of New England. When John J. Williams became Bishop in 1866 there was no French parish in Massachusetts but the following year a French priest from Albany organized the first French Canadian congregation at Pittsfield. Much information on the history of the French Canadian people in the city of Fall River comes from the research of a native son, Father Pierre Lachance, O.P. In the summer of 1868 Father Antoine Derbuel, a French priest came to Saint Mary's Parish to assist Father Edward Murphy, who was ill at the time. Father Derbuel counted about one hundred Canadian families in the city. The next year when Father Murphy was ill again Bishop Williams sent Father Oliver Verdier, another Canadian priest on loan from the Bishop of Quebec. He stayed from April to July 1869. Realizing the need for a second parish the Bishop sent Paul Adrien de Montaubricq, a canon of Bordeaux, who found between five and six hundred Canadian families. He began to celebrate Mass for them at St. Mary's Church and to make plans for a new church. Land was purchased at Hunter and William Streets. Construction proceeded and Father Montaubricq was able to schedule the laying of the cornerstone for March 13, 1870. A severe storm delayed the event for a week and then it was marred by an accident. A platform, on which close to a hundred people had gathered for the ceremony, collapsed when the frozen ground on which it had been constructed began to melt. No one was seriously hurt and the cornerstone was duly laid. But the incident caused Father Montaubricq to change the name of the church. Instead of naming the church for St. Clothilde as he had planned, Father Montaubricq chose to have the church dedicated in honor of St. Anne because he attributed the lack of serious injuries in the accident to her intercession. Bishop Williams blessed the church on November 13, 1870.

Up to the Civil, War New Bedford and Fall River had taken dissimilar paths to growth and prosperity. While textile mills were multiplying in Fall River, the whaling industry was enriching New

The original St John the Baptist Church in New Bedford about 1875

John J. Williams, Bishop of Boston 1866-1907 (Archbishop 1875)

Bedford boat owners and merchants. Whaling reached its peak in 1857; there were 329 vessels worth $12,000, manned by ten thousand seamen, bringing into New Bedford oil and whalebone worth $10,000,000. Ten shipyards in New Bedford, Fairhaven, and Mattapoisett built over a hundred new whalers in one fifteen year period. A gradual decline followed the discovery of petroleum in Pennsylvania in 1856, and the destruction of twenty-eight New Bedford whalers, by Confederate cruisers. For many years New Bedford whalers had called at the port of Horta on the island of Fayal in the Azores. Not only did the ships take on fresh water and provisions but captains also augmented their crews with both experienced Portuguese seamen and young men seeking adventure beyond their homeland. Many of these men, as well as sailors from the Cape Verde Islands, eventually found their way to New Bedford where the popular tradition is that they contributed gold coins to church collections. Some of the Portuguese seamen returned to the Azores and to Cape Verde and came back with brides or wives and families. Others remained; Father McNulty recorded several marriages in the 1840s and the 1850s where the groom was Portuguese and the bride an Irish immigrant. During the early 1860s Portuguese immigrants also began to settle in Provincetown at the tip of Cape Cod; in August of 1861 Father James A. Healy baptized nine children of Portuguese origin. Father McMahon found a significant number of Portuguese in his congregation when he came to New Bedford in 1865. One source puts the numbers at eight hundred. Encouraged, very likely by Father McMahon who was known for his concern for immigrants throughout his life, Bishop Williams sought a priest for the Portuguese. The first to come was Antonio Felisberto Diaz. Unfortunately he became ill and died on September 13, 1866, shortly after arriving in New Bedford. His grave is in St. Mary's Cemetery. A second Portuguese priest known only as Father Noya is said to have come in 1867, but apparently he stayed a very short time. In January of 1869 the Bishop of Angra sent Father Joao Ignacio d'Azevedo Encarnacao from the island of Pico. On the feast of the Epiphany, he offered Mass at St. Mary's Church at Fifth and School Streets and initially registered one hundred-sixty families. On September 10, 1871, Bishop Williams established the first parish for Portuguese-speaking people in North America. It would bear the title of St. John the Baptist, the patron of the founding pastor. In 1872, Father John Ignatius, as he was popularly known to the English-speaking community, purchased land at Fifth and Wing Street for a church. Frustrated by difficulties in establishing the parish, Father d'Azevedo Encarnacao accepted an assignment in Boston in 1873 and returned to the Azores in 1878. Meanwhile the original congregation of old St. Mary's had moved to its new stone church of St. Lawrence on County Street.

6. The End of the Beginning

When John J. Williams was born on April 27, 1822, in the town of Boston John Cheverus was Bishop and John Adams was still alive in Quincy. Ordained a priest in 1845, he served under Bishops Fenwick and Fitzpatrick. It has been said that when he was born his parents could have known virtually every Catholic in Boston and when he died in 1907 at age eighty-five there were two million Catholics and eight dioceses in New England. In 1866 Bishop Williams inherited a rapidly growing diocese with a Catholic population of 300,000. The Diocese of Boston had comprised the state of Massachusetts since 1853. At that time, the state of Vermont was detached to form the Diocese of Burlington and on the same day the Diocese of Portland was established having as its territory the states of Maine and New Hampshire until 1884, when the latter state became the Diocese of Manchester. In 1870 the Diocese of Springfield was created embracing Worcester County and the four counties of western Massachusetts, which today make up the present Diocese. Patrick T. O'Reilly, pastor of St. John's Parish in Worcester was named first Bishop of Springfield. This involved the separation from Boston of 100,000 Catholics, about forty-five priests and fifty-two churches. A final reduction effecting southeastern Massachusetts came about more by force of circumstances than by pastoral necessity. The background was that Francis P. McFarland, Bishop of Hartford for over ten years was seeking some assistance with his responsibilities in his rapidly growing diocese. The Bishops of the New York Province in 1871 supported a division of the Diocese of Hartford. The obvious course was to separate the states of Connecticut and Rhode Island but the objection was raised that Rhode Island was too small an entity to be a separate diocese. This obstacle was overcome when Bishop Williams offered to cede to the Diocese of Providence a portion of southeastern Massachusetts, which is identical with the territory of the present Diocese of Fall River.

On August 13, 1871, Bishop Williams came to New Bedford for the dedication of St. Lawrence Church where Father McMahon had celebrated the first Mass the preceding Christmas. This was in a way a farewell. In six months, the Diocese of Providence would become a reality and the people and parishes of southeastern Massachusetts would pass from the care of the Bishop of Boston. The occasion was undoubtedly a consoling finale for Bishop Williams. This parish traced its roots to Bishop Cheverus, Father Lariscy who built the first church had witnessed the marriage of Bishop Williams' parents at the old Holy Cross Cathedral and Father Byrne, the first resident pastor, had baptized the Bishop. The dedication of this impressive Keely church where thirty years before Bishop Fenwick found a confirmation class of ten and a congregation of two hundred and fifty worshiping in a small wooden church in a poor neighborhood was certainly a cause of thanksgiving and of hope for the future.

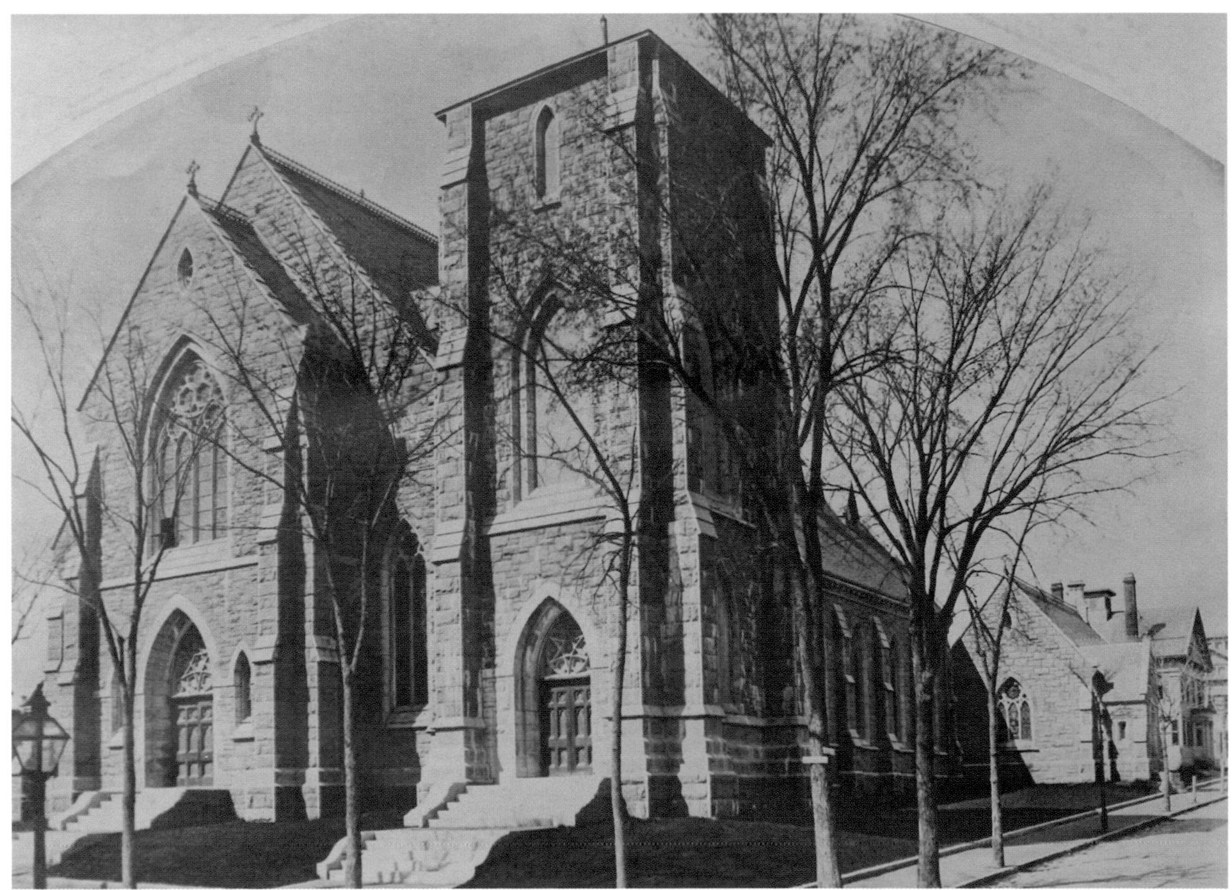

St. Lawrence Church in New Bedford about 1876

Part Three

The Expanding Structure: Under Divine and Earthly Providence

On February 13, 1872, Pope Pius IX established the Diocese of Providence. The new diocese had at total Catholic population of 125,000. The Massachusetts portion numbered 30,000 Catholics. For the next thirty two-years, the church in southeastern Massachusetts would be under the care of the first two Bishops of Providence, Thomas F. Hendricken (1872-86) and Matthew Harkins (1887-1904). It was a time of great expansion for the nation and also of growth for the church. There were now in this section of the new Diocese, 9 parishes and 6 mission churches. There were no Catholic schools, religious houses or charitable institutions. These would all be introduced during the Providence years. In addition, 36 parishes were established; 14 were national parishes, among them the first parishes for Polish and Italian immigrants.

1. Growth in All Directions

Thomas F. Hendricken was ordained Bishop of Providence on April 28, 1872, in the original Saints Peter and Paul Cathedral in Providence by the Archbishop of New York, John J. McCloskey. He was born on May 5, 1827, in the city of Kilkenny in Ireland. He was an excellent student at Ireland's national seminary at Maynooth. His life was changed by a chance meeting with Bernard O'Reilly, the Second Bishop of Hartford. The Bishop was successful in recruiting Thomas Hendricken and had the joy of ordaining him a priest of the Diocese of Hartford at All Hallows College in Dublin on April 25, 1853. The story of Father Hendricken's passage to America aboard the ship Columbia would be pure melodrama if it were not true. The details are given to us by Robert W. Hayman, in the first volume of his history of the Diocese of Providence, *Catholicism in Rhode Island and the Diocese of Providence, 1780-1886.* The captain of the ship was intensely bigoted. When he apprehended Father Hendricken returning from ministering to a dying passenger, having previously prevented the priest from going to the woman, he became enraged. While the crew held his companions, the captain gave Father Hendricken a severe beating. Eventually Samuel Davies, a Protestant minister, was able to break away and seek help. Fifty passengers, all German army veterans, responded just in time to prevent the captain from throwing Father Hendricken overboard. Father Hendricken was taken to his cabin and cared for by the Irish and German passengers who mounted a guard at his cabin door until they reached New York. After serving in various parishes, in 1854 Father Hendricken became pastor of St. Joseph's in Winsted, Connecticut. Eighteen months later, he was appointed pastor of Immaculate Conception Parish in Waterbury where he served with zeal and energy until being named Bishop.

Many Catholics who were the native-born sons and daughters of the earliest Irish immigrants together with some of the more fortunate immigrants were entering professional and upper middle class circles. Employment was available for those who could and would work, but conditions in the mills were often difficult and health threatening. Job opportunities were attracting many immigrants from French Canada. Shortly after the beginning of Bishop Hendricken's ministry, there was a slump in the economy called the Panic of 1873, work became scarce and immigration slowed. Except for Sacred Heart in New Bedford, no new parish was founded between 1874 and 1882. In spite of all the difficulties including debilitating asthma, Bishop Hendricken labored bravely on. He died on June 11, 1886, having established 15 parishes, a hospital and two orphanages in Massachusetts.

His successor was Matthew Harkins, the pastor of St. James Church in Boston. The new Bishop was 42 years old and was consecrated in his Cathedral on April 14, 1887, by John J. Williams who had become the Archbishop of Boston in 1875. Matthew Harkins, the child of Irish immigrant parents, was educated at Boston Latin School, Holy Cross College and the Sulpician Seminary at Paris, where he was ordained on May 22,

Thomas F. Hendricken, Bishop of Providence, 1872-1886

Matthew Harkins, Bishop of Providence 1887-1921

1869. After ordination, he pursued graduate studies at the Gregorian University in Rome at the time of the First Vatican Council. When he returned to Boston, he served in parishes in Arlington and Salem, as well as Boston. When Bishop Harkins succeeded to the See, the Providence Diocese had a Catholic population of 195,000. Bishop Hendricken had established 15 parishes in Massachusetts bringing the total there to 24.

Fall River, Somerset and Taunton

When he first arrived, Bishop Hendricken judged the city of Fall River to be in the greatest need of new parishes. The population had increased by 10,000 in the five years following the Civil War and in one year (1872) fifteen new mills were constructed. Following the Bishop's first visit to the city in June of 1872, three parishes were established, Sacred Heart, St. Joseph's and St. Patrick's. All were divisions of St. Mary's Parish where there were 500 baptisms in 1870. Construction of Sacred Heart Church at Linden and Pine Streets began within a few weeks of the Bishop's visit. It may have been planned as a mission of St. Mary's but when dissatisfaction arose among the people over the location and the plans, the Bishop decided to appoint a pastor in the final days of 1872 and Father Francis J. Quinn was in Fall River for New Year's Day. He stayed only a year. Father Mathias McCabe completed the church which was dedicated on October 7, 1883. At St. Joseph's in the north end of the city, established on April 14, 1873, and at St. Patrick's at Globe Village in the south end, established on April 17, temporary wooden churches were constructed. On May 30, 1885, a gothic church in red brick was dedicated in honor of St. Joseph and a gothic church in native granite, was dedicated to St Patrick on July 22, 1888. Both the work of architect Patrick C. Keely. Catholics of Somerset, across the Taunton River from Fall River, became the responsibility of the pastor of St. Joseph's Parish. Somerset, known to the Indians as Shawomet separated from Swansea in 1790. During the nineteenth century Somerset was an active port. It had an iron works with a rolling mill and nail factory, a shipyard where at one period clipper ships were built. The manufacture of stoneware and pottery also provided employment for natives and immigrants. Father Bric built a small frame church in Somerset, which was dedicated by Bishop Hendricken on November 2, 1873, in honor of St. Patrick. In 1878 the Bishop asked Edouard Norbert the assistant at St. Joseph's in Fall River to take up residence in Somerset that he might more easily take care of the French Canadian community in nearby Warren, Rhode Island. In August of 1887, when he was formally appointed pastor of St. John the Baptist Parish in Warren, James Masterson became the first pastor of St. Patrick's Parish in Somerset, which then numbered 1,200 parishioners. Bishop Hendricken founded two more parishes in Fall River in April of 1882, indicating the return of better times and increased needs. Immaculate Conception Parish was established for 600 English-speaking parishioners who formerly belonged Notre Dame. Their first pastor, Owen Kiernan came with them from Notre Dame where he had been an assistant. A frame church was constructed on Thomas Street and dedicated by Bishop Hendricken on September 14, 1883. The other new parish was in the neighborhood, formerly belonging to St. Mary's Parish, called Rattle Snake Hill or Niagara, after the local volunteer Fire Company. Father Patrick Doyle built a wooden church on Snell Street. Mass was first offered in the unfinished building on November 1, 1882, but the church wasn't dedicated under the title of SS. Peter and Paul until January 12, 1890. Under the second pastor, Bernard F. McCahill Ralph Adams Cram designed a church in Spanish baroque style, which was dedicated on March 25, 1900. St. Louis Parish was created on May 14, 1885, taking its title form the patron saint of the founding pastor, Louis J. Deady.

Saints Peter and Paul Church, in Fall River destroyed by fire 1973

Bishop Hendricken laid the cornerstone of the church on October 8. The mayor, John W. Cummings gave some granite for the foundation, which was left over from a city project. The story is that Father Murphy, unhappy about another division in St. Mary's, called the mayor in and asked. "What's this I hear about your building a church in my parish?" As the story goes, Father Murphy told the mayor he wouldn't be elected again and he wasn't. On July 7, 1887, Father Murphy died on a visit to Ireland. His body was returned to Fall River. Following his Funeral Mass Father Edward Murphy was laid to rest in the church he built in the parish where he presided, most would say ruled for 47 years. Father Murphy's successor was Christopher Hughes, to the annoyance of some parishioners, a priest "they didn't know." Father Hughes was an experienced pastor who decorated the church, installed central heating and electricity and paid off the debt. Finally he arranged to have St. Mary's Church solemnly consecrated by Bishop Harkins on September 7, 1901. It was an extraordinary three-day celebration involving several bishops who were friends of the pastor including Archbishop Michael A Corrigan of New York. A choir of 80 voices and a 27-piece orchestra provided the music for the principal Mass.

Significant growth took place in Taunton too. On November 3, 1872, Bishop Hendricken officiated at the long awaited dedication of St. Mary's Church. The pastor was Edward J. Sheridan, appointed by Bishop Williams in 1871. Maydell Murphy describes Father Sheridan's introduction to his Taunton congregation. Ascending the pulpit on his first Sunday, he announced directly "I am E. J. Sheridan from St. Vincent's Parish in Boston. I am 180 pounds of flesh and a ton of spunk and I don't need any help from any of you." Newspaper accounts report that on the occasion of the church dedication, Bishop Hendricken confirmed six hundred children. No wonder within a few months the Bishop effected the first division of St. Mary's Parish. In April 1873, the Bishop appointed Hugh J. Smyth, pastor of a new parish at Taunton's Weir Village. A wooden church was dedicated to the Sacred Heart on November 15, 1874. Father Smyth was given charge of Holy Family Church in East Taunton as a mission and was also made responsible for the Catholics of Dighton and Myricks. Taunton's third parish, Immaculate Conception was formed late in 1882. The bishop sent Napoleon A. Riviere to take a census in the north end of Taunton where a great many French Canadians had settled near the Whittenton Mill. In January of 1883, James F. Roach who was born in Nantucket and raised in Providence replaced Father Riviere as pastor. A large wooden church was dedicated on May 30, 1885. Father Sheridan protested the division of his parish, appealing to Rome. The Bishop was upheld but Father Sheridan continued to urge the English-speaking members of the new parish to remain at St. Mary's. Under Bishop Harkins Taunton received two more parishes. St. Joseph's was formed from the western portion of St. Mary's on October 23, 1896, and received William H. Curley, a native of Newport as first pastor. In September of 1900, Holy Family Church in East Taunton was raised to parochial status and Charles W. Cullen was appointed first pastor. In 1887, Joseph McDonough established a mission of Sacred Heart Parish in North Dighton, converting a house into the first St. Joseph's Church known to the earliest Catholics as the "Church House." The fourth pastor of Sacred Heart, James L. Smith built a second mission church in Dighton dedicated in honor of St. Peter by Bishop Harkins on December 22, 1901.

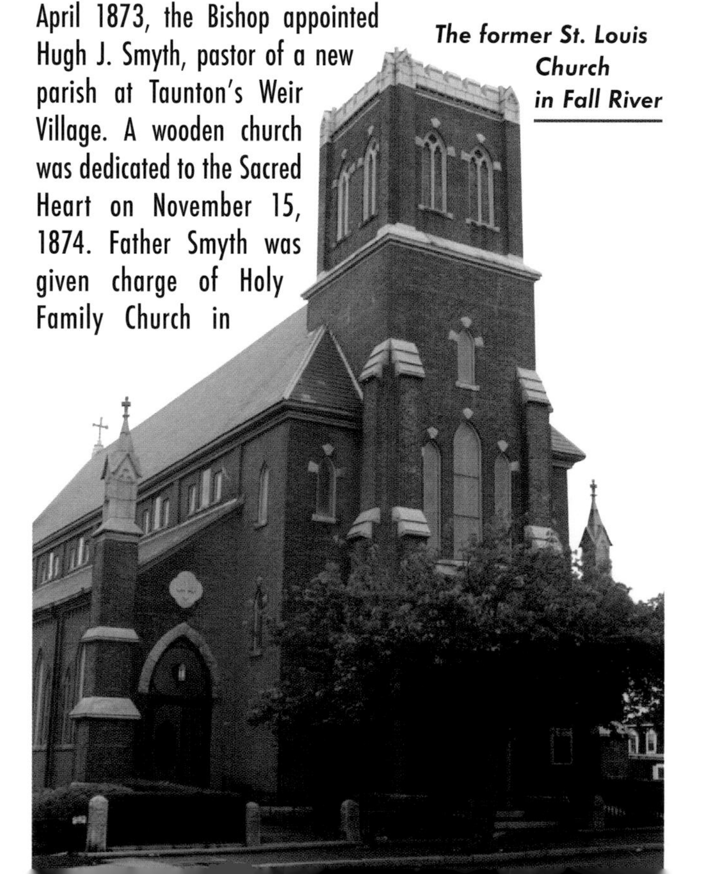

The former St. Louis Church in Fall River

Progress on the Cape

Cape Cod, the eastern most section of the diocese demanded Bishop Hendricken's attention too. In Sandwich, Father Bertoldi was anxious to retire so he could return to Italy. On July 8, 1872, the Bishop sent Henry F. Kinnerny to replace Father Bertoldi. Father Bourgoin relates that Father Bertoldi, a botanist by avocation was remembered for years because of a small edible plant with a purple blossom that covered the fields and yards of Sandwich called "Father Bertoldi flower." Father Kinnerny reported to the Bishop that there were 600 Catholics in Sandwich and 400 in Wareham. Succeeding pastors were Mathias McCabe, Andrew J. Brady and Thomas F. Clinton, a native of Providence, who served from 1880 to 1895 and is buried in St. Peter's Cemetery. James H. Looby a native of Harrisville, Rhode Island followed Father Clinton. During his three years, Father Looby began offering Mass at West Wareham and invited a Polish priest to come to Wareham to preach and to hear confessions for Polish speaking members of the congregation. When Father Looby went to North Easton in 1899, Patrick F. McKenna became pastor. Father McKenna recognized the need of a new church. The second St. Peter's Church, damaged by a storm just after its completion in 1857, sustained a fire in 1887 and was so badly weakened by the gale that sank the steamer *Portland* on November 26, 1898, that part of the front wall fell in to the street in June of 1899. After Sunday evening Benediction on July 6, 1899, the church was closed forever. With considerable aid from parishes throughout the Diocese and the sacrifices of parishioners, a new church was built in the center of town. Father McKenna out of devotion to the Holy Eucharist chose to give the title of Corpus Christi to the new church when it was dedicated by Bishop Harkins on July 7, 1901.

The other centers of Catholic life in Barnstable County were on the lower Cape at Provincetown, and Harwich. In the fall of 1873 the Bishop appointed John Mc Geough, assistant at St. Mary's in Fall River, to replace Father O'Connor at Harwich. He was to concentrate on Provincetown, where he took up residence, and on the missions of Truro and Wellfleet. In the latter town there was small community of French Canadians. Harwich became the responsibility of the priests in Sandwich who also during this period cared for Catholics in a number of other Cape villages, including Hyannis and Falmouth as well as on Martha's Vineyard and Nantucket. Father O'Connor eventually returned to the Boston Diocese where he served as pastor of St. Mary's Parish in Winchester.

Father McGeough, in the spring of 1874, purchased land and planned to build a church in Provincetown but he was replaced by John Maguire on June 4, 1874. Father Maguire proved to be a zealous pastor who set about learning Portuguese and brought the church construction to completion. Bishop Hendricken administered the sacrament of Confirmation and dedicated the Church of St. Peter, the Apostle on October 11, 1874. In December of 1878 James Ward succeeded Father Maguire. Bishop Hendricken had sent Father Ward who was ordained in 1875 to prepare for the priesthood in Portugal, so he could serve Portuguese-speaking parishioners. Unfortunately he was in poor health and was replaced by Thomas P. Elliott in 1886. Father Elliot and his successor, Bernard F. McCahill, a Taunton native appointed in 1889, had their share of difficulties. Some people were unhappy because Father Elliott didn't speak Portuguese. A neighbor contended the ringing of the church bell seriously injured his health and brought Father Elliott to court. A decision was given in Father Elliott's favor and the bell continued to ring. Parishioners and pastor continued to be at odds. Father Elliott admitted some of the complaints were true and the Bishop thought it best to transfer Father Elliott. In July of 1892 the Bishop sent a young priest from the Azores as assistant but he soon accepted an assignment in the

The statue of Our Lady, a memorial to Father Edward Murphy, has inspired devotion outside the Cathedral since 1900.

Boston Archdiocese. Agitation flared again for a Portuguese pastor. A clipping form the *Provincetown Advocate,* which Father McCahill brought to Bishop Harkins on March 23, 1893, told of damage done to a sailboat Father McCahill owned. Some of the more hostile in the congregation had bored holes in the boat and broke the rudder. A later apocryphal account claimed the holes were filled with soap. The inference being that the boat and pastor might sink and the deed is also mistakenly connected with

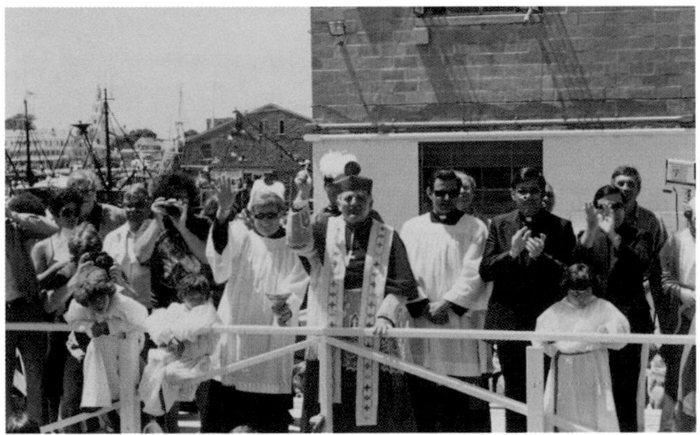

Bishop Daniel A Cronin at the Blessing of the Fleet held annually in Provincetown since 1948

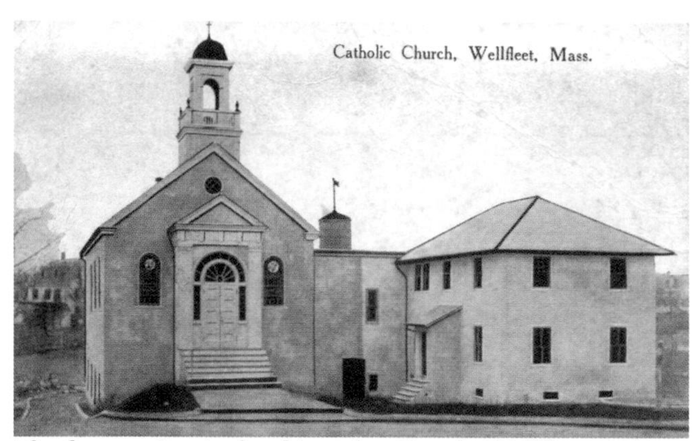

The former Our Lady of Lourdes Church, Wellfleet in 1912

Father Elliott. On August 15, the Bishop transferred Father McCahill to SS. Peter and Paul Parish in Fall River. The Bishop was now able to send to Provincetown the long desired Portuguese priest, the colorful Manuel Candido Terra. Father Terra was born in New Bedford in 1862 of Portuguese parents. He went to school in the Azores and prepared for the priesthood in Montreal and with the Oblates in the Canadian Northwest. In 1890, he was ordained for the Diocese of Providence. He served St. Peter's until his retirement in 1925.

At Woods Hole in the town of Falmouth, the number of Catholics grew. Irish Catholics had found employment at the Pacific Guano Company, a fertilizer plant established in 1863, and after the railroad was extended to Woods Hole in 1872, many wealthy people began to build summer homes. Often, they employed Catholic domestic help. Under Father Clinton, a church was built on Millfield Road, overlooking Eel Pond and dedicated in honor of St. Joseph on June 26, 1882, Jane A. McLaughlin, author of *Saint Joseph's Church, Woods Hole, Massachusetts, A History 1882-1992* relates that while the exterior was typically New England in appearance, built of cedar shingles on a foundation of granite, upon entering one was surprised to find a light interior, the ceiling and walls beautifully decorated by an Italian painter. The following year, Cornelius McSwiney, assistant at St. Peter's in Sandwich became pastor. Father Whelan believes he had been living at the Holy Trinity mission in Harwich and may have continued to live there until the rectory was built in 1888. This Kerry man with a mind of his own traveled up and down the Cape ministering to Catholics at Harwich, Yarmouthport, Hyannis and on Nantucket. Local historian, Father Francis J. Bradley has left us this dramatic picture of Father McSwiney. "He has been known to leave for the island of Nantucket in the teeth of a storm so severe that the people crying on the wharf thought they would never see him again..."

The importance of Mass and the sacraments to Catholic domestic help motivated many non-Catholic employers to be generous to the church. The Sacred Heart Chapel in Yarmouthport is a remarkable example. The Sipmkins family was extraordinarily grateful to Jane A. Byrne, a nurse, for the devoted care she gave the wife of Congressman John Simpkins. Miss Byrne, declining a financial gift for herself, suggested that a chapel be built. Father McSwiney offered the first Mass there in 1899. Bishop Harkins formally dedicated the chapel on September 29, 1902, with the benefactors and Miss Byrne in attendance. By the time of the dedi-cation of the Sacred Heart Chapel, Yarmouth along with the towns of Barnstable, Dennis, Harwich, Chatham, Brewster and Orleans had become part of St. Francis Xavier Parish in Hyannis, founded on January 4, 1902, with Daniel E. Doran as first pastor. Father Moran from Sandwich had tended to the first Catholics in Hyannis. Land for a cemetery on Barnstable Road was purchased in 1870 and in 1874 Father Mathias McCabe built a small chapel named for St. Patrick, as was the cemetery. Father Doran began construction of a church on South Street and made plans for a mission in Osterville where in the summer there were about 400 Catholics.

Meanwhile, in 1899 Father McSwiney completed the construction of St. Patrick's Church on Main Street in Falmouth, another mission of the Woods Hole parish.

Two Brothers for the Two Islands

Bishop Harkins made his first visit to Nantucket, accompanied by Father McSwiney, on July 17 and 18, 1888. The Bishop offered Mass and toured the island. The Bishop's second visit took place in on August 16 and 17, 1892, when he celebrated the sacrament of Confirmation and stayed at the Eschevina home. He also met with Mrs. Richard White and Mrs. William Lawrence who were seeking supporters to join them in requesting a priest be stationed on the island. After visiting the island again in 1895 the Bishop approved plans for a new church. Robert F. Mooney in a parish commemorative history related how quickly Father MacSwiney disposed of the old buildings on the church property including the church, the former Harmony Hall. Father McSwiney was able to offer Mass in the new church on August 4, 1897. After Christmas in 1901 Father McSwiney became pastor of Immaculate Conception Parish in Fall River. James M. Coffee served the Woods Hole parish and its missions from 1902 to1905 and was succeeded at Woods Hole by Thomas F. Kennedy. On May 26, 1903, Thomas J. McGee, became pastor of St. Mary, Our Lady of the Isle

Sacred Heart Chapel in Yarmouthport built in 1899

Parish in Nantucket. On January 15, 1903, his brother Patrick E. McGee had been appointed first pastor of Sacred Heart Parish at Cottage City, now Oak Bluffs on Martha's Vineyard. Both priests, New Bedford natives had studied in Rome and were highly regarded by the Bishop Harkins and his successors.

Martha's Vineyard did not enjoy the prosperity that whaling brought to Nantucket in the early nineteenth century. According to Father Henniss, there were in about 40 Catholics including children on the island in 1857. Father Mc Nulty was probably the first priest to visit the Island on a sick call in 1848. In 1854 Father Henniss records offering Mass at Holmes Hole, now Vineyard Haven and at the Sylvia home in Edgartown; he continued to visit the island semi-annually. In the early 1870s Henry Magetts, a butler for the Drake family bought land for a church and a further gift was forthcoming in his memory from his employer's family. John McGrath, a summer resident from Mansfield, directed it to Bishop Hendricken who asked Father Smyth, recently assigned to St. Lawrence in New Bedford, to take on the task of building a mission church at Cottage City, which was dedicated to the Sacred Heart in 1880. Father Smyth sent some furnishings from St. Mary's Church on Fifth Street including the altar, which had come from the Allen Street church. It is unfortunate that this altar from the first church in the Diocese was discarded in a subsequent renovation. In 1896, Bishop Harkins transferred the Sacred Heart mission to St John the Baptist Parish in New Bedford since the majority of the year round parishioners were of Portuguese background

Upper Bristol County

On January 31, 1874, the zealous founder of the church in Attleboro, Father Philip Gillick retired and died shortly thereafter in New York State. His successor was Edward J. Mongan. In 1877 Father Mongan purchased the Tift estate in North Attleboro. It was "to the surprise of many and to the consternation and chagrin of not a few without the fold that the Catholics were able to secure such a desirable location" reports an early twentieth century historical sketch of St. Mary's Parish. With the property came a curious trio of buildings. An octagonal stone building, when converted, served as the church for eleven years. A circular house called the Round House and sometimes described as looking like a wedding cake became the parish rectory, which housed the parish clergy for over eighty years. In addition there was a famous "Old Red Barn." Since the move from the Falls made it difficult for the Catholics of the east village to attend Mass, Father Mongan began celebrating Mass in Union Hall in the center of Attleboro. Late in

The stone octagon building, which served as the church for North Attleboro Catholics for several years

The laying of the cornerstone of St. Mary's Church in North Attleboro, 1890

1882 Bishop Hendricken formed a new parish to include East Attleboro and Norton. The founding pastor, John O'Connell, who had come to the diocese after ordination from County Tipperary, built a church on North Main Street, which was a fine example of carpenter's gothic. It was dedicated by Bishop Hendricken on September 27, 1885, under the title of Saint John the Evangelist, the pastor's patron. There were at the time about 600 parishioners.

In August of 1875 St. Stephen's Church was dedicated. It was built on land donated by the Hebronville Manufacturing Company between the villages of Dodgeville and Hebronville to serve both communities. The original Catholic community of a few Irish families had grown through immigration from French Canada. In 1880 the mission was transferred from the care of St. Mary's in North Attleboro to St. Joseph's Parish in Pawtucket. This must have been helpful to Father Mongan who was now caring for missions in Attleboro, Mansfield and Norton. By 1885 parishioners numbered 650 and Bishop Hendricken established St. Stephen's as a parish and sent Father Patrick S. McGee, as the first pastor. In addition to the Attleboro villages of Dodgeville and Hebronville, he was given the care of Catholics in parts of Rehoboth and Seekonk.

On June 13, 1893, Thomas Elliott P. Elliott was appointed first pastor of St. Mary's Parish in Mansfield. Father Elliott beautified the former mission church, built a rectory and purchased land for a cemetery. Soon after the foundation of the parish work on the street railway brought the first Italian parishioners to St. Mary's. The Italian community increased significantly; many worked for the railroad, at Lowney's chocolate factory or in other shops and factories.

In North Attleboro attention was centered on Father Mongan. Bishop Harkins laid the cornerstone for the present Church of St. Mary of The Immaculate Conception on May 30, 1890. Shortly thereafter the Bishop began getting complaints about Father Mongan's administration of the parish and his treatment of parishioners. Although the Bishop spoke to Father Mongan who promised to resolve the differences, the situation escalated. After visiting the parish in September of 1896 and hearing all who wished to speak with him and conducting a formal investigation of parish records, the Bishop, in November, asked Father Mongan to resign. When he refused, a formal canonical proceeding was begun which decided in favor of the Bishop and the decision was delivered to Father Mongan on March 25, 1908. Father John A. Hurley became the next pastor.

Belated Growth in New Bedford

Bishop Hendricken established no English-speaking or territorial parish in New Bedford. When Bishop Harkins came he found seven such parishes in Fall River, three in Taunton and only one in New Bedford, where real growth in the textile industry didn't come until after 1880. In the decade ending in 1880 the population rose by only 5000, whereas in the following decade it rose by over 20,000. New mills were being built at the north and south ends of the city. At St. Lawrence Father Hugh J. Smyth had built two schools and completed the tower of the church. Bishop Harkins on December 16, 1888, consecrated the fourteen bells that hang in tower. In 1888 Bishop Harkins appointed Father Smyth Permanent Rector in compliance with the directive of the Third Council of Baltimore that there be a certain number of permanent pastors in each diocese. At the same time, the Bishop announced the division of the parish, which Father Smyth had proposed. The new parish called St. James, again after the patron saint of the founding pastor, James F. Clark. A native of Taunton, ordained in 1876, Father Clark was one of our first native vocations to the priesthood. The focus of parochial life was centered at St. Mary's School within the confines of the new parish. Bishop Harkins on October 25, 1891, laid the cornerstone of the granite lower church designed by P.W. Ford, son-in-law of Patrick C. Keely and Father Clark celebrated the first Mass there on May 15, 1892. Anticipating a parish in the north end, Father Smyth purchased the Earle property on the present Ashley Boulevard and James J. Brady was named pastor of a new parish on January 17, 1896. Father Brady engaged the firm of Kelly and Houghton of New York to design a church to be built of granite in Romanesque style. The parish, which served German, as well as Irish parishioners was fittingly placed under the patronage of St. Kilian, 7th century Irish missionary to the German kingdom of Franconia. The saint was also the patron Father Brady's native parish at Mullagh, County Cavan.

2. French Canadian Struggles

One of Bishop Hendricken's earliest challenges was to provide for an increasing number of French speaking Canadians coming into the diocese. They were most numerous in Fall River where they were settling in the east end of the city known as Flint Village. The neighborhood took its name from one on the recently built mills. The mill owner was John D. Flint who had come from Vermont and prospered dealing in real estate. When the Catholics of Flint Village who had to walk to St. Annes's Church requested a church of their own, the Bishop with the help of a Canadian priest in Rhode Island secured the services of a Montreal priest, Pierre J. B. Bedard. An organizer and a leader, Father Bedard lost no time in obtaining land and building a wooden church. Mass was offered in the unfinished building in November and the cornerstone of the first Notre Dame de Lourdes Church was laid on December 1, 1874. Father Bedard believed it was important for Canadians to maintain a spirit of nationalism and their religious traditions. For him and many of his parishioners the preservation of the French language was essential to preservation of the faith. Bishop Hendricken, while wanting to provide the best pastoral care for immigrants, believed that assimilation was the key to a better life. He felt learning English and becoming part of the mainstream of the church was important for the individual and the church. These two contending outlooks would be the basis for future strife at Notre Dame, which is detailed by Father Hayman and treated thoroughly by Dr. Philip T. Silvia who has called the controversy the "Flint Affair."

The independent Father Bedard with the help of family money, parishioners and the Religious of Jesus and Mary, whom he brought from Canada, soon built a convent, orphanage, school for boys and a commercial high school. The land on which all the buildings except the church stood was in the name of a corporation, of which he was the president. Relations between the Bishop and Father Bedard became strained when the Bishop warned Father Bedard not it interfere in the mule spinners strike in 1879. Irish strikers appealed to the Bishop, fearing Father Bedard would import Canadian workers to take their jobs. On August 24, 1884, Father Bedard died of a stroke at age 42. The Bishop sent as his successor a Canadian priest, Edourad Norbet. After a few weeks, Father Norbert finding the financial and administrative details of the parish so stressful that he asked to return to Warren. Since he had no other Canadian priest to send, the Bishop appointed Patrick Samuel McGee who was born in Canada and spoke French. While some were willing to accept Father McGee the corporation trustees were not and they called upon the Bishop. The Bishop became irritated, reminding them he had sent a Canadian priest who declined to stay and that if he had another Canadian he would send him but he did not, finally telling them Father McGee spoke better French than they did.

The trustees now decided to force Father Mc Gee out. They first evicted him from the rectory, which was owned by the corporation, and on one occasion did some damage at his brother's house where he took up residence. Disturbances were engineered at Mass. Loud coughing would break out as Father McGee began to read the announcements after the Gospel. When the appointment of a young Canadian assistant in December of 1884 failed to appease the opponents, the Bishop transferred Father McGee to Dodgeville. The Bishop now for whatever reason tried to send another Irish priest, Owen Clarke, who was fluent in French and popular at St Anne's. He was not accepted and on February 12, 1885, the Bishop ordered Father Clarke to close the church. During the next ten months the "Flint Affair" affair held the attention of the Catholics of New England, especially those concerned with preserving the Canadian way of life in this country. Appeals were made to Archbishop Williams in Boston and to Cardinal Simeoni at the Propaganda Congregation in Rome. On October 23, 1885, the Cardinal decided the Bishop should be allowed to appoint a pastor of his choice together with a Canadian assistant who would succeed the pastor in due course. This didn't satisfy the discontented but providentially the Bishop was able to secure a distinguished priest from the Diocese of St. Hyacinth, Joseph Laflamme, a wise and sensitive man to take the post of assistant to Father Peter Ferron. He arrived on December 12, 1885, and in March of 1886 became pastor and soon brought a young priest from Canada, Joseph Payan, to be his assistant.

Healing and Growth Continue

One of the chief concerns of Bishop Harkins was the peace and harmony of the French Canadian community especially in Fall River where there had been so much controversy. Within six weeks of his ordination as Bishop, he was at Notre Dame Parish on May 31, 1887, for the celebration of the sacrament of Confirmation. Before the ceremony the Bishop spoke to the congregation in French, telling the people this was his first confirmation ceremony since becoming Bishop. The Bishop's fluency in French, his seminary studies in France and his interest in French-speaking parishioners as a young priest in Salem were seen as positive signs by the Canadians of Fall River. Two further developments took place within Fall River's French Canadian community in the first few months after the coming of Bishop Harkins. The pastoral care of St. Anne's Parish passed to the Dominican Friars and a third parish for Canadians was established at Bowenville, Fall River's north end.

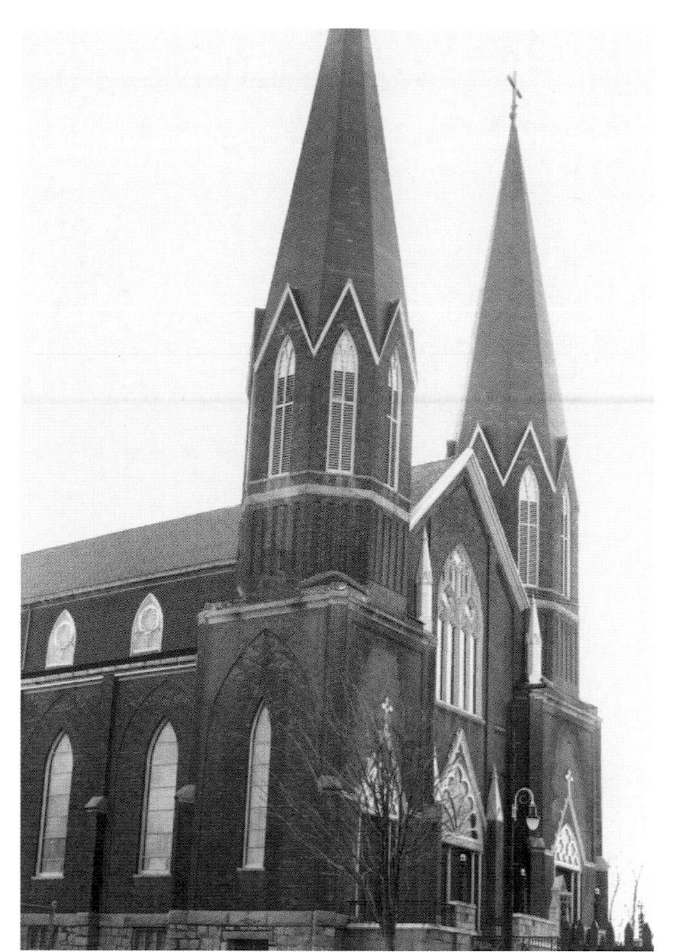

The former St. Mathieu Church in Fall River

From its foundation St, Joseph's Parish embraced a congregation of both Irish and Canadian parishioners. According to one report the number of Canadian families had grown to 300. In the summer of 1887 they requested a separate parish for themselves. One event fresh in people's minds caused everyone to look favorably on the petition. It had become the custom to have High Mass celebrated for the Canadians at nine o'clock and the Irish at eleven. On March 6, 1887, to accommodate the Forty Hours Devotion, Father Boylan had announced there would be one High Mass at half past ten. The Canadians arrived early and occupied the pews for which they paid pew rent. When the Irish parishioners arrived and found the Canadians occupying what they considered their pews, they forced them out, "seizing the women and men by the collar and dragging them to the floor," reported *L'Independent.* One Canadian resisted. The sexton was dispatched by the pastor to settle the disturbance "as best he could." In December, Bishop Harkins appointed Father Payan, assistant at Notre Dame, pastor of the new parish, which was named for the Bishop's patron, St. Matthew, as a gesture of appreciation. The basement of the large brick church was dedicated by Bishop Harkins on April 29, 1888. The bishop blessed the upper church and the new bell on September 20, 1896, and contributed one hundred dollars for a statue of St. Matthew to be placed in front of the church. The church was designed by Louis Destremps, who came to Fall River from Canada as young man to work as a carpenter and builder and went on to study architecture.

At St. Anne's Parish, while many of the people accepted Father Briscoe, there was an abiding desire for a Canadian pastor. Encouraged by the outcome at Notre Dame, St. Anne's parishioners presented Bishop Harkins with a petition for a Canadian pastor. Although not of the same mind set as his predecessor, Bishop Harkins felt he had no qualified Canadian priest to send and he began to consider the possibility of a religious order. The Bishop knew that Bishop Healy in 1881 had welcomed to Lewiston, Maine Dominican Friars, who harassed by the anti-clerical government in France, were eager to make foundations in Canada and New England. In October of 1887 Bishop Harkins promoted Father Briscoe to the parish of St. Patrick in Providence. Shortly thereafter, the French Dominicans agreed to take St Anne's Parish on trial for a year. Their ministry began on November 22, 1887, and would prove to be enduring and fruitful. The first pastor and superior was Francois Bonaventure Esteva, O.P. Charles. Bernard Sauval, O.P. succeeded him in 1891. The Dominicans were soon founding missions and schools in the southern sections of the city.

The first of these was at Townsend Hill where the Dominicans built a combination church and school dedicated to St. Dominic on November 10, 1889. In 1892 Bishop Harkins made St. Dominic's a separate parish and appointed L. Octave Massicotte, pastor. Deserie V. Delemarre, a French born priest who succeeded Father Massicotte in 1901, asked the Bishop's permission to build a new church according to plans drawn up by Louis Destremps. On July 4, 1902, Bishop blessed the cornerstone of the new building, which would have the title Church of the Blessed Sacrament.

An additional Canadian community had grown up in the Maplewood section of Fall River. The basement church of St. Jean Baptiste was blessed on Thanksgiving Day, November 25, 1897. In January of 1898 Father Sauval had started a school in the basement church. The mission became a parish on February 6, 1901 with Joseph S. Fortin the first pastor. The outstanding in event of Father Fortin's brief pastorate of one year was the celebration of the feast of St. John the Baptist on June 24, 1901. A parade of twenty different societies marched to the church grounds where a Solemn Mass was celebrated at an outside altar with a congregation of two thousand people and the participation of various choirs. The celebration attracted sufficient attention to be reported in the Montreal newspapers. Henry J. Mussley, a former Belgian Redemptorist replaced Father Fortin when he went to Woonsocket. Father Mussley received permission to build a school and in 1903 secured the services of the Sisters of St. Joseph.

In April of 1899 a fourth French Canadian parish was established in Fall River and a church constructed on Pine Street on land purchased from the Granite Mills. J. A. Theodule Giguere was appointed first pastor. Father Giguere suggested the parish be given the title of St. Roch, the patron of his place of birth, in the Province of Quebec. Louis Destremps designed a large wooden building that would accommodate school classrooms on the first floor with the church on the second floor. Bishop Harkins laid the cornerstone on July 4, 1899, and Father Christopher Hughes blessed the new bell on September 24.

This development of new parishes indicates the rapidly growing Canadian population. One estimate puts the number at

The former Blessed Sacrament Church in Fall River

The former St. Rock Church and School in Fall River

Notre Dame de Lourdes Church, Fall River

Interior of Notre Dame de Lourdes Church, Fall River

20,000 in 1890. In the older parishes of St. Anne and Notre Dame improvements continued to be made. At Notre Dame, ill health caused Father Laflamme to retire in August of 1888. During his brief pastorate of a little more than two years, he purchased land on Stafford Road for a cemetery in 1887 and the same year the Religious of Jesus and Mary began construction of a new convent and boarding school.

In October of 1888 Jean A. Prevost, the pastor of Sacred Heart Parish in New Bedford, succeeded Father Laflamme. Father Prevost was born in St. Charles -de- Bellechasse, Quebec in 1849 and was ordained a priest of the Diocese of St. Hyacinth on September 21, 1879. For the next 37 years, he would preside over an extraordinary parochial complex, which would include a magnificent church, parish elementary school, private girls academy and orphanage. Shortly after his death, a boys' junior and senior high school for which he made plans, became a memorial bearing his name. Father Hayman's evaluation of Monsignor Prevost is telling. He remarks that unlike Father Bedard, who wished to retain intact the Canadian tradition of parochial administration with no provision for the customs of the American church, Father Prevost wisely balanced two traditions, giving the laity a say in the temporal concerns of the parish, but also fostering a good relationship between himself and his bishop, especially by being financially accountable to him; and the parish prospered as never before. Meanwhile, Father Prevost had been planning for a new church. Louis Destremps would be the architect. The plans were for a church in classic baroque style to be built of native granite. The stone came from two nearby sites, one of which was owned by the parish. Bishop Harkins blessed the cornerstone on May 30, 1892.

Saint Anne's Church and Shrine

In May of 1892 Father Sauval purchased land at South Main and Middle Streets for a new church. The cost was $19, 000. Plans for a monumental church were drawn by architect, Napoleon Bourassa of Montreal. Father Sauval hoped that the church would not only provide for the needs of the parish but would also become a shrine where pilgrims would come to honor St. Anne. On October 6, 1895, the Friars were able to occupy their

St. Anne's Shrine, Fall River

Bishop Daniel A. Cronin celebrated the final Mass for St. Hyacinth's Parish in 1977

The interior of St Anthony of Padua Chruch in New Bedford

new brick residence at South Main and Middle Streets and to use the basement of the new church. In 1901 a relic was received from the Church of St. Anne at Apt in France and on July 14, 1902, the cornerstone of the church was blessed. Before this could take place, on April 30, 1901, Father Charles Bernard Sauval, O. P. suffered stroke and died the next day. A Canadian, Ange-Celistin Cote, O. P. was appointed pastor on May 25, 1901, however his pastorate was to be brief. In July, a new provincial was elected who supported the position that houses founded by French Dominicans should remain under their direction and a new pastor, A. Raymond Grolleau, O. P. was proposed and was appointed by Bishop Harkins after Father Cote resigned.

On October 16, 1890, St. Hyacinth Parish, New Bedford's second for French Canadians, was established and Antoine Berube appointed the first pastor. It had been a mission of Sacred Heart Parish since October of 1887. The lower church was blessed on September 16, 1888, and the upper church was dedicated by Bishop Harkins on December 10, 1893. Another parish for French Canadians in the north end of New Bedford came into being in September when Homisdas Deslauriers was appointed first pastor of St Anthony's Parish. Father Deslauriers found a congregation of 300 families when he began offering Mass in a rented hall. Soon he purchased a very acceptable parcel of land at Acushnet Avenue and Nye Streets and built a wooden building, which contained a church on the first floor and school classrooms on the second. The first St. Anthony's Church was blessed on March 8, 1896. Plans were drawn for a large stone church, which although it took several difficult years to build, turned out to be a worthy rival to the grandeur of Notre Dame and St. Anne's. Other communities of French Canadians were being served in various ways at Westport Factory, Taunton, Attleboro and North Attleboro. They would all have parishes in due time.

Monsignor Jean A. Prevost, P.A.

3. Additional Portuguese Parishes

As Bishop Harkins started his ministry, second among non-English-speaking Catholics were Portuguese immigrants. There was one Portuguese parish, St. John the Baptist in New Bedford. The church had been dedicated by Bishop Hendricken on June 24, 1875, during the pastorate of Antonio de Mattos Freitas. In 1885 Father Freitas acquired land for cemetery on Allen Street and the next year retired to the island of Sao Jorge to be succeeded in 1886 by Antonio da Silva Neves. A significant number of Portuguese were in the congregation at St. Peter's in Provincetown and Portuguese parishioners had also begun to settle on Martha's Vineyard and Nantucket.

The need for a parish in Fall River was becoming apparent. Jobs in the textile mills had been drawing Portuguese immigrants, some from New Bedford. As early as March of 1875 a Lenten mission for Portuguese residents was preached by a certain Father Hayes at St. Mary's Church. A year later, on March 10, 1876, the Portuguese Catholic community, calling itself the Portuguese Congregation of St. Anthony came together under the leadership of Father Freitas, pastor of St. John's in New Bedford. Father Hayman explains this step forward was made possible by the presence of a second priest in New Bedford, F.B.M. Bettencourt. The two priests alternated in offering Mass in Fall River once a month for about two years. When Father Bettencourt left St. Johns, the monthly Masses in Fall River were discontinued. It would be ten years before any efforts were made at organizing the Portuguese Catholic community again. On January 1, 1888, the St. Joseph's Benevolent, Protective and Charitable Society was formed. The members were quick to request Bishop Harkins to reestablish the mission in Fall River. The Bishop asked Father Neves, now pastor in New Bedford to meet with the St. Joseph Society members, which he did on January 12, 1888. Fortunately Father Neves soon received a young assistant from the island of Pico, Candido d'Avila Martins. He began offering Mass in Fall River, first in the Hibernians' Hall at Spring and South Main Streets. Shortly after, the small First Baptist Church at the corner of Columbia and Canal Streets became available and was purchased by a businessman, Francisco Machado da Silva, in March of 1889 and presented to Father Neves. The building was in need of repair and the first Mass was not offered in the church until September. There were now an estimated 1,500 Portuguese in Fall River. In September of 1890 Manuel C. Terra, the future Provincetown pastor, now assistant in New Bedford began saying Mass every Sunday. As pleased as some people may have been with the progress that had been made many would not be satisfied until they had a resident priest. In July of 1892 two more young priests came from the Azores allowing Bishop Harkins to provide the Fall River congregation with a priest. After talking with Father Terra, the Bishop appointed Father Martins pastor of the new Portuguese parish in Fall River. Mr. Silva wanted to name the church for St. Joseph but Father Neves knowing that the members of the congregation were almost exclusively from the island of Sao Miguel decided that that the title of the Fall River Parish should be Senhor Santo Christo dos Milagres. The title commemorates the devotion of the faithful of Sao Miguel to the suffering Christ centered around a statue of Ecce Homo or Santo Christo, a gift from Pope Paul III to the Poor Clare Nuns who wished to establish

Bishop Aurilio Granada Escudeiro, retired Bishop of Angra in the Azores leads the Santo Christo Procession.

In Fall River the procession takes place on the last Sunday in June

a convent in the Azores in the sixteenth century. Father Martins immediately recognized the difficulty the parishioners, especially the children, who lived in the north end had in reaching Santo Christo Church. Late in 1895 Father Martins began celebrating Mass for them in a hall. Once Santo Christo Parish seemed to be firmly established, the Bishop permitted Father Martins to construct a stone basement church in the north end, which the Bishop placed under the patronage of St. Michael when he laid the cornerstone on May 10, 1896. Father Martins was a dedicated pastor but he was not trained for administration. His situation was also complicated by poor health. Finally, the Bishop asked him to resign. He went to live with Father Neves in New Bedford as his assistant and he died there on November 27, 1898. Father Francisco Silveira Mesquita, a native of the island of Pico replaced Father Martins. During his pastorate on February 28, 1902, St. Michael's mission was formally given parochial status. The first pastor was Francisco Jose Constantio Flores, from the island of Terceira. Father Flores and had served in his native parish, in New Bedford, Provincetown and at Santo Christo. Unfortunately Father Flores died of a ruptured appendix on December 2, 1902. His successor was Manuel Cipriano Grillo. He was known as a good speaker and he traveled to various places where Portuguese people had settled, such as Rehoboth and Little Compton, giving missions in an attempt to keep people in rural communities in contact with the church. Unfortunately at St. Michael's Father Grillo showed a facility for becoming involved repeatedly in controversies with parishioners. Meanwhile a Portuguese community in Flint Village was growing in numbers and in January of 1903, through the hospitality of Father Prevost at Notre Dame, Father Mesquita began saying Mass at St. Joseph's Hall on Bassett Street.

Rededication of the renovated Our Lady of Mt. Carmel Church in New Bedford, 1990

In New Bedford, there was more diversity in Portuguese community than in Fall River. The original immigrants from the island of Fayal were joined by settlers from the other islands in Azores group, often called the Western Isles, and later by people from Madeira and Cape Verde. St John the Baptist Parish now had about 7,000 people. Parishioners in the southern part of the parish requested the Bishop to divide the parish. At first Father, Neves supported the proposal but later had reservations. He had saved over $20,000 hoping to replace the original wooden church and he realized it would be more difficult to raise funds within a smaller parish and he would be required to share a portion of the parish savings with the new parish. Bishop Harkins presented the proposal to the diocesan consultors and when they approved the Bishop went ahead and appointed Joseph D. Nunes, an assistant at St. John's, pastor of the new parish on September 5, 1902. A controversy ensued which greatly disturbed the Bishop. Ultimately, thirteen members of the parish brought a civil complaint and the judge issued a temporary injunction against the transfer of funds until the case could be heard before a court appointed master. The Bishop now with the full cooperation of Father Neves consulted civil and canon lawyers. The case was heard in November of 1903, the decision was made in favor of the Bishop and upheld on appeal to the Supreme Judicial Court of Massachusetts. Meanwhile, Father Nunes had begun saying Mass in a hired hall and found he had over 600 families. He soon had plans for a Romanesque church to be built at Rivet and Bonney Streets and engaged Michael Houlihan, a Providence architect and builder. Father Nunes received the Bishop's permission to begin work on the basement church. Bishop Harkins blessed the cornerstone and placed the church under the patronage of Our Lady of Mount Carmel on July 4, 1903. In Taunton where it was estimated in 1902 that the Portuguese community numbered 2,500, the leaders sought the help of Father Smith at Sacred Heart and Father Coyle at St. Mary's in presenting their needs to the Bishop. On April 2, 1903, Bishop Harkins appointed Alexander F. Louro pastor of the first Portuguese parish in Taunton. Father Louro, a native of Terceira came to the diocese in 1901 and had been serving rather unhappily as Father Terra's assistant in Provincetown. Father Louro acquired a house for a rectory where the Bishop directed him to celebrate daily Mass. The pastor soon found a hired hall on Trescott Street provided more room for Sunday Mass than did the Perkins house on Weir Street, which had been purchased for a church by a parishioner, John Rosa of Dighton. The new parish served the Portuguese speaking faithful of Dighton, Rehoboth and Seekonk as well as Taunton and was named in honor of St. Anthony.

4. Polish and Italian Parishes

The final years of the nineteenth century saw an increase in Catholic Poles and Italians in Fall River and New Bedford. In 1898 some Polish Catholics in the south end of Fall River formed a corporation and purchased an old Methodist Episcopal church on Globe Street and asked Bishop Harkins for a priest. The Bishop had pre-viously declined the offer of a priest while recognizing the need. With these new developments, the Bishop now accepted Paul Guzik, a priest who came from Buffalo with good recommendations and sent him to Fall River to live with Father Hughes at St. Mary's. On December 10, 1898, the Bishop established a parish for the Poles of Fall River and Somerset. Land for a permanent church was purchased on Rockland Street. On June 25, 1899, Bishop Harkins laid the cornerstone of the church, which he dedicated in honor of St. Stanislaus seven months later on January 28, 1900. Father Guzik because of difficulties with the parishioners decided to give up the parish, and in March of 1902, Joseph Ziemba, a member of the Congregation of the Resurrection, came but he was recalled by his community after serving a few months. On August 28, 1902, Bishop Harkins accepted Peter Basinski, a priest recommended by the Bishop of Chicago, and sent him to St. Stanislaus. In spite of the fact that some Poles chose to set up their own church on West Globe Street, dedicated to Blessed Virgin Mary, Father Basinski found it necessary to enlarge the church and Bishop Harkins blessed the reno-vated church on December 13, 1903. In New Bedford a sizeable number of Polish Catholics lived in the north end around the original Weld Square and they attended Mass at St. Kilian's Church. Another Polish community lived in the south end. In 1902 Adalbert Marion Dynia came to New Bedford with credentials which prompted Father Brady to allow him to offer Mass a to preach in Polish at St. Kilian's. Father Dynia did not stay in New Bedford but returned shortly and began to organize a parish without any consultation with Father Brady or Bishop Harkins. When he did ask permission, it was denied. The Bishop advised Father Brady to neither recognize nor publicly repudiate Father Dynia who sadly ended up in trouble with the law. Bishop Harkins then accepted Edward A. Uminski, a priest who had served in the Diocese of Hartford. Father Uminski was expelled for his activities on behalf of Polish independence in territory ruled by the Russian Czar. The Bishop first sent him to Fall River to assist Father Basinski and then as assistant to Father Brady in New Bedford. The Polish people persisted in their requests for a parish and the Bishop at Father Brady's urging appointed Father Uminski pastor. Late 1903 he began offering Mass in the Chapel of the Guardian Angels, on Acushnet Avenue with the permission of the pastor of Sacred Heart Parish and he rented a house on Washburn Street for temporary rectory. This community would become the parish of Our Lady of Perpetual Help.

St. Stanislaus Church destroyed by fire in 1991

Church of Our Lady of the Holly Rosary of Pompeii, Fall River

In 1898 the Italian community had grown in numbers significant enough for Bishop Harkins to ask the Dominican Fathers at St. Anne's if they could provide a priest to minister to Italian immigrants. At the same time, Father Christopher Hughes at St. Mary's Church in Fall River expressed his concern for the Italian immigrants. Father Hughes arranged with the Scalabrini Fathers from Providence to preach a mission in Italian and the Bishop placed the Italian community in the care of Father Hughes for the time being. In August of 1900 probably the first expression of Italian patriotism was manifested in Fall River. It was occasioned by the assassination of King Umberto. Three societies took part, The Society Italiana, the Italian American Naturalization Society of Fall River and the Fartellanza di Mutuo Socorro of Newport. Listed in the program were M.A. Clorite, Vittorio de Nadal, Nicholas Ziroli and Gabriel Sisca. A procession of carriages, led by Mayor John H. Abbott and marshal, Pietro Barsi, with Storey's Band, accompanied a hearse covered with flowers bearing a picture of the King from Pleasant and Sixth Streets to St. Mary's Church where the bearers placed the casket before the altar beside the portrait of the king and an eloquent address was delivered in Italian by Father Hughes. After 1900 many Italian immigrants began to settle in the east end of Fall River. Some were stonecutters brought to work in the quarry of William Beattie, others settled in the Slade Street area of the south end. In 1902 the Bishop found himself with an available Italian priest, Roberto Parrillo. In 1901 Father Parrillo received permission to come to this country to join his parents who had immigrated to North Providence. On December 6, 1902, Father Parrillo came to Fall River and found lodgings with Gabriel Sisca on Bedford Street. Father Giguere graciously offered St. Rock's Church as place for the Italian community to gather for the celebration of Mass and the sacraments. Land was purchased on Beattie Street facing Colt now Wall Street. On December 6, 1903, according to the Italian custom, the blessing of the first stone to be laid, with Father Hughes officiating. Romualdo Vioni a member of the building committee was able to hire skilled workmen from the parish community who built a basement-church of Fall River granite, that won the admiration of all upon its completion.

5. The Religious Sisters and the Spiritual Life of the Parish

March 19, 1873, is a significant date in local church history. On that day the Sisters of Mercy opened a convent in St. Lawrence Parish in New Bedford, establishing the first house for Religious in the future Diocese of Fall River. The Sisters, who had been in Providence since 1851, came to New Bedford not to open a school but a hospital. Mrs. Ada Baker, a generous woman concerned about health care, hoping the Bishop would permit the Sisters to open a hospital had purchased the Charles Russell mansion at Pleasant and Campbell Streets. The large stone building has some additional local fame, as the childhood home of the eccentric and avaricious Hetty Howland Robinson Green, reputed to be the richest woman in the world when she died in 1916. The Bishop accepted the gift and placed the project in the hands of Father McMahon. The hospital opened in June of 1873. The chief consulting physician was Dr. Stephen W. Hayes, an immigrant from County Cork, who came to this country as a boy, graduated from Harvard Medical School in 1870 and became one New Bedford's earliest prominent Catholic laymen. Despite a contract with the United States marine hospital service for the care of disabled seamen and the donated services of physicians, the hospital, which admitted many indigent cases free, was forced to close in 1887 for financial reasons. The Sisters had not limited themselves to their nursing ministry but readily accepted Father McMahon's invitation to direct the Sunday school for girls, which was conducted both at St. Lawrence Church and old St. Mary's Church. In the summer of 1888 two of the Sisters cared for General Philip H. Sheridan and were at his bedside when he died on August 5, at Nonquitt in Dartmouth.

About the time the first religious community was getting settled in New Bedford, in October of 1873 five Paulist Fathers came to Fall River to conduct a mission at St. Mary's Church in Fall River. The report that they made to their community was reprinted in a Paulist Publication under the heading of Mission Memories in 1990 and is a revealing glimpse of parish life among the Irish immigrants of the day. The Mission Fathers reported that "from working in the noisy mills, almost everyone is deaf and this kind of mechanical slavery tends to debase and degrade the operatives both mentally and morally". They go on to speak of "profanity and smuttiness of speech which is the language of cotton mills" and among the girls of "snuff rubbing" about the interior of the mouth which caused partial intoxication. Among boys and girls there was also the problem of drunkenness but it was not as serious as in other cities, perhaps due to the enforcement of strict state laws. Apart from the social conditions and the temptations the people were exposed to, the missionaries report on the lack of understanding some have of the Catholic faith. The Fathers found over 100 young people under the age of 18 who lacked the most basic knowledge, "several not knowing how to make the sign of the cross, nor indeed what the cross meant, did not know how many Gods there were or who Jesus Christ was." The best the priests could do, was to form a class to be instructed by one of the assistant pastors. Among the adults, they were able to hastily form a confirmation class and Bishop Hendricken came to administer the sacrament to 270 people before the end of the mission. The Paulists concluded, "never could there be a place that needed more a thorough mission. If it could have been done the whole city ought to have been missioned at one time and temperance societies and pious societies formed on the spot." Perhaps the situation the missionaries found can be partially explained by the Irish Catholic experience of the time. Up to the Great Famine in the mid nineteenth century, the church in many places in Ireland was still showing the effects of the penal laws of the eighteenth century, although Catholic emancipation had taken place. Some of the clergy were poorly trained, although improvement had come through the founding of the Maynooth Seminary in 1795. Many people were ignorant of the church's teaching and often influenced by superstitious and pre Christian traditions. Many of the early immigrants and their offspring would have been in this mold. Later immigrants brought to this country a strain of Catholicism, which was marked by pietism, obedience and extraordinary financial generosity due to the "Devotional Revolution" directed by the authoritarian Cardinal Paul Cullen who became Archbishop of Dublin in 1852. The Sisters of Mercy who came here in the early 1870s not only had an impact in the classroom but also organized the societies for children and young people called for in the mission Fathers' report. Since the Sisters of Mercy were founded in Ireland to care for the sick and the poor as well as to teach, they were able to reach out to the needy and the suffering in their homes. There was no scarcity of suffering among many of the immigrants whether from Ireland, England or Canada. Many lived in mise-rable crowded tenements. Mill operatives were paid no more than $1.75 a day.

This chalice and paten of extraordinary workmanship now in our Diocesan Archives was an ordination gift in 1923 to the late Msgr. John A. Chippendale

Women and children as well as the men worked in the textile mills in conditions hazardous to health and at jobs dangerous to life and limb. Well aware of the poverty of his people Father Murphy established a conference of the St. Vincent DePaul Society in 1871. St. Mary's Conference numbered twenty men who not only concerned themselves with the material needs of the poor but also tended to their spiritual needs by assisting with the Sunday school classes. Since the abuse of alcohol was a major contributor to poverty and misery in the family there was a revival in the Catholic temperance movement and new temperance societies were organized. In addition to supporting temperance among the members, they provided opportunities for recreation and socializing. Some had cadet and band units that practiced and took part in holiday parades and celebrations. Some temperance societies provided benefits for the widowed and orphaned and other benevolent societies were formed also for that purpose.

In Massachusetts, the state law required that children between the ages of 10 and 15 attend school for at least three month each year. The child laborers were usually divided in to four groups by the overseer and sent to the factory school, one group every three months. No child could be employed without presenting a school certificate. Sadly, it is known that parents motivated by poverty or greed lied about their children's ages in seeking employment for them. In 1874, legislation was passed limiting the employment of women and minors under 18 years old to ten hours a day. In December of 1882, Father Edward Murphy spoke at the Sunday Masses at St. Mary's Church in Fall River of the "unfriendly attitude" of the Fall River School Committee toward children attending the parochial school. The school committee had refused to accept certificates signed by the Sisters testifying to the requisite period of attendance at school for children seeking to work. Father Murphy called this treatment "flagrant injustice" since the Catholic schools functioned with the approval of the School Committee.

6. The First Schools and Charitable Institutions

An early attempt at Catholic education was made by Father Murphy in Fall River. He had once opened a school in the basement of St. John's Church, hiring a lay teacher, Michael Hanrahan. The school was of short duration. In Sandwich, when the school attended by most Catholic children closed in 1892, Father Clinton thinking this an injustice rented space, outfitted a classroom with books and supplies and engaged a teacher from Boston, Miss Mary Murphy. The school was very successful but it functioned for only one year. The Jarvisville School reopened. The parish couldn't afford a long term commitment and apparently Father Clinton's point had been made.

Catholic Schools flourished with the coming of religious Sisters and Brothers. The Sisters of Mercy and the Sisters of the Holy Union of the Sacred Hearts were pioneers in the English speaking parishes. The Sisters of Mercy opened a school in their convent soon after their arrival in St. Mary's Parish in Fall River in 1874. The Holy Union Sisters came to Sacred Heart Parish in Fall River in 1886. Among the French Canadians the Religious of Jesus-Mary arrived first, coming to Notre Dame Parish in Fall River in 1877. The were followed by the Holy Cross Sisters who replaced two French speaking Sisters of Mercy at St. Anne's School in Fall River in 1883, the Dominican Sisters of St. Catherine of Siena who came in 1891 from Carrolton, Missouri to St. Dominic's in Fall River, while still a mission of St. Anne's and the Sisters of St. Joseph who came from France to St. Rock's Parish in Fall River in 1902. The Sisters of Charity, the Grey Nuns, came from Quebec to care for orphans, but they taught briefly in schools also.

A few of the schools began with lay teachers before the coming of religious Sisters and Brothers. At Notre Dame Parish, the school began a year before the Sisters came and in 1882, Father Bedard began a school for boys with a layman in charge. In 1893 the Brothers of Christian of Christian Schools began teaching the boys there and two years later at St Anne's Parish in Fall River. In 1885 the French-speaking community in Fall River's north end with the permission of Father Boylan at St. Joseph's, established a school prior to the founding of St. Mathieu Parish and at St. Jean Baptiste mission in Fall River a school was started in 1898 which was staffed by lay teachers.

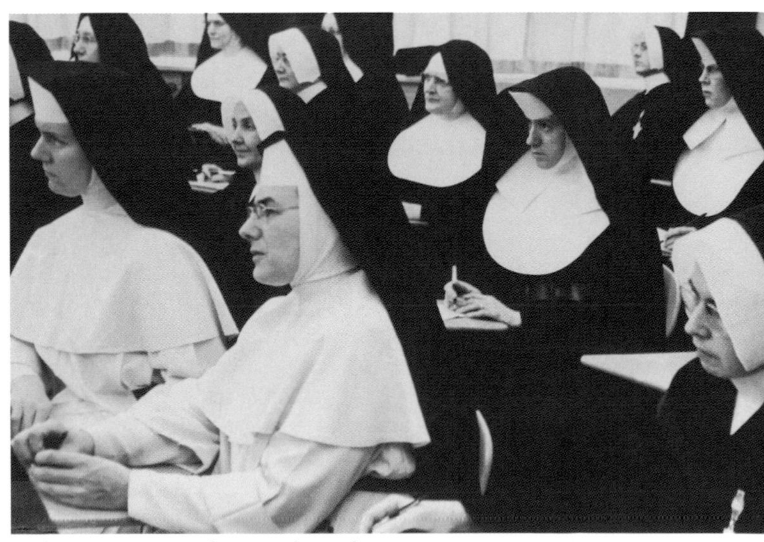

Religious Sisters of several teaching communities at a convention about 1960

The present St. Vincent's Youth Residential Education Center

In addition to the academy established at Notre Dame Parish in Fall River in 1877 by the Religious of Jesus-Mary, two other schools for girls were established in the city. The Holy Union Sisters opened Sacred Hearts Academy in 1886 and the Dominican Sisters of St. Catherine began Dominican Academy when they moved into their new convent on Park Street in 1895. Henceforth the community was familiarly known as the "Park Street" Dominicans. In St. Lawrence Parish in New Bedford, St. Joseph's High School began in 1884 with two classes and the first graduation took place in 1887. The school was succeeded by The Holy Family High School in 1904. In 1897 the Brothers of the Christian Schools opened St. Anne's Commercial School in Fall River.

The Sick and the Orphan

There were no Catholic charitable institutions in southeastern Massachusetts until St. Joseph's Hospital in New Bedford opened in 1873 in the first year of Bishop Hendricken's ministry. The next institution was an orphanage at Notre Dame Parish in Fall River. At first the Religious of Jesus-Mary cared for orphaned children from both Canadian and Irish families in their convent beginning in 1881. Two years later Father Bedard provided a separate building to house the children. On January 1, 1890, the Sisters of Charity of Quebec better known as the Grey Nuns took over the care of the orphans. Father Prevost built a new building called St. Joseph's Orphanage, which was dedicated on July 16, 1893. Children from the French Canadian parishes in the entire Diocese of Providence were cared for here. In September of 1885, St. Vincent's Home opened in Fall River under the care of the Sisters of Mercy. Bishop Hendricken purchased Forest Hill Gardens, a picnic grove and summer resort

The former Holy Rosary Church and School in New Bedford built as the Guardian Angels Day Nursery.

along the Taunton River in the Steep Brook section of the city. The Sisters sold some of the buildings. They kept the hotel and out buildings and with discarded lumber built a two-room school building. Bishop Harkins took great interest in St. Vincent's and directed that income from the Catholic cemeteries, which he reorganized, should go to home. In June of 1894 a new building was dedicated. St. Mary's Home was established in New Bedford with the support of the pastors of St. Lawrence, St. John the Baptist and St. James Parishes. The Franciscan Sisters of Glen Riddle, Pennsylvania, agreed to staff the home whose new building was dedicated by Bishop Harkins on September 30, 1894. The home was to be financially supported by a diocesan collection for the orphans taken up each year on Easter Sunday. The Sisters cared for a small number of elderly men and women as well as children from the English and Portuguese speaking parishes of New Bedford. In November of 1896 the Asylum of the Guardian Angels, a day

St Anne's Hospital nursing students with Bishop Connolly seated between Mother Pierre Marie, O.P. and Sister Madeleine Clemence, O.P.

nursery for pre-school children with the Holy Cross Sisters in charge, was opened by Father Charles Gaboury in Sacred Heart Parish in New Bedford to assist mothers who had to work. It was situated in a two story wooden building on Acushnet Avenue near the Wamsutta Mill. The first floor accommodated the nursery while the second floor became a chapel. In later years this work was also carried on by the White Sisters, more formally, the Daughters of the Holy Spirit, who came from Brittany to St. Mary's Parish in Fall River in May of 1903, where they also began their wonderful work of nursing the sick in their homes. To materially assist the White Sisters, the Bishop established a local affiliate of the Association of the Queen's Daughters. At the same time, Saint Anne's Hospital, another great institution of charity was being planned. On April 17, 1902, Bishop Harkins met at St. Anne's Friary with Father Grolleau and a group of about 20 Catholic physicians who wished approval to investigate the possibility of a Catholic hospital in Fall River. The Bishop gave guarded approval stating all pastors must be supportive. A committee comprised of Doctors Dolan, Cummings, Keily, Bane and Rosa was formed to meet with the pastors. On February 24, 1903, the Bishop again approved of the project as long as St Anne's Parish was not financially liable. In April of 1904 Father Grolleau obtained the services of the Dominican Sisters of Charity of the Presentation of the Blessed Virgin Mary whose motherhouse is at Tours in France. In September of 1905 the Sisters arrived to begin their blessed ministry, which happily endures to the present.

7. The Parting of the Ways

The geography of the Diocese, with territory in two states, invited periodic rumors about a division. In 1886 when nominating candidates for the vacant See of Providence, the question of a division was brought up and two years later when Cardinal James Gibbons, Archbishop of Baltimore, stopped in Providence the press thought sure the creation of a new diocese with its See in Fall River was in the offing. On one occasion in 1896 Archbishop Williams and Bishop Harkins discussed the matter and tabled it waiting for better economic times. In 1903 Matthew Harkins was 58 years old and had been Bishop for fifteen years. In these years, he had shown himself a tireless and zealous shepherd. He was consistently available to his priests and he treated them with respect and patience. He made his way around the Diocese, visiting parishes; he traveled usually by train but often in the cities he made his way on foot between various rectories and convents for visits and meetings. In southeastern Massachusetts he had established 20 parishes, encouraged parish schools, was concerned about the care of orphans and the elderly and supported plans for a hospital. Bishop Harkins was particularly solicitous in his care of Religious Sisters, frequently making himself available to them for spiritual direction and the sacrament of Penance. He showed equal and edifying concern for his own spiritual life, going regularly to the Dominican Friary in Fall River for what he refers to in his diary "monthly retreat" or what we might call a day of recollection. He avoided national church controversies but he wholeheartedly supported the Catholic University at Washington and he was loyal to the Sulpician Fathers who had trained so many American priests. In January of 1903 he brought up the question of the division of the Diocese of Providence again with Archbishop Williams and with the Archbishop's approval the question was placed on the agenda of the spring meeting of the Bishops of the Boston Province scheduled for April 15. There were now 295,000 Catholics in the diocese and a total of 86 parishes. The Bishops supported the petition and Bishop Harkins prepared formal documents, which he presented to the Apostolic Delegate in June. In September, Archbishop Williams was requested to submit a list of names of possible candidates for the office of bishop of the new diocese. In accordance with the procedure laid down by the Third Council of Baltimore, Archbishop Williams called the Diocesan Consultors and Father Hugh J. Smyth, Permanent Rector of St. Lawrence in New Bedford to meet with him in Providence on October 6, 1903, in order to receive from this body the names of three possible episcopal candidates. On October 13 the Bishops of the Province met to draw up their slate of candidates, all to be sent to the Apostolic Delegate. The press now began speculating. The list of potential candidates included Fathers Thomas P. Grace of St. Mary's in Providence, William Stang of St. Edward's in Providence, Jean A. Prevost of Notre Dame de Lourdes, Fall River, as well as Father Smyth, and Auxiliary Bishop John Brady of Boston. On February 22, 1904, the Congregation of the Propagation of the Faith voted to recommend to Pope Pius X the Diocese of Fall River be established and that William Stang be named its first Bishop. The "great amputation" as the wags in Providence liked to call it had taken place.

Father Stang, as a seminarian at the Catholic University of Louvain in Belgium, had responded to an appeal made by Bishop Hendricken for priests to come to the Diocese of Providence to care for German immigrants. William Stang, the son of Francis Joseph and Frances (Bellm) Stang, was born on April 21, 1854, at Langenbrucken in the Grand Duchy of Baden near the town of Bad Schonborn in the present German state of Baden-Wurttemberg, south of Heidelberg. Shortly after his ordination on June 15, 1878, Father Stang came to Providence. He served at SS. Peter and Paul Cathedral until 1885, when he was appointed pastor of St. Ann's Parish in Cranston. After two years, he came back to the Cathedral as Rector. In 1887 he became the Bishop's principal assistant in preparing for the Third Synod of Providence. All the while he was providing pastoral care for German-speaking parishioners in Providence and beyond. In 1885 he gave a mission in New Bedford to German speaking immigrants who had found employment there as textile workers and glass blowers. Early in 1892 Bishop Harkins placed Father Stang in charge of the fund-raising campaign for St. Joseph's Hospital in Providence and the Bishop relied on him to see to many of the details involved in the establishment of the new institution. In 1894 Bishop Harkins received a request from the Rector of the American College at Louvain in Belgium to allow Father Stang to return to his alma mater to serve as Vice Rector, but because of his responsibilities connected with the new hospital, the Bishop declined to release him until the hospital was completed. Within a week of the dedication of the Hospital on March 19, 1895, Father Stang set sail for Europe. At the American College, he served as vice rector and taught a course in Pastoral Theology for which he wrote a textbook and not in the customary Latin but in English. The work remains today an object of interest to those studying the history of seminary education. In 1898 Father Stang was appointed professor of fundamental moral theology at the University. He served in this capacity for one year when Bishop Harkins called him home, feeling the need of his assistance in the administration of the Diocese. Returning in June of 1899 Father Stang was appointed chancellor and secretary to the Bishop. Father Stang also encouraged Bishop Harkins to establish a diocesan mission band devoted to preaching missions to Catholics and non-Catholics. Known as the Providence Apostolate, the first band was made up of four priests including Father Stang, the superior. The Apostolate took its inspiration from the work of the Paulist Fathers. In November of 1901 Father Stang was appointed pastor of St. Edward's parish in Providence but he continued to serve as the superior of the Apostolate. In connection with this work Father Stang wrote a popular exposition the Catholic faith called *Spiritual Pepper and Salt For Catholics and Non Catholics.* William Stang was engaged in these good works when in March of 1904, he was named first Bishop of Fall River.

Crosier presented to Bishop Stang by the people of St Edward's Parish in Providence

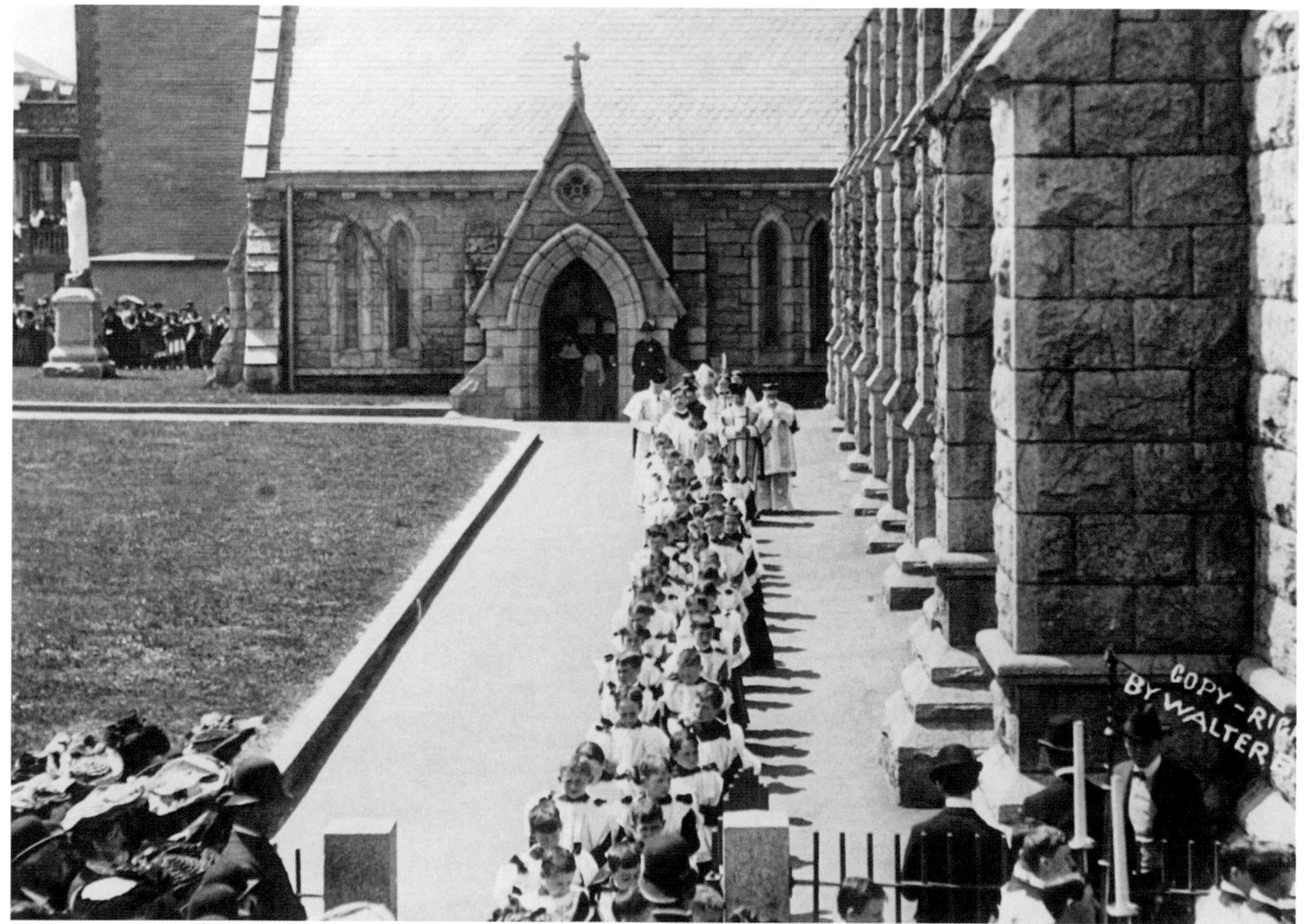

Bishop Stang entering St. Mary's Cathedral to take possession of the Diocese, May 8, 1904

Part Four

The New Diocesan Church: Fall River, Now Sister to Crete and Ephesus

On Sunday, May 1, 1904, William Stang was ordained a bishop in the Cathedral of Saints Peter and Paul in Providence by Matthew Harkins assisted by Michael Tierney, Bishop of Hartford and John Brady, Auxiliary in Boston, in the presence of the Archbishop, John J. Williams and three other bishops, Henry Gabriels of Ogdensburg, John S. Michaud of Burlington and William H. O'Connell of Portland. The preacher, James Coyle, pastor of St Mary's Parish in Taunton eloquently proclaimed..."and so brethren, the long ago is again here... as Titus was appointed to the see of Crete and Timothy to that of Ephesus, so today ...another pontiff begins his reign. Ephesus and Crete across the ruined centuries salute Fall River, as a sister diocese and the name of its first ordinary is now written as indelibly as that of Titus and Timothy in the archives of the Church of God... We have unquestionably come to the parting of the ways. The old guides, the old friends will be sadly missed... we part with a prelate whom we revere, a clergy that was the apple of our eyes but we bear away with us the sturdiest of champions, the priestliest of priests, the toilers of toilers-Fall River's first and honored Bishop."

Bishop Stang on the day of his consecration in Providence May 1, 1904. At the left with co-consecrators Bishops Michael Tierney and John Brady.

Bishop Stang from the reviewing stand at the old St. Mary's Rectory greeting members of organizations marching to welcome him on May 8, 1904

1. All Too Short: The Ministry of Bishop Stang

On May 2, Bishop Stang celebrated Mass at St. Edward's Parish where two weeks before the parishioners had presented their pastor with his crosier. At that time, he responded "I trust the great Spirit of God will not only fill me with the strength and light of God, but give me what I need now, joy and cheerfulness. For I am not only going to be a bishop but the Bishop of a new diocese... I shall carry this crosier after it has been blessed to Massachusetts where in time many men will take the crosier now lying before you and look back to the first one who used it and the example set by him." On Wednesday, Bishop Stang arrived in Fall River to take up residence at St. Vincent's Home referred to simply as Forest Hill on the Bishop's stationery. On November 4, the Bishop was able to move into the former Baptist Parsonage at Winter and Cherry Streets that Bishop Harkins had purchased for a Bishops' Residence. On the Sunday following his ordination, May 8, 1904, Bishop Stang took possession of his Diocese with the celebration of a Solemn Pontifical Mass at St. Mary's Church now the Pro-Cathedral. The decree establishing the Diocese was read by Bernard F. McCahill, pastor of Saints Peter and Paul Parish in Fall River who also preached the sermon. Bishop Stang spoke briefly at the end of Mass before bestowing his blessing. In the afternoon, what the newspapers called a "Monster Demonstration" took place. This was a parade of Catholic societies and parishioners numbering several thousands, which the Bishop reviewed with clergy from a stand set up in front of St. Mary's Rectory then on the east side of Second Street. The newspapers further report that about 25,000 people came from beyond Fall River by train and trolley to join in welcoming the new Bishop; about 10,000 from the Providence area, 5,000 from New Bedford, nearly 4,000 from Taunton and another 4,000 from Newport. The first act of the new Bishop had been to confirm the faculties granted to the clergy by the Bishop of Providence and to appoint Father Hugh J. Smyth, Permanent Rector of St Lawrence parish in New Bedford, Vicar General of the new Diocese and Father James E. Cassidy, assistant at St. Mary's Parish in North Attleboro, Chancellor and Secretary to the Bishop. Shortly thereafter the Bishop asked the priests to submit names of priests for possible appointment as diocesan consultors. On June 1, the first meeting of the Board of Consultors took place; the members were Fathers Smyth, Charles Gaboury, Christopher Hughes, James Coyle, James F. Roach and Jean A. Prevost. Michael J. Cooke was appointed Defensor Matrimonii of the Diocesan Tribunal. Bishop Stang had the advantage of being thoroughly familiar with the clergy and parishes of the new diocese, since the territory had been part of the diocese of which he had been a priest for over twenty- five years.

Bishop William Stang

Bishop Stang took his motto from the Book of Sirach, 39:17 which is translated Bear Fruit By Streams of Waters.

Getting Started

The Bishop could without breaking stride take up where Bishop Harkins left off and there were numerous projects in various stages of progress. In addition to the administration of the sacrament of Confirmation, there were also churches to be blessed. The first such blessing, together with the confirmation of 130 children, was celebrated on May 12, 1904, at the newly constructed basement church of the Sacred Heart in Taunton, which the Bishop thought quite beautiful. There followed on June 5, the laying the cornerstone of St. Anthony's Church in New Bedford after the Bishop reviewed a

Monsignor Hugh J. Smyth, P. R.

parade of 2,800 marchers. The dedication of the basement church of Our Lady of the Holy Rosary of Pompeii in Fall River took place on July 10, complete with brass band and on July 16, the Bishop blessed Our Lady of Mt. Carmel Church in New Bedford. On August 7, the dedication of St. Francis Xavier Church in Hyannis took place and near the end of the year on November 24, Bishop Stang dedicated Blessed Sacrament Church in Fall River.

The constantly growing population demanded the division and addition of parishes. At a certain point, Bishop Harkins felt it proper to leave these decisions concerning Massachusetts parishes to the bishop of the new diocese. The first parish to be established in the new Fall River Diocese was Espirito Santo, on July 8, 1904, to care for the needs of the Portuguese people of the east end of Fall River. Bishop Stang would establish a total of 11 parishes, 2 for Portuguese, 3 for French Canadians, 1 each for Germans and Cape Verdians and 4 territorial parishes. In addition he sent a resident pastor to Holy Trinity Church in Harwich Center where no pastor had resided since 1873. The Bishop appointed George Maguire pastor with the care of several mission stations on the lower Cape. The Bishop later remarked in reference to the material situation there, that he had been deceived. The majority of Father Maguire's parishioners were Cape Verdian immigrants who found work in the expanding cranberry industry. One parishioner became the center of a sad chapter in local history. Frank Pina, father of nine children was diagnosed with leprosy and separated from his family. When vigorous public protests to a leper colony in Brewster were made, the Commonwealth of Massachusetts purchased Penekese, one of the Elizabeth Islands, in Buzzards Bay. Cottages and a hospital building were built and in November of 1905. Frank Pina and four other lepers were brought to the island. They were well cared for but completely isolated from family and friends. Father Stanislaus Bernard. SS. CC. from Our Lady of the Assumption Church in New Bedford and state officials were the

The first Our Lady of Assumption Church, New Bedford

only visitors. Fifty patients lived there between 1905 and 1921, when the patients were transported to Carville, Louisiana where a leprosarium had been established by the Federal government. About the only visual reminder of the leper colony is the small cemetery of 16 graves.

The first priest of the Diocese of Fall River, Edward F. Coyle was ordained by Bishop Stang in his home parish, St. Mary's in Taunton on June 26, 1904. Father Coyle spent his entire priesthood as a seminary professor in the Society of St. Sulpice. He died in 1954, the year of his Golden Jubilee and that of the Diocese. On December 11, 1904, the Bishop ordained Pierre Louis Damase Robert of Montreal in St. Mathieu Church in Fall River. The two remaining priests to receive ordination from Bishop Stang, John B. deValles, a native of St. Michael in the Azores who had grown up in New Bedford and Joseph P. Lyons of North Easton were ordained at St. Mary's Pro-Cathedral on June 22, 1906. In Lent of 1905 the Bishop accompanied by Mortimer Downing, chaplain at St. Vincent's Home and director of Diocesan Charities made a canonical visitation of parishes, noting in each the condition of sacred furnishings, the altar, tabernacle, sacred vessels and confessionals, as well as the sacramental registers and financial account books. After Easter, the Bishop on May 12, 1905, announced the convocation of a Diocesan Synod to promulgate legislation for the guidance of the clergy and faithful of the young diocese. The priests were invited to send suggestions to Fathers James Coyle and Raymond Grolleau, O.P. The formal session of the synod took place at St. Mary's Pro- Cathedral. On June 28, 1905, one hundred ten priests participated including ten Dominicans and three Sacred Hearts Fathers.

Bishop Stang knew the Sacred Hearts Congregation in Belgium. The community had sought a foundation in the Diocese of Providence. When their friend became the Bishop of Fall River, he was very happy to welcome the community to the Diocese.

The former St. Boniface Church, New Bedford

An attractive piece of property, seven acres and a spacious house for a residence, had been purchased in Fairhaven and in May of 1905, three priests and two brothers arrived. The Bishop imme-dia-tely placed three new parishes in the care of the Sacred Hearts Fathers, St. Joseph's in Fairhaven, and two in New Bedford, St. Boniface for the small German community and Our Lady of the Assumption for immigrants from Cape Verde. From Fairhaven, the Fathers also began to celebrate Mass in Mattapoisett where a former Advent chapel became the first St. Anthony's Church in 1908.

First-Born of a Saint

Not long after the synod, on August 7, 1905, Bishop Stang embarked on his *ad limina* visit to the tombs of the apostles, Peter and Paul in Rome and to make a report of his stewardship to the Holy Father and then to visit his home in Germany and to spend some time at the University of Louvain in Belgium. On September 7, 1905, Bishop Stang was received by the Holy Father, Pope Pius X. The Bishop described the audience in a letter to the priests of the Diocese. He wrote that when he reminded Pius X the Diocese of Fall River was the first established by the Pope in the United States, the Holy Father replied, "you are my very dear child because you are my first born."

When the Bishop arrived home on November 12, 1905, he took up his residence in a new home at 394 Highland Avenue. The purchase of the red brick residence built by Job Leonard the "Iron King" took place on June 29, 1905, at 2:00 p.m. according to Bishop Stang's journal and the price was $18,600. The Bishop apparently had second thoughts concerning the house for in September he cabled Father Cassidy from Lisbon, the laconic message, "Sell Leonard mansion" and a few weeks later on October 10, he wrote from Germany that he had not changed his mind, however apparently bowing to the inevitable, he cabled his approval to sell the Winter Street property on October 20. On October 23, Father Cassidy notified the priests that the Chancery Office would be located at 394 Highland Avenue beginning, October 25, 1905, and on November 3, Dr. P.E. Truesdale opened his first hospital at 163 Winter Street. Bishop Stang noted his arrival home in his journal, writing"... found the chancellor busy working." The busy and determined chancellor had been rewarded with a photograph personally autographed by the Holy Father, Pope Pius X, and the Vicar General shortly after the Bishop's return was honored with the dignity of domestic prelate, which was formally conferred on Monsignor Smyth at a Solemn Pontifical Mass celebrated at St. Lawrence Church on January 16, 1906.

Other significant events followed throughout 1906. On February 4, Bishop Stang blessed St Anne's Hospital founded and financed and still under the dedicated direction of the Dominican Sisters of the Presentation of Mary. On July 4, Archbishop Diomede Falconio, OFM, the Apostolic Delegate came from Washington to officiate at the dedication of St. Anne's Church. A few months later on November 30, Notre Dame de Lourdes Church was dedicated by Bishop Harkins with Bishop Stang celebrating of the Solemn Pontifical Mass.

Shepherd and Scholar,

Amidst this pastoral activity, Bishop Stang never overlooked his responsibility as chief teacher in the local church. He wrote three Lenten pastoral letters, *The Christian Family* in 1905, *Christian Marriage* in 1906 and *Christian Education* in 1907, published after his death. In April of 1905 Pope Pius X released his encyclical *Acerbo Nimis* on Catechetics and in response to and in support of the Holy Father two month's later Bishop Stang published a pastoral entitled, *The Teaching of the Catechism.* Bishop Stang's interests were universal in scope and both academic and practical. In addition to his previous writings, he found time as Bishop to translate a life of Martin Luther, write a manual of Moral Theology in Latin and a book contrasting Socialism and Christianity. He was a teacher, a missionary, writer and a pastor. He heartily endorsed the American Federation of Catholic Societies, a group recently founded to bring together Catholic laity and Catholic societies to better promote and protect Catholic interests in education, charity, social justice and civil rights. The Bishop also hoped this Federation might be able to bring together Catholic societies separated along national and ethnic lines. In November, he invited Bishop James A. McFaul of Trenton, a founder of the Federation to address an assembly of 2500 men at the Bijou Theatre in Fall River. Also at this same time, the Bishop was very concerned for the many people suffering the devastating effects of a strike of textile mill operatives. It had begun in July when a 12.5% cut in wages was announced. Eventually 71 mills were closed and 25,000 people were out of work. In the fall, the Bishop met on separate occasions with the committee of manufacturers and union leaders, Thomas O'Donnell and James Tansey. Bishop Harkins allowed the St. Vincent de Paul Society of Fall River to seek donations from the priests and faithful of the Diocese of Providence and on October 23, 1904, Bishop Stang, preached an appeal on behalf the poor and suffering in the Providence Cathedral. Through the intervention of the Governor the strike ended in January of 1905 with ultimately no gain for the workers except there was work for all who had remained in the city. Philip T. Silvia remarks that this was the first time Catholic priests openly sided with the workers. Bishop Stang refrained from commenting on the strike itself but in his book, *Socialism and Christianity,* in the chapter entitled, *Not Socialism, But Social Reform,* the Bishop wrote "is there no human weapon with which he (the working-man) may defend himself against a cruel, greedy employer? As long as the cause is just, he has the right to strike... At present they (strikes) are frequently the only power in the hands of the working people to restrain the despotism of capital."

The Bishop's concern for "the material and spiritual growth and development" of the Diocese led him to request Archbishop Williams to cede the remainder of Plymouth County excepting Hingham to the Diocese of Fall River. The copy of the Bishop's letter is undated but in May of 1906 both Bishop Stang and Bishop Harkins mention in their journals that the 84-year-old Archbishop did nor receive the proposal favorably.

Amid his many activities Bishop Stang remained a loyal supporter of the American College at Louvain and its alumni. He was also devoted to the interests of German-American Catholics in the Diocese and beyond. Once, his arrival at St. Lawrence Rectory in New Bedford coincided with a sick call from a German-speaking parishioner to which the Bishop responded at once. On occasion, he heard the confessions of German parishioners at St. Kilian's Church, as indeed he regularly heard confessions in his Cathedral Church.

In the latter part of 1906, he admits in his journal to feeling unwell. After medical consultation in Fall River and Boston, it was decided he should undergo surgery at the Mayo Clinic. He remained active up to the moment of his departure. On January 16, 1907, he attended a festive banquet hosted by the Knights of Columbus. The next day he recorded the final entry in his journal, "said Mass and left for Minnesota." The Bishop was accompanied by his friend Monsignor Thomas F. Doran, Vicar General of Providence. The surgery took place on January 21. Dr. William J. Mayo reported the removal of a tumor of the sigmoid intestine which he believed to be "a diverticulitis non-malignant." Initially the Bishop was reported as progressing well, but in the days before anti-biotics, infection could be fatal, and the Bishop died on Saturday, February 2, 1907, at St. Mary's Hospital in Rochester, Minnesota. When his body reached Fall River on Monday evening, it was escorted by 1200 men through falling snow, which during the night turned into a howling blizzard, which prevented the attendance of the venerable Archbishop Williams at the Funeral. Bishop Harkins celebrated the Mass in the presence of William H. O'Connell, coadjutor of Boston, Archbishops Louis Begin of Quebec and Paul Bruchesi of Montreal, and Bishops Thomas D. Beaven of Springfield, Michael J. Tierney of Hartford, Louis S. Walsh of Portland, Edward P. Allen of Mobile, Camillus Maes of Covington, and John Brady, Auxiliary of Boston Father James Coyle who preached so eloquently less than three years before at Bishop Stang's ordination, now had the sad duty of pronouncing the eulogy, which was equally eloquent. He said, "Fall River mourns as well she may her mitred prince and dons the sable of personal sorrow. Her heirloom for many cycles to come, will be the example and teaching of him whose career was all to short, her first Bishop."

Sede Vacante

For five months Monsignor Hugh J. Smyth served as administrator of the Diocese. The vacancy would have an impact on the beginning of the new Bishop's tenure. Two events made the period memorable. A controversy arose over the administration of St. Patrick is Cemetery in Fall River. It seems that Father Mathias McCabe, pastor of Sacred Heart Parish, took the opportunity of the vacancy to exert his authority at St. Patrick's Cemetery. While he had originally established the cemetery, Bishop Harkins had reorganized the administration of the cemeteries so the income would benefit St. Vincent's Home. Bishop Stang had appointed Father Cassidy director of cemeteries, and he reacted swiftly to Father McCabe's intrusion on his authority. Monsignor Smyth tried to remain aloof from the controversy, but when drawn into it, he acted by appointing Father Michael J. Cooke of St. Patrick's Parish director of the cemetery, instructing Father Cassidy to turn over all cemetery records to Father Cooke. Father Cassidy did not comply maintaining that he never received any such order. All these events were fully treated in the daily press. The second event of notoriety concerned the transfer of several priests occasioned by the deaths of two pastors. When James Clark, the pastor of St James in New Bedford, died on May 24, 1907, and Bernard McCahill, pastor of SS. Peter and Paul Parish in Fall River, died on June 25, Monsignor Smyth filled these vacancies, making transfers affecting the pastors of the parishes of St. Kilian's, in New Bedford, St. Francis Xavier in Hyannis, Immaculate Conception in North Easton, Corpus Christi in Sandwich and assistants at Sacred Heart in Taunton and St. Lawrence in New Bedford. Some of the appointments were made after press dispatches considered reliable by most, reported the appointment of a new Bishop, Daniel Francis Feehan, a priest of the Diocese of Springfield and pastor of St. Bernard's Parish in Fitchburg.

Picture autographed by Pope Pius X for Father James E. Cassidy at the request of Bishop Stang

2. Strength in Numbers: Before and After the First World War

Daniel F. Feehan, the son of William and Joanna (Foley) Feehan had lived his entire life in Worcester County except for his college and seminary years. He was born in Athol on September 24, 1855, but when Daniel was 3 years old his father, a blacksmith, moved the family to Milbury where he attended school. Here, he became the friend of the future President of the United States, William H. Taft, who would come from Ohio during the summer to visit his grandparents. Following graduation from St. Mary's College in Montreal, Daniel Feehan entered St. Joseph Seminary in Troy, New York where he was ordained to the priesthood by Bishop Francis McNeirny of Albany on December 20, 1879. His first assignment was assistant to Philip J. Garrigan, pastor of St. Bernard's Parish in Fitchburg. In October of 1886, Father Feehan was appointed pastor of St. Anthony's parish in West Boylston. Two years later in the fall of 1888 Father Garrigan was asked to take the post of Vice Rector of the Catholic University in Washington. Father Feehan was sent back to St. Bernard's to be administrator for one year and the Permanent Rector for the next eighteen years. The Brief naming Father Feehan second Bishop of Fall River was dated July 2, 1907. Given the state of affairs in Fall River, the Bishop-Elect was encouraged to assume jurisdiction before his consecration and so he presented his credentials to the Board of Consultors on July 31. The Bishop's consecration, the first episcopal ordination to be celebrated in St. Mary's Cathedral, took place on September 19, 1907. Bishop Thomas D. Beaven of Springfield was the consecrating prelate, assisted by Bishops Matthew Harkins of Providence and Michael Tierney of Hartford. The preacher was Bishop Feehan's former pastor and predecessor in Fitchburg, Philip J. Garrigan, then Bishop of Sioux City. The new Bishop's mother, sister and aunt were also present to share in the joy of the occasion.

Bishop Daniel F. Feehan

While Bishop Feehans's tenure is the longest of any Bishop of Fall River, his personality remains elusive. From newspaper accounts at the time of his promotion, we learn he was highly regarded in Fitchburg as a priest dedicated to his parishioners and to the good of the community. Under his care, St Bernard's Parish became known for its beautiful liturgical ceremonies enhanced by an outstanding choir. The soft-spoken pastor was known as a good preacher, equally capable in French and English; and his devotion to the children and to the parochial school was extolled by all. Civic leaders praised his strong support of temperance, his ministry at the Fitchburg jail and his efforts in the work of reforming juvenile offenders.

On the day he assumed administration of the Diocese, the Bishop-Elect wrote to the priests of the Diocese saying "I come with no new message to you. I come to correct no abuses, to institute no reforms, to punish no guilty persons, but to encourage a holy and united priesthood and through this priesthood to endeavor to spread the kingdom of God in the Diocese." He began at once to take up the ministry laid down by Bishop Stang, administering confirmation, visiting parishes, and blessing new churches. However, the Bishop apparently felt he could make no appointments until he resolved the question of the pastoral appointments made during the vacancy of the Diocese.

Having consulted canon lawyers and the Apostolic Delegate, he embraced the opinion that without the authorization of the Holy See, the administrator had acted unlawfully. Rather than ratifying the appointments, Bishop Feehan in December directed the pastors to return to their former parishes and the assistants to be prepared for other assignments. The priests obediently complied, but all appealed their cases to Rome. On January 1, 1908, the Bishop announced various appointment including new diocesan consultors and the retention of Father Cassidy as chancellor, but no Vicar General was named. A month later on February 8, Bishop Feehan took formal possession of St. Mary's Cathedral announcing that the title Pro-Cathedral was no longer to be used implying that he had no plans to build another Cathedral as had been Bishop Stang's desire. At the same time the Bishop announced he had reluctantly accepted the retirement of the ailing Father Christopher Hughes and was appointing Father Cassidy rector of the Cathedral in his place. Father Cassidy remained chancellor while the recently ordained Louvain graduate, Edward J. Carr became secretary to the Bishop. Near the end of 1908, Father Cassidy asked to be relieved of the office of chancellor and was succeeded again by Father Carr. A few weeks later, on January 11, 1909,

Bishop Feehan with co-Consecrators Bishops Matthew Harkins and Michael Tierney and master of ceremonies Father Thomas J. McGee

Bishop Feehan appointed Father Cassidy Vicar General, ending a year of speculation among the clergy, laity and press. Concerning the controversial pastoral appointments, the final note was sounded on January 31, 1910, when the press reported that a decision of the Congregation of the Council had been approved by the Pope. Two questions had been submitted to the Congregation. To the first question, whether diocesan administrators in the United States have the authority to appoint pastors, no formal answer was given; to the second, whether the decision of the Bishop should be upheld, an affirmative answer was given.

The beginning of Bishop Feehan's ministry coincided with a period of prosperity. Textile manufacturing flourished in Fall River and New Bedford and continued to attract immigrant workers and the children of immigrants who had settled in rural areas of New England. By 1920 the population reaches almost 130,000 in each city. At the same time in Taunton, the population was close to 40,000. Long a manufacturing center for the iron industry, whose citizens could proudly boast that a Taunton locomotive drew the train that carried the body of Abraham Lincoln across the country, stoves continued to be made here, as well as fine silverware. Attleboro, where the jewelry trade flourished, became a city in 1914 and soon had a population of 20,000 people. Fall River had in 1910 the highest percentage of residents of foreign birth or with one foreign-born parent of any Massachusetts city, 86.9%. These figures would obviously be reflected in the church's pastoral activity. Bishop Feehan established 38 parishes, 8 for

Church goers traveled in style to St. John the Baptist Church in Westport

French Canadians, 7 for Portuguese, 4 for Polish people, 2 Maronite parishes, 1 Italian parish, and 16 territorial parishes. The list testifies to the abiding needs of non-English-speaking people as well as the growing population beyond the cities. The electric streetcar and the automobile made it possible for more people to stay in the countryside or to move there from the cities. The venerable missions at Wareham and Norton were raised to parochial status and Wellfleet, Swansea, Dighton, Westport, Seekonk, Acushnet, and Osterville welcomed their first resident pastors. A few of the parishes in the towns were national parishes and others had a prevailing ethnic strain but Holy Ghost Parish in Attleboro had to be unique for on the day of the dedication Father Patrick S. McGee from neighboring Hebronville spoke in English, French, Portuguese, and Italian. In need of Polish priests, Bishop Feehan welcomed the Franciscan Conventual Friars to the Diocese in 1922.

As parishes were multiplied so did the number of Catholic schools increase. By the end of Bishop Feehan's active years, there were 34 elementary schools, 2 parish high schools, Holy Family High School in New Bedford and St. Mary's High School in Taunton established in 1911 and four private girls academies, Jesus-Mary, Sacred Hearts, Dominican in Fall River and Sacred Hearts in Fairhaven. The Fathers of the Sacred Hearts had hopes of establishing a college in Fairhaven. They constructed one building and had plans drawn for another. The college never became a reality, but for a few years beginning in 1908, they conducted a boys' academy known as Fairhaven College. On Christmas Day, 1922, Bishop Feehan announced at the Cathedral he intended to build a high school in Fall River on recently acquired land opposite the Superior Court on North Main Street. Plans were drawn for a fine coeducational school but for some reason they were never carried out. Possibly the parcel of land proved too small for the projected school.

The Blessing of St. Kilian's Church in New Bedford by Bishop Feehan in 1927

Sacred Heart Home, New Bedford

Spreading the Kingdom of God Near and Far

Bishop Feehan with years of experience as pastor of a city parish was quick to recognize the many social and material needs of working people. When he came to the Diocese, he found three orphanages. Under his guidance the Bethlehem Home was opened on Summer Street in Taunton to care for infants and young children. The home, dedicated on October 4, 1909, was placed in the care of the Sisters of Mercy. In 1913 Bethlehem Home was enlarged to care for 60 children. A chapter of the Queen's Daughters was formed in 1914, numbering 250 women, and the maintenance of Bethlehem Home became their special apostolate. In 1928 a decision was made to close the home in favor of placing children in private homes. The Bishop Stang Day Nursery in Fall River was dedicated to the Bishop's memory on August 14, 1910. It was adjacent to the convent of the White Sisters who cared for the children. St. Francis Guild, a residence where women working away from home could find safe and comfortable lodging, was established on Whipple Street in Fall River in 1912 and placed under the supervision of the Franciscan Missionaries of Mary. The Sisters came first to New Bedford in 1906 at Bishop Stang's invitation to do catechetical work among Portuguese-speaking children. In 1910 the Sisters came to Fall River taking up residence in the former Mercy Convent of St. Catherine on Second Street. In the fall of the year they began their long and fruitful teaching apostolate in the new Espirito Santo School, the first school founded in a Portuguese-speaking parish in the United States. The Sisters of Charity of Quebec also established a residence for workingwomen in New Bedford in 1917, but in 1920 they received permission to discontinue this work in order to devote themselves to the care of the elderly in what would become The Sacred Heart Home. Another Diocesan facility, Cathedral Camp was originally organized as a parish program for youngsters by Father Francis McKeon, assistant at St. Mary's Cathedral. After a few seasons in various locations near Fall River, including Horseneck Beach, the summer camp found an excellent site on Long Pond in East Freetown in 1919. This became permanent when the Diocese purchased the former trolley park the next year. A chapel and retreat house was soon added to the complex, and the first retreats for the clergy were conducted there in May of 1923.

Bishop Feehan assisted by Msgr. Jean A. Prevost laying the cornerstone of St. Patrick's School, Fall River in 1915

The First World War and the terrible influenza epidemic of 1918 brought special concerns. Eight diocesan priests served as chaplains during the war. Monsignor Osias Boucher, later pastor Blessed Sacrament in Fall River, was decorated for bravery in France and after the war served as a chaplain in the Reserves attaining the rank of Brigadier General, but it was Father John B. DeValles who received the most popular acclaim. He was awarded the Croix de Guerre for bravery at Apremont in April of 1918 and the Distinguished Service Cross. News of the latter award arrived from Washington and was communicated to him about a half hour before he died at St. Luke's Hospital in New Bedford on May 12, 1920. His funeral was the occasion for a great demonstration of respect and patriotism. The only chaplain to die on active duty before the Armistice was also a Fall River priest. Father Simon O'Rourke assigned to the Boston Navy Yard died of influenza in Fall River on September 20, 1918. Within a month, three other young priests succumbed to influenza, Fathers James C. J. Ryan, assistant at Immaculate Conception Parish in North Easton, Matthew D. Lowney, assistant at Sacred Heart Parish in Taunton, and Francisco L. Jorge, assistant at Our Lady of Mt. Carmel in New Bedford. At the height of the epidemic in October of 1918, Bishop Feehan excused the faithful from the obligation of attending Mass on two Sundays and forbade the celebration of public Mass. He placed church facilities at the disposal of public authorities for use as emergency hospital wards, and priests and Sisters responded heroically in caring for the sick.

Knowing that not every need could be taken care of by a charitable institution. Bishop Feehan wished to provide for the multiple needs of families and individuals, many of them temporary. To this end, he announced the formation of a central Catholic Charities bureau under the direction of Father Charles A. Donovan with offices in Fall River and New Bedford. The Bishop hoped the bureau would be of assistance to priests in the parishes in providing solutions for difficult cases through "able leadership and methodical effort in the field of Catholic social service." In the report given for the first eight months of 1926, we learn that 640 families were received as clients and 412 of the cases had been resolved and closed.

Bishop Feehan showed his great concern for spreading the kingdom of God beyond his own diocese by permitting Fall River priests and seminarians to respond to the call of a missionary vocation especially as Maryknoll Missioners or to serve as seminary professors often in the Sulpician Society. The first to be ordained for Maryknoll was John J. Toomey from Holy Name Parish in New Bedford, who entered Maryknoll in 1918. Ordained in June of 1922, Father Toomey left for the Far-East in September. He described his voyage and arrival at his mission in South China in a fascinating letter to Bishop Feehan. The Bishop also permitted two young priests to join Maryknoll. Father Antonio Paulhaus, assistant at Notre Dame Parish, who went to China with Father Toomey and Father John E. Morris, assistant at St. Joseph Parish in Fall River. Sent to Korea, Father Morris served from 1930-1936 as Prefect Apostolic of Peng-Yang, which later became the Diocese of Pyongyang. He lived to be 98 years old, dying at Maryknoll in 1987. Other early Maryknollers from the Diocese were Fathers William Fletcher, John J. Considine, and autority on mission work, and first director of the American Bishops Latin American Bureau, and two future bishops, Frederick A. Donaghy, who was detained by both the Japanese and the Chinese Communists and after being expelled from the Diocese of Wuchow, spent many years as a missionary in Taiwan, and Joseph W. Regan, Prelate of Tagum in the Philippines, who delighted congregations with his stories when he came home to make mission appeals. Many were to follow these pioneers. The Maryknoll Sisters also received many vocations from the diocese as well, among them Sister Rita Marie, Bishop Regan's only sibling. In the band of six Sisters who left for China in 1921, two were from Fall River, Sister Mary Lawrence Foley and Sister Mary Monica Moffatt.

Father John B. DeValles standing second from left with fellow World War I chaplains

About the same time Archbishop Austin Dowling of St. Paul, Minnesota was in need of priests to teach in his seminary. Bishop Feehan released three men about to be ordained priests for this work, William O. Brady, James L. Connolly, and Francis J. Gilligan. They were quickly dubbed by their students "the three wise men from the east." Father Brady would become the Archbishop of St. Paul, Father Connolly the Bishop of Fall River, and Monsignor Gilligan, a respected advocate of racial equality. After retiring as a pastor, he served as the Director of the Propagation of the Faith in St. Paul until his death at 98.

As he reached his mid seventies, it seems Bishop Feehan began to develop what was called hardening of the arteries or senility. He celebrated the complete liturgy of Holy Week and Easter for the last time in 1929. In March of 1930 the Vicar General, Monsignor James E. Cassidy, was named Auxiliary Bishop and consecrated on May 27 at St. Mary's Cathedral by the Apostolic Delegate, Archbishop Pietro Fumasoni-Biondi, assisted by Bishops George A. Guertin of Manchester and Joseph J. Rice of Burlington. As evidence of Bishop Feehan's growing incapacity, on October 3, 1930, Bishop Cassidy was appointed Apostolic Administrator. On the evening of July 19, 1934, Bishop Feehan died at a summer home at Cataumet on Cape Cod. Bishop James Anthony Walsh, Superior General of Maryknoll, was the eulogist at the funeral Mass, which was celebrated by Bishop Cassidy on July 23, at the conclusion of which Bishop Feehan was laid to rest in the Cathedral churchyard beside Bishop Stang.

Perhaps the best insight into the heart and soul of Daniel F. Feehan can be found in his own words written on June 1, 1925, concerning the newly founded Catholic Charities Bureau. "Cognizant of my own responsibility before God towards those of my children, who stand in greatest need of love and encouragement... I have set my mind and my heart to the work of organizing the charities of the diocese. It is my desire to make the Office of Catholic Charities a sanctuary where the poor and the helpless may bring their burdens and through their Catholic religion receive aid, both spiritual and temporal, that will restore them to normal Christian living."

3. Courage and Sacrifice: Depression and War

Although it was learned on July 12, 1934, that Bishop Cassidy had been appointed Coadjutor with the right of succession, Bishop Feehan died before the proper documents arrived from Rome and the appointment really never took effect. Consequently Bishop Cassidy was appointed third Bishop of Fall River by Pope Pius XI on July 28, 1934, and the Bishop formally took possession of the See on September 2, when in a simple ceremony he presented the letter of appointment to the Diocesan Consultors at a Mass celebrated at St. Mary's Cathedral.

James Edwin Cassidy was born in Woonsocket, Rhode Island, on August 1, 1869, to Irish immigrant parents James and Mary Ann (Burns) Cassidy. He graduated from Woonsocket High School in 1888 and in 1890 entered St. Charles College in Maryland to prepare for the priesthood. From 1893 to 1896, he studied at St. Mary's Seminary in Baltimore completing two years of philosophy and one of theology while taking courses in chemistry, physics, and biology at Johns Hopkins University. With this background, he began teaching science at New York's St. Joseph Seminary at Dunwoodie in the fall of 1896 at the same time continuing his own theological formation. On September 8, 1898, the seminarian-professor was ordained to the priesthood in Providence by Bishop Harkins. At the conclusion of the academic year of 1899, Father Cassidy was given a summer assignment at St. John's in Attleboro, after which he spent a year at the Sulpician House in Rome taking courses in moral theology at the Propaganda University and in dogmatic theology at the Minerva. Upon his return in the summer of 1900 he was appointed assistant at St. Mary's Parish in North Attleboro until Bishop Stang appointed him chancellor of the new Diocese of Fall River in May of 1904.

Bishop James E. Cassidy

Vigorous Notions of Life

The influence of James E. Cassidy on the Diocese of Fall River in the first fifty years of its existence was singular. He served successively as chancellor, rector of the Cathedral, Vicar General, Auxiliary Bishop, Apostolic Administrator and Diocesan Bishop. He is quoted as saying once to a gathering of parishioners "I have always had very vigorous notions of life. I have always tried to measure up to my place in the organization, which God has set up." His convictions were deeply held, and since he was a person of action who seemed to thrive on competition, he often advanced his causes by public debate. An early indication of his indepen-dence took place in September of 1905 at the laying of the cornerstone of the first St. Joseph's Church in Fairhaven. Father Cassidy gave the sermon. Without mentioning specific names, he chose to draw a comparison between the humble wooden combination church and school the Sacred Hearts Fathers were building and the magnificent gothic church being built nearby for the Unitarian congregation by Fairhaven native, philanthropist and Standard Oil executive, Henry Huttleston Rogers.

The one he described as "built of the wealth and surplus of the mighty rich... a great Goliath, typical of the power and pride of individual exaltation. And in its shadow rises the new born infant, David, humble and lowly and unassuming erected to the honor of the sacramental Christ... (built) of the hard earned pennies of the laboring poor." The chancellor went on to say while it would be shameful not to love and hand on cherished customs and memories of the old country. He called the present a transition period in which people need churches where various languages are spoken. Father Cassidy maintained that "if in this country we are to be the power God intends we must be united in faith, we must be united in energy, we must be one in tongue and that tongue the language of the nation." The talk created a sensation. The newly arrived Sacred Hearts Fathers were embarrassed before their neighbors. The French and Portuguese clergy were annoyed over the language issue. Throughout his pastoral ministry at St. Mary's Cathedral 1908-1913 and then as pastor at St. Patrick's Parish in Fall River 1913-1934, Bishop Cassidy became well known by his powerful public statements on moral and social issues, many of them caught up in national and local politics. The address to departing troops in World War I, entitled *What Fight Ye For?*, brought a complimentary letter from former President Theodore Roosevelt, but on another occasion he so angered the Mayor of Fall River, John T. Coughlin, that he journeyed to Washington in 1910 to complain about Father Cassidy to the Apostolic Delegate. A lifelong advocate of temperance, he vigorously opposed the licensed saloon and each time the issue appeared on the ballot he spoke forcefully from the pulpit and the platform at temperance meetings that sometimes drew over two thousand men. In this, he would have had the support of Bishop Feehan, a less vehement but equally ardent temperance man. When Monsignor Cassidy was named a prelate in 1912, Bishop Feehan noted the honor was "in large measure a recognition of his courageous attitude on matters pertaining to the general morale and public good of Fall River."

The years of his episcopal ministry spanned the decline of the textile industry, the great depression, and the Second World War. In 1928 cotton operatives in Fall River and New Bedford were the lowest paid in the state. For example, the average weekly wage in February of that year was $17.10 in Fall River, 19.74 in New Bedford, 24.04 in Attleboro and 25.37 in Taunton. A 10% reduction in wages had induced a devastating strike in New Bedford. Very likely hoping to spare his people in St Patrick's Parish, 90% of whom were mill people whose wages had also been cut, the effects of a disastrous strike, he wrote a 22 page paper, *Americanization or Africanization Which shall It Be? A Study of Industrial Peonage In The Cotton Industry.*

One of several windows by John LaFarge obtained for the former St. Patrick's Convent in Fall River

Diocesan School Supervisors, Sister Miriam O'Neil R.S.M., and Sister Felicita Heffernan, R.S.M.

Monsignor James Coyle

The masterful study describes in stark detail the attempt of a mill operative to support a wife and family of three children on $15 a week, discounts the value of a strike because it is wanting in one essential aspect, hope of success, and calls for a congressional investigation. When the full force of the depression struck, the Bishop urged people to have confidence in the banks, in the President, in themselves, above all in God. The Bishop called for a conference of the St. Vincent de Paul Society to be established in every parish and directed that the parish conferences receive the proceeds of the collections taken up at holy day Masses. In February of 1932 a Catholic Conference on Industrial Problems, one of several held around the country, but the first to deal with the textile industry, was hosted by Bishop Cassidy in New Bedford. One of the speakers was Father John A. Ryan, of the Catholic University and director of the Social Action Department of the National Catholic Welfare Conference.

Catholic Education

In June of 1932 the Apostolic Administrator made his first diocesan appointments. Father James J. Gerrard succeeded Father Edmund J. Ward as Chancellor, and in November Father Henry J. Noon, pastor of St. James Parish in New Bedford was named Vicar General. Father Edward J. Gorman was appointed superintendent of schools. This marked the beginning of the Catholic School Department. Father Gorman's predecessors, Fathers Francis J. Bradley, Edward J. Carr, and Damase Robert, called supervisors of schools, directed a far less centralized organization. Other significant developments took place in the education field about this time. The Bishop broke ground for a high school to be built on the former Bethlehem Home property in Taunton in March of 1932. The school was named for Monsignor James Coyle, recently deceased pastor of St. Mary's Parish in Taunton, whose dream it was. The School staffed by the Brothers of the Holy Cross opened in September of 1933 with 160 students in four grades; sixty upperclassmen transferred from St. Mary's High School, which would continue as a girls' high school. Three other secondary schools opened during Bishop Cassidy's time. In 1934 the Brothers of Christian Instruction added high school grades at Monsignor Prevost School in Fall River, in 1940 a parish high school staffed by the Holy Cross Sisters was begun at St. Anthony's Parish in New Bedford, and in 1946 the Sisters of Mercy opened an academy for girls at Mt. St. Mary's Convent in Fall River. In June of 1934 the Sacred Hearts School of Education, a normal school for Religious teaching in schools, was opened under the auspices of the Holy Union Congregation with Father Gorman as its director. Bishop Cassidy who had received an honorary degree from Notre Dame University in 1932 was pleased to welcome the Holy Cross Fathers from Notre Dame into the Diocese a year later when they purchased the former Crary Hospital property on Tucker Road in Dartmouth. Here in September of 1934 they opened their college seminary. A year later in October of 1935 the Ames estate in North Easton was acquired by the Congregation. The seminary eventually moved there and the novitiate and mission house were located in Dartmouth. In 1948 at the North Easton site, the Congregation of the Holy Cross opened Stonehill College with an enrollment of 140 students and Taunton native, Father George P. Benaglia, C.S.C., as first president.

The Sick and Old and the Youth

On August 2, 1932, the Dominican Sisters, Servants for the Relief of Incurable Cancer opened the Rose Hawthorn Lathrop Home at the former Bay View Sanatorium, which had been purchased in their name for $ 1,000 by Bishop Cassidy in January. This was the beginning of an extraordinary ministry to the sick and a witness to Christ-like charity. Soon the Catholic Memorial Home came into being. The Misses Ellen and Julia Sullivan bequeathed the sum of $71,000 to provide a home for the aged in Fall River in memory of their parents, Michael and Julia Sullivan. In April of 1937 the Bishop called the clergy together to enlist their help in providing the balance of the cost of a home, which was then estimated at $175,000 exclusive of the chapel. A Diocesan Drive was conducted from June 6 to June 16 that year under the direction of Father Raymond T. Considine and over $200,000 was raised. The drive was a forerunner of the annual Catholic Charities Appeal begun in 1942. The handsome colonial style building overlooking the Taunton River was blessed on June 30, 1939. The home and its residents were placed in the care of the Carmelite Sisters for the Aged and Infirm. In 1945 the Sisters took on another commitment here when Bishop Cassidy purchased the former Tabitha Inn in Fairhaven and converted it into a home for the aged to be known as Our Lady's Haven.

Stonehill College, North Easton

Young people especially underprivileged children had always been a concern of Bishop Cassidy. The camp on the Westport Adamsville line operated by St. Anne's Hospital for children with special needs was turned over to the St. Vincent DePaul Society in the summer of 1938. Bishop Cassidy was a supporter of Scouting and in March of 1938 he appointed Father James E. Gleason Catholic Scout Chaplain and on the feast of Christ the King in 1939 the Bishop blessed flags and insignia at the Cathedral. The event was to become an annual one for boys and girls in Scouting and Camp Fire programs. About the same time the Catholic Youth Organization was established locally, also with Father Gleason as chaplain. The Anawan Hall, originally the property of the Young Men's Irish American Catholic Benevolent and Temperence Society, was purchased by the Diocese for a

Catholic Memorial Home, Fall River

Our Lady's Haven, Fairhaven

Catholic Community Center. Auxiliary Bernard J. Sheil of Chicago, the founder of the CYO, was guest speaker at the dedication in December of 1940.

Bishop Cassidy inaugurates the basketball court at the Taunton CYO Center

The End of an Era

On September 21, 1938, New England was struck by a hurricane and accompanying storm surge. Loss of life and property was extensive in the coastal communities of the Diocese. Father George Jowdy, pastor of New Bedford's Maronite Parish of Our Lady of Purgatory, drowned at his nephews' summer cottage at Sconticut Neck in Fairhaven. Two churches were lost, St. Mary's in New Bedford and the St. Rose of Lima Chapel at Horseneck Beach in Westport. The Bishop reported the Diocese suffered a loss of $100,000 from the hurricane and the cost of lowering the damaged spires of Notre Dame Church would be $25,000.

As the years went on, Bishop Cassidy continued to crusade on behalf of temperance asking confirmation candidates to take a pledge to abstain from intoxicating liquor until age 21. When confirming in national parishes, he would usually concede that wine could be taken safely in the cultural atmosphere of the old world; he is quoted as saying "there is no harm in a glass of beer or a glass of wine in proper surroundings, but over indulgence is at the base of many crimes and accidents. The Bishop also warned of the evils of divorce and birth control, calling them the new" fifth column." He sponsored lectures on the dangers presented by the Communist party in this country and on the Civil War in Spain. The motion picture industry came in for sharp criticism from the Bishop in a campaign against indecent "talkies" launched in Lent of 1934. After a referendum on the ballot in 1938 to allow pari-mutuel betting on horse and dog racing was successful, the Bishop made unusual personal appearances at public hearings to voice his opposition to the possibility of horse racing in Westport and dog racing in Wareham.

The Bishop's ad limina visit to Rome in 1939 caused him to be present at the coronation of Pope Pius XII and to be one of the first Bishops in the world to be received by the new Pope. The Pope on his visit to this country as Vatican Secretary of State in 1936 did not formally visit the Diocese of Fall River, but he did visit Cape Cod privately with Bishop Francis J. Spellman. The proprietress of the little Italian restaurant where the prelates dined preserved for many years the chair on which the future Pope sat. In the very same year, another Cardinal did make a visitation of the Diocese. In September of 1936 the Patriarch of Lisbon, Cardinal Manuel Goncalves Cerejeira, visited the various Portuguese parishes and was joyfully received by the clergy and faithful. The Cardinal's visit was closely followed by two other events of importance to the Portuguese community. On December 10, 1939, Bishop Cassidy was honored by the government of Portugal, which conferred upon him the Crimson Cross of a Grand Official of the Order of Christ at a ceremony held in St. Anne's School Auditorium. The next year, the 800th anniversary of Portuguese independence was celebrated with a service at St. Mary's Cathedral on September 22, 1940. The Bishop appealed for more Portuguese American vocations to the priesthood and religious life saying "The priests that Portugal and the Azores have sent us are worthy of their high calling. The priests who have been ordained from among the Portuguese living here are a great glory to God, to His priesthood, and to the parents who have offered them. But they are too few and the immediate future cries for more native-born Portuguese priests." Europe was now at war and Bishop Cassidy urged everyone to pray daily for the protection of Portugal, which stands today alone as the peaceful nation in Europe.

Msgr. Antonio P. Vieira is congratulated on the 75th anniversary of his ordination in 1963 by Cardinal Richard J. Cushing together with Bishop Gerrard and Bishop Connolly

The Bishop had returned from abroad in the spring of 1939 realizing the threat of another war hung over Europe, and he was very much against any American involvement. With many other Americans, the Bishop was to alter his opinion in the months ahead. Even before Pearl Harbor, the former Music Hall on Franklin Street in Fall River, which the Diocese had purchased became a USO facility under the National Catholic Community Service for the benefit of the growing number of servicemen. It was inaugurated on November 21, 1941, with Bishop John F. O'Hara, C.S.C. Auxiliary to the Military Vicar, the principal speaker. The Bishop turned Cathedral Camp over to the government for a military police base. He visited nearby military bases, celebrating Mass and administering Confirmation. His thoughts on the war were set forth in a twelve page paper, *Japan's War on the United States,* printed and distributed in churches on January 18, 1942. Drawing on his own impressions and experiences during a trip to the Far East to take part in the Eucharistic Congress in Manila in 1937, he outlined Japan's long planned treachery against the United States. The piece attracted the attention of the Boston papers and a surprising number of people wrote seeking copies of the booklet. Another notable expression of patriotism was the dedication of the monument to George Washington, which is located directly across Highland Avenue from the Bishop's residence. The Bishop announced the plan in May of 1940. Extolling the gift of religious freedom Americans enjoy and lamenting the absence of monuments to Washington and Lincoln, the Bishop said "the founders, those who gave... everything they possessed for this land are not honored in Fall River. Yet some who gave us nothing are monumentalized and memorialized." The Bishop said he would appeal to the children of the Diocese to contribute ten cents a month to finance the monument. In fact, he refused to accept contributions from adults. By the time the monument was finished the whole country was deeply involved in the war. The dedication took place with a good deal of fanfare on the beautiful afternoon of July 4, 1942, in the presence of civic and military officials including Governor Leverett Saltonstall and Senator David I. Walsh. Archbishop Francis J. Spellman of New York was the principal speaker. Twenty priests had volunteered to serve as chaplains. One made the supreme sacrifice. Captain Arthur C. Lenaghan died on January 7, 1944, from wounds

Priests of the Diocese serving as chaplains in World War II

The George Washington Monument in Fall River, dedicated July 4, 1942

received on the battlefield in Italy. His body was returned home and Bishop Cassidy celebrated his funeral Mass at St. Mary's Cathedral on January 31 with Archbishop Spellman, the Military Vicar, in attendance. Just before the end of the war in Europe, it was announced that Bishop Cassidy was to receive the assistance of a Coadjutor Bishop with the right of succession, Fall River native, James L. Connolly, Rector of the Seminary in St. Paul, Minnesota. On May 24, Archbishop John Gregory Murray ordained Bishop Connolly in St. Paul. The new Bishop celebrated a Solemn Pontifical Mass in St. Mary's Cathedral on June 7, in the presence of Bishop Cassidy and Archbishop Richard J. Cushing of Boston. Archbishop Murray gave the sermon. Later in the year, Bishop Connolly was appointed pastor of Sacred Heart Parish in Fall River, and following the death of Monsignor Henry J. Noon in 1947, he became Vicar General. Bishop Cassidy continued to be active, only gradually ceding responsibilities to Bishop Connolly. On May 8, 1945, V-E Day, Bishop Cassidy offered a Low Mass in the Cathedral, overflowing with grateful worshipers. On V-J Day, August 14, people streamed to an evening Holy Hour at the Cathedral one half hour after victory over Japan was announced. The next morning on the feast of the Assumption Bishop Cassidy preached at the Solemn Pontifical Mass offered by Bishop Connolly. A month later on September 18, Bishop Cassidy offered a Solemn Pontifical Requiem Mass for the 700 servicemen from the Diocese who died in the war.

Bishop Cassidy following a Confirmation celebration within a few days of his death

On November 1, 1950, the Bishop presided at a Pontifical Mass, commemorating the solemn definition of the dogma of the Assumption by Pope Pius XII, celebrated by Bishop Connolly in the Cathedral dedicated under the title of Mary's Assumption. The Bishop was very aware this church would soon celebrate its hundredth anniversary and was in need of renovation. He had formed a committee to study the project, and on Easter Sunday, March 25, 1951, the Bishop announced the need to provide "a new garment for the mother church of the diocese." It was a work that was close to his heart. As rector, he had supervised the previous renovation completed in 1913, which gave the Cathedral substantially the appearance it has today. The oak wainscoting, pews, Bishop's cathedra, and sanctuary windows date from that time. After Easter, the Cathedral was closed and work began in earnest. The pews and furnishings were removed so the floor could be taken up to examine the foundation. The remains of Father Edward Murphy and his nephew, Father James Murphy, buried beneath the side altar near the Lady Chapel were re-interred in the Bishop's Crypt under Bishop Cassidy's personal supervision. The remains of a third priest, Father Thomas Kealey, who had died visiting here, could not be found, causing some anxiety. Finally, his remains were discovered on Tuesday, May 15, and on Wednesday buried in St. Patrick's Cemetery with Bishop Cassidy present. That night shortly after retiring the Bishop became ill and at 1: 15 on Thursday morning, May 17, 1951, Bishop Cassidy died. Bishop Connolly, Father Considine, and the Bishop's physician, Dr. Joseph Norman, were at his bedside. Bishop Connolly celebrated the funeral Mass on Tuesday morning, May 22, 1951; it had to be at Sacred Heart Church since St. Mary's Cathedral was closed. Archbishop Cushing gave the eulogy and at the conclusion of the Mass the cortege proceeded to St. Mary's Cathedral crypt where Cardinal Spellman officiated at the committal rite.

4. A Time For Hope: World Peace and The Second Vatican Council

James

James Louis Connolly was born in Fall River on November 15, 1894. His mother Agnes McBride was the second wife of his father, Francis Connolly. It was a family of five sons and two daughters. James graduated from St Patrick's School in 1909 and from Durfee High School in 1913, the same year Monsignor Cassidy became the Connolly family's pastor. Originally considering an engineering career, the future bishop decided to follow his brother Bernard on the path to the priesthood. After studies at St. Charles College, St. Mary's Seminary in Baltimore, and the Theological College of the Catholic University in Washington, James L. Connolly was ordained by Bishop Feehan on December 21, 1923. He spent the summer of 1924 as assistant at Our Lady of Lourdes Parish in Wellfleet and was formally transferred to the Archdiocese of St. Paul in August of that year, before being sent by Archbishop Austin Dowling to the Catholic University of Louvain for graduate studies. In 1928, Father Connolly earned the degree of Doctor in Historical Sciences. His dissertation on Jean Gerson, fifteenth century reformer, mystic, and chancellor of the University of Paris, is still highly regarded. Father Connolly returned to serve in the minor and major seminaries of St. Paul until he was called home in 1945 to be Coadjutor Bishop. Several hours after Bishop Cassidy's death, Bishop Connolly presented the Papal Brief naming him Coadjutor with the right of succession to the Board of Diocesan Consultors, thereby becoming the fourth Bishop of Fall River.

Bishop James L. Connolly, Sc.H. D.

Post War Expansion

The years of Bishop Connolly's tenure were years marked by great activity in the life of the church running parallel to the post war expansion and prosperity in society in general. The church's great concerns were the threat of communism and the dangers presented by a rising secularism, as well as a new wave of anti-Catholic sentiment, perhaps inspired by the fear of a Catholic Church with a rising number of well-educated and affluent members. As one involved for many years in higher education, a recurrent theme in Bishop's Connolly's preaching and writings in his early years as Bishop, was the responsibility of those in academic life to develop ideals rather than to question them, creating cynicism and skepticism. In 1954 he received the George Washington Medal from the Freedoms Foundation in Valley Forge for a sermon he gave warning against the threat to freedom from those in academia who would espouse a philosophy at odds with our religious and social heritage. The post war activity of the Communist party in the area was dramatically revealed in the testimony of Armando Penha, counterspy for the FBI on March 19, 1958, before a special session of the U.S. House of Representatives Committee on Un-American Activities in Boston. Mr. Penha, a member of St. Mary's Parish in Fairhaven, recounted that he was able to persuade leaders from carrying out a bomb plot to kill author and lecturer, Louis Budenz, former editor of the Communist Daily Worker who had returned to the Catholic Church, as he sat on the stage of New Bedford High School. The occasion was a lecture sponsored by the Holy Family High School Alumni Association on November 28, 1954. Five hundred people were in the audience and six people were on the stage with Mr. Budenz including Monsignor James J. Gerrard, Vicar General of the Diocese.

Bishop Connolly was able to preside over two significant anniversaries. The hundredth anniversary of the construction of St. Mary's Cathedral was observed of October 8, 1952, with Archbishop Cushing presiding and preaching. The Golden Jubilee of the Diocese of Fall River was observed in 1954. By happy coincidence, the founder of the Diocese Pope Pius X, was canonized a saint that same year on May 29. On June 2, a civic reception was held at St. Anne's School. Archbishop Cushing was the principal speaker. Bishop Connolly spoke on behalf of the clergy and religious and Judge Joseph L. Hurley for the laity. The following morning Bishop Connolly celebrated the Solemn Pontifical anniversary Mass in honor of St. Pius X. Fall River native, Bishop William O. Brady of Sioux Falls and later Archbishop of St. Paul preached the memorable sermon.

CCD and The Lay Apostolate

In the six years he was Coadjutor Bishop and pastor at Sacred Heart Parish, Bishop Connolly was able to get to know the younger priests and the pastoral needs of the diocese. The Bishop also brought to his new ministry knowledge and experience of pastoral life and practice in the mid-west, gained during his time in Minnesota. His first concern appropriately enough for a former seminary rector was for vocations to the priesthood. Within a month the Bishop called for a novena of prayer and the following spring, he instituted the custom of gathering high school students and eighth graders for an annual Mass of the Holy Spirit for Vocations and later promoted the introduction of the Serra Club to foster and encourage vocations in families and schools. To further involve the laity in the mission of the church the Bishop welcomed the Legion of Mary, founded the Family Life Bureau to provide the

New Bedford Knights of Columbus 50th anniversary banquet in 1946

Delegation from the Diocese at the convention of the National Council of Catholic Women in Pittsburg in 1979

Pre-Cana seminars for engaged couples and the Cana programs for married couples, and organized a Diocesan Council of the National Council of Catholic Women. The Council was inaugurated on June 3, 1953, at the first evening Mass celebrated in the Diocese of Fall River. The Bishop asked Carolyn B. Manning of New Bedford to be the first President. Mrs. Manning had served several years as National Regent of the Daughters of Isabella. During the same period, Catholics in various professions showed a desire to organize themselves into societies and guilds to foster their own spirituality and to promote apostolic works. Among them were the Guild of St. James, which played a key role in organizing a national guild of Catholic Pharmacists, and the St. Luke's Physicians' Guild formed in 1953. A Catholic Nurses Guild had existed since Bishop Feehan's time, as well a Guild for the deaf and hard of hearing. In 1951 Bishop Connolly founded the Catholic Guild for the Blind, which was incorporated in 1954 with chapters in Fall River, New Bedford, Taunton, and Attleboro.

The Bishop, convinced of the necessity of involving the laity in the work of religious education, especially of public school students, was ever a firm supporter of the work of the Confraternity of Christian Doctrine. Bishop Stang in his 1905 pastoral letter had endorsed the Confraternity, and in 1938 Father Gorman, the Superintendent of Schools, was named director of the Confraternity by Bishop Cassidy and proceeded to draw up a diocesan curriculum. Two communities of religious women were devoted to catechetical work. The Victoryknoll Sisters came in 1953. Their convent was in West Harwich, but the scope of their activity extended to Chatham and Wellfleet. In this work, they joined the Missionary Servants of the Blessed Trinity, who began doing catechetical work at Holy Ghost Parish in Attleboro in 1939 and subsequently opened cenacles in Wareham, Osterville, Hyannis, and at Holy Name Parish in Fall River. To further this important work, Bishop Connolly appointed Father Joseph L. Powers Diocesan Director of CCD independent of the Diocesan School Department in 1957. Training sessions were provided for lay catechists, and in 1960 Bishop Connolly directed the CCD executive board be established in every parish. The Bishop also encouraged the building of parish centers to provide the best possible setting for CCD classes. The Diocese hosted the New England CCD Congress in 1954 and 1965. At the same time modern communications began to be used locally as a vehicle for spreading the church's message. A limited radio apostolate was begun with a brief news commentary by Father John E. Boyd and also the recitation of the rosary by Bishop Connolly. A decade later, when WLNE-TV Channel 6 was established in New Bedford, the Sunday Mass began to be televised. The celebration of Mass, which was carried live from the studio for several years, began on September 24, 1963. Meanwhile a diocesan newspaper, *The Anchor*, began publication on April 24, 1957. The paper was managed by Fathers Daniel F. Shalloo and John P. Driscoll with Attorney Hugh J. Golden as the first editor. It was to become in terms of circulation the largest weekly in southeastern Massachusetts.

Ministry In Parishes, The City Center, Among the Spanish - Speaking

As the Catholic population continued to increase, new parishes and new churches were needed. Immigration from the Azores increased dramatically. A series of volcanic eruptions and earthquakes in the islands near Fayal in 1957 and on Sao Jorge in 1960 and 1964 caused legislation to be passed admitting the victims of these disasters to the United States. Since immigration had been minimal for the past few decades due to restrictive quotas and the uncertainties caused by depression and war, some parishes had to begin again to care for considerable numbers of immigrant parishioners. On June 20, 1957, at a formal banquet at Lincoln Park, the Portuguese ambassador on behalf of his government conferred the Crimson Cross of a Grand Official in the Order of Christ on Bishop Connolly.

From 1951 to 1969, in addition to reopening St. Mary's Parish in New Bedford, which was closed in April of 1939 after the loss of the church in the 1938 hurricane, Bishop Connolly created

Our Lady's Chapel in downtown, New Bedford

St. John the Baptist Ukrainian Church Fall River

St. Anthony of the Desert Maronite Church, Fall River

16 new parishes. In addition, 12 new parish schools were opened, 6 new school buildings replaced older facilities, and 15 parish centers were built.

For decades, the Dominicans at St. Anne's Shrine had provided the people of Fall River during the week with a convenient schedule of Masses, confessions, and devotions. In 1956 at Bishop Connolly's invitation, the Franciscan Friars opened Our Lady's Chapel in downtown New Bedford, and four years later they built a new friary and chapel just to the north of the original chapel on Pleasant Street. The congenial friars soon had many coming to daily Mass and to the sacrament of Penance. That the friars became particularly popular with men is clearly indicated by the reception into the Third Order of 104 men together with Bishop Connolly in January of 1958. The next year the Bishop was honored by being granted affiliation with the First Order in August of 1959.

By the early 1960s the Puerto Rican population had become significant. On February 8, 1961, Bishop Connolly appointed Father Regis Kwiratkowski, SS.CC. "City Missionary" to provide pastoral care for the Spanish-speaking community and a month later the Regina Pacis Centro Catholico opened on South First Street in New Bedford. Masses for Spanish-speaking parishioners also began to be celebrated soon thereafter at St. Mary's Church in Taunton and a few years later at St. Joseph's Church in Attleboro.

The new parishes were mostly in suburban settings, including four on Cape Cod and two on Martha's Vineyard. At the same time, an extraordinary number of older parishes were building new churches. Thirty-three churches were built under Bishop Connolly's supervision, almost one third of the churches in the diocese. The economically minded Bishop revived the plans originally drawn for St. Joseph's Church in North Dighton and used them for several of the new churches. The brick of the original was replaced by white shingles, and with the distinctive colonial cupola, they were quickly named the "Howard Johnson" churches. In 1966 when a diocese was established for Maronite Rite Catholics in the United States, the Lebanese parishes of St. Anthony of the Desert in Fall River and Our Lady of Purgatory in New Bedford were transferred from the jurisdiction of the Bishop of Fall River. A third Eastern rite parish, St. John the Baptist in Fall River founded in 1914 to serve Ukrainian Catholics has always been under the care of the Byzantine Rite Bishops, first in Philadelphia and since 1956 in Stamford, Connecticut.

Our Lady of Purgatory Maronite Church, New Bedford

St. Anne's Hospital, Fall River

Diocesan High Schools and the Nazareth Schools

The most ambitious project of the era was the long-range plan to build four diocesan high schools, one after the other. Each was preceded by a well-organized fund-raising campaign directed by a priest of the area with the assistance of clergy, a lay chairman, and volunteers in all the parishes. The first campaign began in the fall of 1957 in the New Bedford area, and Bishop Stang High School in Dartmouth was dedicated by the Bishop Connolly on November 11, 1959. The Sisters of Notre Dame de Namur had agreed to staff the school. Bishop Feehan High School in Attleboro opened in 1961 under the direction of the Sisters of Mercy. In Taunton, Bishop Cassidy High School for girls was dedicated on May 3, 1963, by Cardinal Spellman. The school replaced St. Mary's High School, but the Holy Union Sisters continued to teach in the new school. Bishop Connolly High School for boys, staffed by the Society of Jesus, opened in September of 1966 in temporary quarters at St. William's Parish Center. The completed school complex was dedicated by the Apostolic Delegate, Archbishop Luigi Raimondi, on October 20, 1967. In May of 1968, fire destroyed Monsignor Prevost High School, and the Brothers of Christian Instruction and their students were accommodated at Bishop Connolly High School. The last class to receive Prevost diplomas graduated in 1972, and the Brothers remained as part of the Connolly faculty. Provision was also made for special education. The first school, Nazareth Hall, opened in Fall River in 1957 under the direction of Sister Maureen Hanley, R.S.M. Two other "Nazareths" opened subsequently in Hyannis in 1960 and in Attleboro Falls in 1969. The Nazareth Schools were major beneficiaries of the annual Bishop's Charity Ball inaugurated in 1956.

Recreational opportunities for youth in a Catholic atmosphere were not neglected. While Fall River and Taunton were provided with CYO centers, New Bedford had none. Bishop Connolly remedied this lack with a $250,000 gift from Ambassador Joseph P. Kennedy and in September of 1957 the Lieutenant Joseph P. Kennedy, Jr., Center was dedicated. Cathedral Camp except in the

Bishop Stang High School, North Darmouth

Bishop Connolly accompanied by Msgr. Humberto S. Medeiros and North American College student, Joseph P. Delaney was received by Pope John XXIII in 1959

Bishop Connoly, High School, Fall River

Bishop Feehan High School, Attleboro

very early years had been exclusively a boys' camp, but in 1960 Our Lady of the Lake Camp, a day camp for girls, opened in East Freetown. In Westport at St. Vincent De Paul Camp, services were expanded to give the Nazareth students an opportunity to experience summer camp.

Hospitals and Homes

Care of the sick and the elderly was advanced also. The homes for the aged in the beginning were more like today's assisted living facilities. Bishop Connolly realized that many residents of our homes as time went on were in need of increasing care and he wished to provide it, beginning with what he called a wing for the chronically ill at the Catholic Memorial Home blessed in 1958. Additions and improvements were also made at Sacred Heart Home and at Our Lady's Haven. Care for the elderly was further expanded with the opening of Marian Manor in Taunton late in 1961 and Madonna Manor in North Attleboro early in 1966. Both homes were staffed by the Presentation Dominicans, and in both instances the Diocese was able to transform former hotels into attractive homes under the direction of Monsignor Raymond T. Considine. At the Rose Hawthorn Lathrop Home, a new convent with a chapel for both sisters and patients was built in 1956. The Bishop had great respect for the competence of Mother Pierre Marie, O. P., for 22 years administrator at St. Anne's Hospital, and

Bishop Connolly wrote on the back of the picture, "some favorite friends from Nazareth Hall, Fall River"

Marian Manor, Taunton

Madonna Manor, Attleboro

together they brought the hospital into a new day. A significant indication of this progress was the appointment in 1969 of Sister Madeleine Clemence, O.P., Ph.D. dean of the nursing school at Southeastern Massachusetts University, now the University of Massachusetts at Dartmouth. In 1962, a community new to the diocese, the Sisters of the Resurrection began the St. Saviour Day Nursery in New Bedford. The Sisters soon became beloved for their devoted care of the children.

Bishop Gerrard

Auxiliary Bishop James J. Gerrard

Early in 1959 Bishop Connolly received the welcome assistance of an Auxiliary Bishop.

In spite of his matter of fact demeanor, Bishop Connolly found the demands of his office at times stressful. In an interview with Everett S. Allen of *The Standard-Times* at the time of his twenty-fifth anniversary as a bishop, he answered a question about the weight of responsibility with candor that was typical "it's a big load if you worry. I've had a couple of breakdowns from lack of sleep but basically you just do what you can." Monsignor James J. Gerrard was consecrated Titular Bishop of Forma by Bishop Connolly on March 19, 1959. Bishop Gerrard, a native of St. James Parish and a graduate of Holy Family High School in New Bedford, was ordained to the priesthood by Bishop Feehan on May 26, 1923. He served as an assistant to Bishop Cassidy at St. Patrick's Parish in Fall River and was named chancellor in 1932 and rector of St. Mary's Cathedral in 1939. Bishop Connolly appointed Father Gerrard Vicar General in 1951 and pastor of St. Lawrence Parish in New Bedford in 1956.

The Council

The latter half of Bishop Connolly's episcopate was focused on the Second Vatican Council, its preparation and implementation. The Bishop attended all four of the sessions of the Council, which opened on October 11, 1962. The chancellor, Monsignor Humberto S. Medeiros, accompanied him as his peritus. Bishop Gerrard attended the final session, as did Monsignor John H. Hackett, Bishop Connolly's secretary and later chancellor. The effects of the Council were felt in the local church in two particular areas, liturgy and ecumenism, before its formal conclusion on

Bishop Frederick A. Donaghy, M.M with Bishop Connolly and Bishop Gerrard at the Second Vatican Council in 1965

December 8, 1965. One of the first evidences of a new spirit of ecumenism fostered by Pope John XXIII was the presence of a delegation of non Catholic clergy at the Mass celebrated by Bishop Connolly at St. Mary's Cathedral following the death of the Holy Father on June 3, 1963. Bishop Connolly established a diocesan Commission for Christian Unity in 1965 and appointed Monsignor Henri A. Hamel chairman. Interim Directives for Ecumenical Activities were drawn up and approved early in 1966. Ecumenical groups and Clergy associations began to take shape in many communities.

Modern liturgical renewal actually began under Pope Pius XII. In 1953 he made the first modifications to the Eucharistic fast allowing water and medicine to be taken before Holy Communion and reducing the fast to three hours from food and one hour from liquids when attending evening Masses. In 1956, the Pope approved the Restored Rites for Holy Week. Just before the third session of the Council convened, English was introduced into the liturgy in this country on September 14, 1964, beginning with the celebration of the sacraments and sacramentals. On the First Sunday of Advent in 1964, the vernacular was introduced at Mass, and its use increased in stages until the Eucharistic Prayer was prayed in English for the first time on October 22, 1967. Certain changes were introduced into the rite of the Mass beginning in 1965, for example, the celebrant facing the people at the altar, the Prayer of the Faithful, and the presentation of the bread and wine by the people.

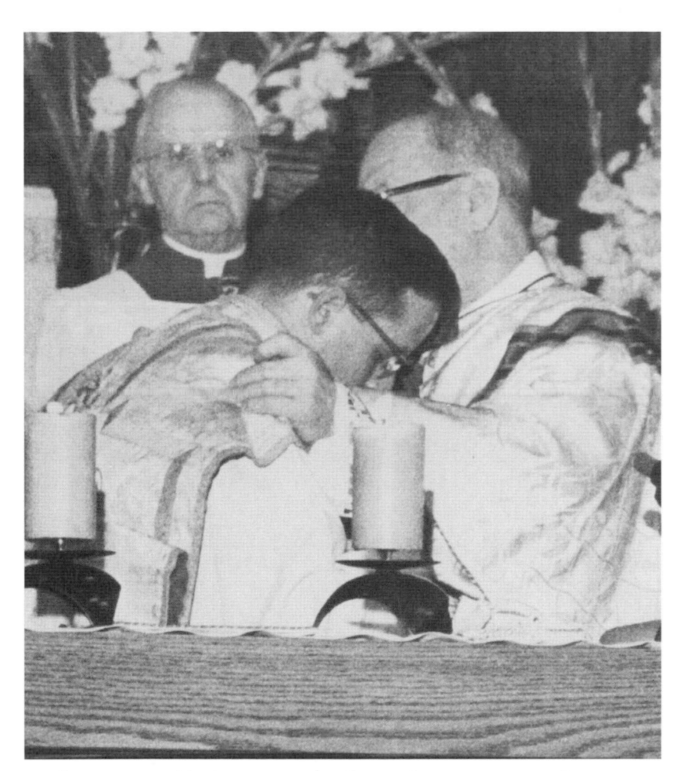

Bishop Connolly bestows the kiss of peace on Father Thomas C. Lopes at the first Ordination Mass celebrated facing the people, February 13, 1965

This led to the new Missal of 1970. Before all these changes careful instruction was given to the clergy. The Bishop had written to Bishop Regan in the Philippines in the spring of 1964 "We are trying to give a good account of ourselves in carrying out the decisions of the Council." At the same time, Bishop Connolly was insistent that priests not exceed the limits of the liturgical directives set down by the Holy See and the Conference of Bishops noting "some unusual and unlawful liberties taken by an overly enthusiastic few." In the whole area of implementation of the Council's directives everyone benefited from the scholarship and organizational skills of Monsignor Medeiros and Monsignor Hackett. To them in large measure, we owe the firm and balanced foundation given to conciliar renewal in the Diocese of Fall River.

Other post-conciliar developments included parish summer assignments in 1966 for deacons approaching the priesthood, the inauguration of the Senate of Priests in the fall of 1966, as well as a Diocesan Pastoral Council made up of 5 laymen and 5 laywomen together with the 22 members of the Priests' Senate. On November 4, 1966, Bishop Connolly directed that Pastoral Councils be set up in every parish. The Bishop did not overlook religious communities. At a meeting at Bishop Stang High School on June 13, 1968, he proposed the formation of a Diocesan Representative Board of Sisters and Brothers. The Bishop who could express profound truths in a clear and almost offhand way

The Shrine Church of Our Lady of LaSalette, Attleboro

reminded the religious the Apostles impressed all converts with the fact that they were community... "I am persuaded no one, priest, religious or layman will ever save his soul alone. We can do a lot of good when we identify with Christ; without Him, no one of us would have much to give, as an individual, but we all have much when we are part of total dedication in community... Let me assure you I have no desire to interfere but to sustain, encourage and help..." In 1966, the first contemplative community of nuns was welcomed into the Diocese. The Discalced Carmelites purchased the formed Sol-e-Mar Hospital in South Dartmouth, and the Monastery of Christ Crucified and Our Lady Mediatrix was blessed in June. In the original community was Sister Agnes Lewin, a native of St. Kilian's Parish in New Bedford, who entered the Roxbury Carmel in 1915.

Lay spirituality was an important concern in the post-conciliar years also. Retreats had been promoted at Cathedral Camp through the Our Lady of Good Council Retreat League and in 1968 the New England Jesuits acquired Round Hills in Dartmouth, the former Colonel Green estate, and for a few years retreats were conducted at this extraordinary site on Buzzard's Bay. In Wareham the Sacred Hearts Community had possessed a house for many years also in a beautiful seaside setting which has been used successively as a seminary, novitiate and retreat house. In Attleboro, where the Missionaries of LaSalette had established a seminary and shrine, in 1942, and the Provincial House of the Immaculate Heart Province in 1946, an attractive retreat center was built in 1964. The first Cursillo was introduced here in November of 1964 by four laymen who had lived Cursillo at the Passionist Retreat House of St. Gabriel in Brighton. From that time, thousands of men and women have lived this experience of spiritual renewal. A few years later, the Cursillo began to be offered at the Holy Cross Retreat House in North Easton.

Archbishop William O. Brady died in Rome in 1961 preparing for Vatican II

In the spring of 1966 the Bishop announced his intention to convene a Diocesan Synod, which no Bishop had done since Bishop Stang. Early in 1967 various commissions were announced and some preliminary work was done, but the synod was never convened. On August 15, 1968, the Bishop promulgated a body of Pro-Synodal Statutes to regulate Catholic life in the Diocese for the foreseeable future. It seems likely the loss of Monsignor Medeiros and Monsignor Hackett dictated this change. In the spring of 1966 came the joyful news that Pope Paul VI had named Humberto S. Medeiros, chancellor and pastor of St. Michael's Parish in Fall River, Bishop of Brownsville. He was ordained by Bishop Connolly at St. Mary's Cathedral on June 9, the feast of Corpus Christi. Six months later on December 6, John H. Hackett who had succeeded Bishop Medeiros as chancellor died of heart disease at age 40. In spite of the loss of these valued collaborators, the Bishop continued on. Eager to encourage and to reward lay participation, in 1968 Bishop Connolly established the Marian Award Medal for service to the local church. Still given annually, it is cherished by the recipients. The next year the Bishop announced plans for a new cottage style St. Vincent's Home to be located on Highland Avenue.

***Monsignor George W. Coleman presents the Marian Medal to Miss Alma Foley** (Courtesy of the Fall River Herald News)*

The late sixties saw the questioning of authority and challenges to the establishment amid anti-war protests. A bit of the same spirit of dissatisfaction was felt in the local church although public dissent over the encyclical *Humane Vitae* never became a pressing issue. The Bishop attempted to address some of the concerns. Discussions were initiated on a pension plan for priests and a personnel board was established. The priests respected the Bishop's age and his abiding good will, even those who felt the need to resign from active ministry. Bishops, and brother priests, lamented the departure of several talented priests from their ranks. An occasion for genuine rejoicing was provided by Bishop Connolly's twenty-fifth anniversary as a bishop in 1970. The actual anniversary, May 24, happily fell on a Sunday and a beautiful May day too. The Cathedral was filled with well wishers, clergy, religious and faithful. Bishop Medeiros was the homilist. It was in a sense a last hurrah. The Bishop was already 75 years old and the previous November had submitted his resignation to the Holy Father. Its acceptance was announced on November 10, 1970, together with the name of his successor, Bishop Daniel A. Cronin, Auxiliary to Archbishop Humberto S. Medeiros who in a surprising and pleasing turn of events had succeeded the ailing Cardinal Cushing on October 7.

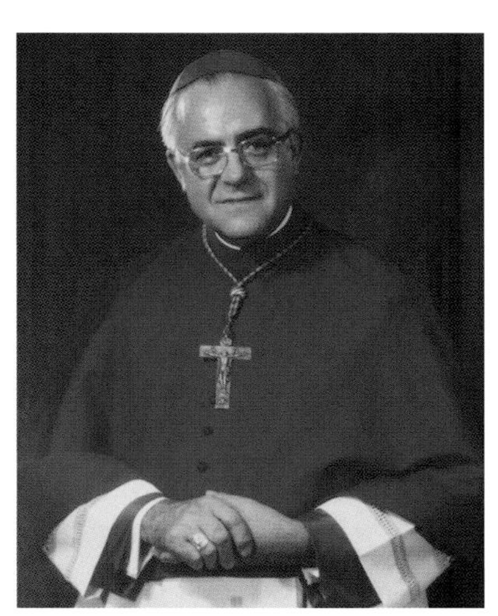

Cardinal Humberto Sousa Medeiros, S.T.D. ordained a priest, June 15, 1946, and a bishop June 9, 1966, at St. Mary's Cathedral

5. The Challenge: Renewing a Changeless Church in Changing Times

The new Bishop, a native of St. Peter's Parish in Cambridge was born on November 14, 1927, the oldest of four sons of Daniel G. and Emily (Joyce) Cronin. After graduating from Boston College High School, he prepared for the priesthood at Boston's St. John's Seminary and in Rome at the North American College and the Gregorian University and was ordained at the Lateran Basilica on December 20, 1952. After two short parish assignments in Salisbury and Lynn, he was sent back to Rome for studies leading to the degree of Doctor of Sacred Theology in 1956. His dissertation has remained timely in the constant discussion concerning the ordinary and extraordinary means of sustaining life. Returning to a parish assignment in Waltham in 1956, he was asked a year later by Archbishop Cushing to fulfill a request of the Holy See for an American priest to assist the Holy Father's representative in Addis Ababa, Ethiopia. Monsignor Cronin was serving in the office of the Vatican Secretary of State when he was named Auxiliary Bishop in Boston. Cardinal Cushing ordained Bishop Cronin on September 12, 1968, at the Holy Cross Cathedral and appointed him pastor of St. Raphael's Parish in Medford. Having presented his Apostolic Letter of appointment to the diocesan consultors on December 15, 1970, Bishop Cronin was formally installed in St. Mary's Cathedral the following day. The Apostolic Delegate,

Archbishop Luigi Raimondi presided in the presence of Archbishop Medeiros and a score of Bishops including Bishop Connolly and Bishop Gerrard. Bishop Cronin began at once with great energy to get to know the diocese. He met with the priests in each deanery and began to visit as many parishes as quickly as he could. One veteran pastor said of the new young Bishop "he would wear you out listening." In his first curial appointments in February of 1971, the Bishop appointed Luiz G. Mendonca, a second Vicar General and Thomas J. Harrington chancellor.

Bishop Daniel A. Cronin, S.T.D.

Against a background of increased opposition to the war in Vietnam, distrust of government induced by Watergate and its fallout, and the Roe v. Wade decision legalizing abortion, the local church continued to carry out its saving mission in the 1970s and 80s, shepherded by Bishop Cronin. The Bishop's first pastoral letter issued on the feast of the Holy Family dealt with the sacredness of unborn human life and the dangers threatened by the relaxation of laws against abortion. This was a full two years before the Supreme Court decision, which denied to such life the protection of the law. The Bishop made his position clear also in a forthright letter under the date of May 2, 1975, addressed to Senator Edward M. Kennedy, in which the Bishop lamented the senator's opposition to an amendment to a law, which would have prevented the spending of government funds for abortion, and to his leadership in the senate debate. The Bishop said "I would be less than true to my duty as Bishop were I to mislead, by my silence, anyone into thinking that I agree with the stance taken in this question by you."

Education, Social Service and Family Ministry

The plight of Catholic schools was high on the list of concerns. Over the years, only modest tuition if any had been charged in parish schools. As the number of religious teachers declined, parishes and parents were not prepared to cope with increased costs. In 1966 Father Patrick J. O'Neill, who had succeeded Father Gorman, with Bishop Connolly's approval had established a Diocesan School Board to offer advice and help formulate policy. In 1968 Bishop Connolly initiated a plan requiring parishes without schools to pay a small subsidy for each parishioner attending a school in another parish. A year later, the Bishop announced that the proceeds of the Easter collection would henceforth go to assist needy children in elementary schools and to provide increased salaries and health insurance for religious teachers. In spite of these efforts, the first school closings were on the horizon. Bishop Cronin approved a plan that had been developed by Father O'Neill to take effect in the fall of 1971. It provided for the merger of Coyle and Cassidy High Schools in Taunton and the establishment of a middle school at the former Coyle High School site, at the same time allowing five parish schools in the city to eliminate the three upper grades. Approval was also given for the merger of Jesus-Mary, Dominican, and Mt. St. Mary's Academies in Fall River. The new school located at the Mount would be called Bishop Gerrard High School. In New Bedford where the Sisters of Mercy had been engaged in secondary education for almost a hundred years, the Institute announced its intention to terminate its commitment at Holy Family High School at the close of the 1974 school year. The school continued however until 1985 under lay administration. In 1978 St Anthony's High School closed, not without some public protests. Two years later the remaining girls' academy, Sacred Hearts in Fairhaven, announced its closing. Studies were made calling for the closing and merging of several elementary schools in Fall River. The plan did not receive popular support and was withdrawn. A similar study was made in New Bedford. Bishop Cronin soon decided that no plan would be imposed by the diocese. Schools would close when they had to, and mergers would take place when there was local support. As time went on, the end result was frequently similar to recommendations made by the various studies. In a reorganization process in 1973 the Catholic School office and the Religious Education office were brought together again with a new office of Adult Education to form the Department of Education. One of the chief benefits was to come from the office of Adult Education in the attention given to continuing education of the clergy. In 1974 an annual Theology Institute was first held, which brought nationally and internationally recognized scholars in theology, scripture, liturgy, and history to the LaSalette Center each spring.

Students at Coyle and Cassidy High School

Bishop Cronin joins scouts from St. Mary's Cathedral Parish having offered Mass at a Catholic Scouting retreat

Bishop Cronin and Cardinal Terence Cooke meet with Pope Paul VI in 1972

In another departmental reorganization, the Catholic Welfare Bureau became the Department of Social Services in August of 1974. Father Peter N. Graziano became the director and also coordinator of Special Apostolates, chief among them, the ministry to Spanish-speaking people estimated to number 7,000 in the Diocese. In New Bedford, the Regina Pacis Center moved to St. Hyacinth Church in 1972 and now the apostolate passed from the pastoral care of the Sacred Hearts Community to the Franciscans of the Immaculate Conception Province. In Taunton and Attleboro, the ministry continued to be carried out from St. Mary's and St. Joseph's Parishes respectively. In 1975 the apostolate was greatly enhanced by the arrival of Sisters from Mexico, Missioneras Guadalupanas del Espirito Santo, who dedicated themselves to catechetical work and to home and hospital visitations. In 1977 the important ministry of the spiritual care of the sick in hospitals, hitherto the responsibility of the clergy of various parishes, was transferred to a new Department of Pastoral Care of the Sick headed by Father Edmund J. Fitzgerald, chaplain at St. Anne's Hospital. Virtually all the hospitals now had a full-time priest chaplain, the larger hospitals having a team of two. The Office of Family Ministry was established in September of 1979 with Father Ronald A. Tosti, the first director. By 1981 the former convent at Bishop Stang High School had been transformed into the Family Life Center. To this office, we owe the marriage preparation program and the Diocesan Marriage Guidelines first approved by Bishop Cronin in November of 1982, the ministry to separated and divorced, the promotion of natural family planning, and the annual recognition of couples celebrating significant wedding anniversaries, which began in 1980.

Bishop Cronin receives a gift for charity from St. Vincent de Paul Society members in 1991

Post-Conciliar Renewal Continues

Meanwhile, the important work of carrying out the Second Vatican Council's decrees and post-conciliar directives went on. Although Bishop Cronin was not a Council Father, he was in Rome during the entire Council, serving at the Vatican Secretariate of State and he was committed to authentic renewal in the spirit of Pope Paul VI who named him a bishop. On April 19, 1976, when he received the Lantern Award from the Massachusetts State Council of the Knights of Columbus in Boston, the Bishop spoke clearly of his regard for the work of the Council.

He praised the Knights for their understanding of the role of the bishop as expressed in the Directory on the Pastoral Ministry of Bishops, "to teach the word of God with authority and bear witness to it, to faithfully guard it and to authentically interpret it" Bishop Cronin then continued, "the Vatican Council permitted the Bishops from throughout the world to do this by helping them to read the signs of the times and in interpreting them in the light of the Gospel... I am acutely aware of the painful difficulties, which the institutional church has encountered in the post-conciliar age. I certainly would hope to be honest enough to admit them and even to assume some responsibility for them. Nonetheless, let not unwanted results cause rejection of the inspired process that occasioned them... The Church's witness is not frozen to a particular age or manner... The Church gathered up her Sacred Scriptures and her Tradition and proudly proclaimed that she was ready and able to lead and shepherd the men of the year 2000 and beyond as she had done for the past 20 centuries."

New liturgical rites were introduced for the sacraments of Anointing of the Sick and for Penance as well as new Funeral rites. In June of 1973 Bishop Cronin commissioned the first Special Ministers of Holy Communion and in November of 1977, receiving Holy Communion in the hand became an option for the faithful of the United States. Beginning in 1976 several priests have been delegated to assist the Bishop as extraordinary ministers of Confirmation, allowing the sacrament to be celebrated in parishes every year. In the same year, the Priests' Senate recommended the ministry of the Permanent Deacon be introduced into the diocese

Members of the Legion of Mary from the Hispanic Community in Attleboro gather for the annual Acies in 1982

Permanent Deacons following their ordination, May 24, 1997

and shortly thereafter in June of 1976, the Bishop appointed Father John F. Moore Director of the Permanent Diaconate. The first class began formation in the fall of 1977 and was ordained on June 7, 1980. To all assembled on that occasion at St. Mary's Cathedral Bishop Cronin said, "You and I have just lived history. We are in the tradition of making all things new at the same time as the Lord and his Church remain unchanged." Another liturgical development appreciated by both priests and people was the permission to celebrate the Chrism Mass earlier in Holy Week rather than on Holy Thursday morning, when few priests could take part. Since 1973 a great number of clergy has gathered for the celebration at which the Chrism and Holy Oils are blessed and the priests together with the Bishop renew their commitment before a large congregation of religious and faithful.

The pioneer consultative bodies set up by Bishop Connolly according to the directives of the Council were reorganized and redefined. In 1977 the Senate of Priests reorganized itself into a Priests' Council, which by mutual agreement, would meet only with the Bishop and would serve as his principal advisory body. A Sisters' Senate was set up in 1973, and in 1977 Bishop Cronin reactivated the Diocesan Pastoral Council appointing three priests two religious women and a layman and a laywoman from each deanery. In 1990, the Bishop promulgated statutes governing Parish Pastoral and Finance Councils. In September of 1983 the first Convocation of Priests was held. All diocesan priests and religious in parish assignments gathered on Cape Cod for two days of prayer, discussion, and recreation together. Two subsequent convocations were held under Bishop Cronin's patronage both in the month of October, in 1987 and 1991.

In December 1975 the Cursillo movement observed its 10th anniversary in the Diocese. At the same time, the Charismatic Renewal was also flourishing. Father Richard Sullivan, C.S.C. conducted a prayer service at the Diocesan Priests' Retreat in 1974, and shortly thereafter Bishop Cronin appointed Father Cornelius J. O'Neill liaison with the Renewal; there were now about 10 prayer groups meeting in the Diocese. Other priests became active in promoting Life in the Spirit Seminars, including Pierre Lachance, O.P., who was also much involved in a healing ministry at St. Anne's Shrine in Fall River. An assembly of prayer groups was held at the Cathedral in 1975 and in succeeding years on Pentecost. A coordinating committee was installed in 1979, which became the Diocesan Service Committee the next year

Significant Celebrations

A number of noteworthy events in the life of the local church were celebrated in the 1970s. Early in 1973 Archbishop Medeiros was named to the College of Cardinals. The next month the new Cardinal offered Mass at St. Mary's Cathedral, receiving the congratulations of his many former parishioners and friends in the Diocese of Fall River. In October, the fiftieth anniversary of ordination to the priesthood was observed by both Bishop Connolly and Bishop Gerrard. This occasioned another celebration at the Cathedral with Cardinal Medeiros as principal celebrant. In February of the Holy Year of 1975, Bishop Cronin led a pilgrimage to Rome and in October the largest gathering since Bishop Stang's installation took place. Many were concerned about political conditions in Portugal and the increasing influence of the Communist party and the fear of a left wing dictator succeeding the right wing dictator defeated the year before. The Bishop was approached about a procession in honor of Our Lady of Fatima and a Mass for Peace. The day chosen was Columbus Day and final plans called for a candlelight procession from St.

Bishop Cronin and Ambassador and Mrs. John A. Volpe with Diocesan pilgrims in Rome for the Holy Year of 1975

Priests gather with Bishop Cronin and Bishop Joseph Gerry, O.S.B. following the celebration of the Eucharist at St. Elizabeth Seton Church, North Falmouth during the 1991 Convocation of Priests

Archbishop Fulton J. Sheen at the Diocesan observance of the Nation's Bicentennial in 1976

Mary's Cathedral to Kennedy Park where Bishop Cronin would be principal celebrant and homilist at the Mass for Peace. To the satisfaction and amazement of all, about 30,000 prayerful people took part. The procession and Mass continues as an annual celebration, but for many years the Mass has been celebrated in St Anne's Church for a congregation taxing the church's capacity.

On Memorial Day of 1976 the Diocesan observance of the Bicentennial of the Nation took place. Bishop Cronin was the principal celebrant of an outdoor Mass at Bishop Stang High School at which Archbishop Fulton J. Sheen was the homilist. The year 1978 was made momentous by the death of Pope Paul VI, the brief one-month pontificate and untimely death of Pope John Paul I, followed by the election of Pope John Paul II. Locally history repeated itself. Bishop Cronin left for Rome just after the Pope's election for his scheduled *ad limina* visit and, like Bishop Cassidy in 1939, was present for the solemn celebration of the inauguration of the new Pope's ministry. In 1979 the seventy-fifth anniversary of the Diocese of Fall River involved a year-long observance. Archbishop Jean Jadot, the Apostolic Delegate came from Washington for the principal celebration in March. The occasion also marked the reopening of the newly refurbished Cathedral. The principal modifications were the relocation of the Cathedral at the center of the apse, new lighting, painting of the interior, and the creation of a cross aisle. One of the Jubilee events was an exercise in evangelization, an adaptation of a national program called *We Care We Share.* The goal was to visit every home, Catholic and non-Catholic. Census cards were left at Catholic homes, and all were invited to a variety of Advent programs. Fallen away Catholics were encouraged to "Come home for Christmas." There were 10,130 visitors, and 165, 959 households were visited, about a third of them non-Catholic homes. On October 1, 1979, everyone's attention was centered on the arrival of Pope John Paul II in Boston and his welcome to the United States by Cardinal Medeiros.

In 1971, Bishop Cronin was able to dedicate two churches, which were under construction when he was appointed, St. Mark's at Attleboro Falls and St. Julie Billiart at North Dartmouth. In the next several years, new churches were built by many long established parish communities, St. Anthony's in Mattapoisett, St. John of God in Somerset, St. John the Baptist in Westport, Our Lady of Mt. Carmel in Seekonk, St. Joan of Arc in Orleans, and St. Mary's in New Bedford. In Assonet, St. Bernard's Parish was able to virtually acquire an instant church and rectory through the purchase of the First Christian Church and parsonage. The Church, which Bishop Cronin dedicated on December 20, 1981, was built in 1832 and is now the oldest church building in the Diocese. Three churches were built in newly founded parishes. St. Elizabeth Seton Church in North Falmouth was dedicated by the Apostolic Delegate, Archbishop Jean Jadot on July 17, 1977, Bishop Cronin dedicated St. John Neumann Church in East Freetown on October 10, 1988, and Christ the King Church in Mashpee on the patronal feast day November 1989.

Archbishop Jean Jadot, Cardinal Medeiros and Bishop Cronin assemble for the celebration of the 75th Anniversary of the Diocese in 1979

The baroque interior of the former Saints Peter and Paul Church in Fall River

Notre Dame Church, Fall River, May 11, 1982

Three new churches replaced churches destroyed by fire. On the evening of April 10, 1973, just before Holy Week, fire broke out at SS. Peter and Paul Church in Fall River. As flames lit the night sky, horrified parishioners watched as the copper dome fell into the burning church. Nine years later on the afternoon of May 11, 1982, a spark from a workman's torch started a fire in the roof of Notre Dame Church in Fall River, and whipped by wind into a virtual firestorm, it destroyed the church and 26 homes and businesses in a 5 block area, providentially not taking a single life. In a few hours the church famed for its copper spites, painted ceiling, and French stained glass was a granite ruin reminiscent of an ancient abandoned monastery. At SS. Peter and Paul an attractive church was created on the ground level of the school; it was dedicated by Bishop Cronin on April 27, 1975. The new Notre Dame Church was dedicated on December 13, 1987. On Sunday morning, April 21, 1991, a fire broke out at St. Stanislaus Church in Fall River, causing no injury but destroying the edifice. Ultimately, substantial modifications to the school building allowed the former auditorium to be transformed into a new and beautiful parish church. The Diocese endured another tragic accident on October 11, 1983, when a backhoe used in excavating a drainage system ruptured a gas line at the Provincial House and Novitiate of the Dominican Sisters of the Presentation in Dighton. One Sister was killed and another seriously injured in the explosion.

Gains and Losses

During the 1980s three priests with ties to this local church were called to serve the church beyond the Diocese in important posts. In 1981 Joseph P. Delaney, former assistant at Sacred Heart Parish in Taunton, assistant superintendent of schools, and for several years a priest of the Diocese of Brownsville, was named Bishop of Forth Worth. Two years later, Maurus Muldoon, OFM, director of Hispanic ministry in New Bedford was appointed Prelate in Olancho, Honduras and in 1984 he was ordained a bishop. In 1983 Daniel F. Hoye, priest of the Diocese, became the General

A cherished memory: the magnificent ceiling of Notre Dame Church, the work of Ludovic Cremonini

Secretary of the National Conference of Catholic Bishops and the United States Catholic Conference. There were losses too. Cardinal Medeiros died suddenly after heart surgery and was laid to rest in St. Patrick's Cemetery in Fall River on September 23, 1983, with the Apostolic Delegate, Archbishop Pio Laghi, officiating at the Committal Rite. Just three years later on September 12, 1986, Bishop Connolly died at age 91. Bishop Gerrard, who retired as Auxiliary Bishop in 1976 and lived for many years in quiet retirement at the Catholic Memorial Home died there on June 3, 1991, a few days short of his 94th birthday. Another kind of loss was experienced too in the decreasing number of religious and the departure of communities, many a vital part of our Catholic life for decades. In 1972 the Daughters of the Holy Spirit, the beloved White Sisters, closed their Second Street convent in Fall River. In 1978, the Dominican Friars, while remaining at the Shrine and Priory, gave up the administration of St. Anne's Parish and the Bishop appointed Father John R. Folster pastor. Between 1987 and 1991, The Sacred Hearts Community, concerned for the needs of their overseas missions, withdrew from six of the ten parishes they had staffed for many years on Cape Cod and in the New Bedford-Fairhaven area.

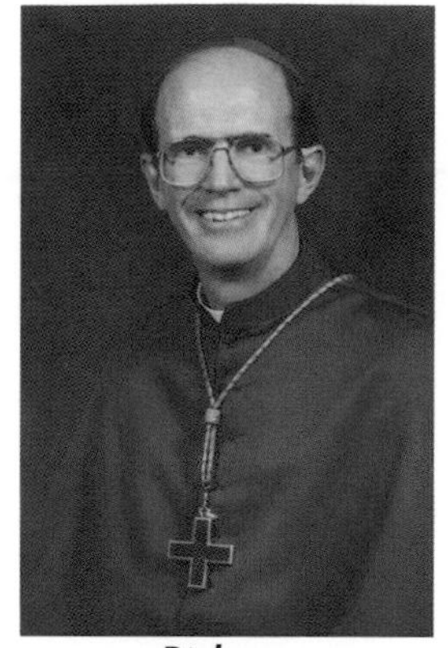

Bishop Joseph P. Delaney

On December 10, 1991, it was announced that Pope John Paul II had chosen Bishop Cronin to be Archbishop of Hartford, bringing to completion a ministry of 21 years as Bishop of Fall River. The new Archbishop was installed in St. Joseph Cathedral in Hartford on January 28, 1992. Two days later the Diocesan Consultors elected Monsignor Henry T. Munroe, Diocesan Administrator.

6. Where There Is Darkness, Light: Coping with Crisis

On June 16, 1992, word came that the Bishop of St. Thomas in the Virgin Island, Sean O'Malley, O.F.M. Cap. had been named Bishop of Fall River. At a press conference later that day, the new Bishop, referring to his friar's habit and sandals, which would become so familiar, quipped "central casting has not sent you a conventional looking bishop." Bishop O'Malley was born in Lakewood, Ohio June 29, 1944, the son of Theodore and Mary Louise (Reidy) O'Malley. Baptized Patrick, he entered the Order of Capuchin Franciscans as a young man, taking the religious name Sean and was ordained a priest on August 29, 1970. The future Bishop studied at the Catholic University in Washington, where he received a Ph.D. in Spanish Literature, becoming fluent in Portuguese as well as Spanish. From 1973 to 1984 he served in the Archdiocese of Washington as director of the Spanish Catholic Center and as Vicar for priests serving in Hispanic ministry. In 1984 Father Sean was named Coadjutor Bishop of St. Thomas in the Virgin Islands and was ordained there on August 2, 1984 by Bishop Edward J. Harper, C. SS. R., whom he succeeded the following year. Bishop O'Malley was installed sixth Bishop of Fall River in St. Mary's Cathedral on August 11, 1992, the feast of St. Clare, by the Archbishop of Boston, Cardinal Bernard F. Law, together with the Apostolic Nuncio, Archbishop Agostino Cacciavillan. Present also were Archbishop Cronin, Cardinal James F. Hickey, Archbishop of Washington, and his predecessor in Washington, Cardinal William W. Baum, a member of the Roman Curia.

Bishop Sean O'Malley, O.F.M. Cap

The Bishop came prepared to shepherd a diocese troubled by scandal. In May of 1992 multiple allegations of sexual abuse of minors was made public. The accused was James R. Porter, a diocesan priest who had resigned from active ministry over twenty years before. The Bishop made the healing of this suffering a priority. He met with the victims and set about to establish policies and a review board to deal with misconduct of clergy and diocesan employees. James Porter was ultimately convicted and received a prison sentence. In spite of the great amount of time and attention Bishop O'Malley devoted to this important pastoral concern, he began to get to know the diocese and the needs of the local church. He began with the priests gathering them together on September 10 for Mass at St. John Neumann Church in East Freetown and for dinner at the adjacent Cathedral Camp. Two subsequent events were of special importance to the priests, the Emmaus program, a national program of spiritual renewal encouraging participation in on-going support groups, which was conducted in the fall of 1994 and the renovation of the former Jesuit Community residence at Bishop Connolly High School into a facility for retired priests. The Cardinal Medeiros Residence was dedicated by his successor, Cardinal Law on September 18, 1996.

At the Bishop's invitation several new religious communities came into the Diocese. Mother Teresa's Missionaries of Charity were welcomed to St. Lawrence Parish in New Bedford on December 19, 1992. About the same time the Franciscans Friars of the Immaculate reopened Our Lady's Chapel in New Bedford replacing the Franciscans of the Holy Name Province who had withdrawn in June of 1992. In January of 1995 the community now known as the Franciscans of the Primitive Observance began a ministry to the poor in New Bedford. In 1993 the Good Shepherd Sisters who have been in Boston since 1867 opened a convent for the contemplative branch of their congregation in Harwichport.

Caring for The People of God

Various apostolates were updated. An AIDS Ministry Office, directed by Krysten Winter-Green opened on October of 1993, and a year later the Presentation Dominican Sisters established Hope House, a hospice for AIDS patients. The Office of Youth Ministry was reorganized under its director, Father George E. Harrison, in November 1993. The Youth Apostles, an institute of clerics and laity, were welcomed by Bishop Sean, and four of their members have been ordained to the priesthood here. Priests of the Fraternity of Charles Borromeo came to the diocese too and became involved in Campus Ministry. From 1995 to 2001 they cared for St. Louis Parish in Fall River succeeding the Franciscans, moving to St. Joseph Parish in Attleboro when St. Louis Parish was closed. The Pro-Life apostolate was important to Bishop O'Malley. Each January he led a delegation to Washington to take part in the annual events observing the anniversary of the Roe v. Wade decision, and in October the Bishop customarily took part in the walk for life in Boston. In 1997 Cardinal John J. O'Connor of New York was celebrant and homilist at the opening Mass of the annual Pro-Life convention.

Bishop Sean with adults and young people witnessing for life in Boston

In 1994 Arlene McNamee became the first lay executive director of the Department of Catholic Social Services. Bishop O'Malley was eager to work with the Department in reaching out to the poor. In 1995 the former St. Mathieu Convent in Fall River became St. Mathieu Residence for women, succeeding the St. Francis Residence maintained by the Franciscan Missionaries of Mary until 1989. In Hyannis St. Clare House opened in January of 1998 providing housing for women making the transition from the house of correction to the community. In New Bedford Donovan House was established in St. James Parish to offer shelter to women and children in difficult situations, and in the North End an old-fashioned rooming house was transformed into the Talbot Apartments providing simple but comfortable accommodations to men in a substance and alcohol free atmosphere. These recent facilities join the shelter and midday soup kitchen which has been conducted for twenty years in downtown New Bedford by Sister Rosellen Gallogly, R.S.M. with the approval of her community and with support of the Department of Public Welfare, local parishes, community organizations and private donations.

Throughout the 1990s the number of Spanish-speaking people in the diocese continued to grow. On July 31, 1993, Bishop O'Malley established the parish of Nuestra Senora de Guadalupe in New Bedford at St. Hedwig's Church, and Father Paul E. Canuel was appointed pastor of both the new parish and of St. Hedwig's Parish. On June 26, 1996, priests of the Institute of the Incarnate Word, who had come from Argentina in 1994 to assist in the Hispanic ministry, were given the care of St. Kilian's Parish in New Bedford, succeeding the Franciscan Friars. Ministry to the Brazilian community began in St Francis Xavier Parish in Hyannis. In the summer of 1991 a census was taken and a report made to Bishop Cronin. Fifty-two households were visited, and there were almost 200 registered parishioners. Various priests were called upon to offer Mass in Portuguese. In the summer of 1992 Father Freddie Babisczuk was assigned to the parish with the explicit direction to care for the Brazilian community. As the numbers increased, the ministry expanded, so that Mass is offered for Brazilian congregations in Hyannis, Falmouth, Fall River, and on Martha's Vineyard and Nantucket.

Bishop O'Malley set up a committee to present a proposal for the reorganization of the Diocesan Curia or office of central administration, and in September of 1994 George W. Coleman, pastor of Corpus Christi Parish in Sandwich, was named Moderator of the Curia and Vicar General. A month later, eight cabinet secretaries were appointed to oversee the work of various offices and apostolates. Father Michael K. McManus, the diocesan financial officer, was appointed Chancellor the following June, succeeding Monsignor John J. Oliveira, appointed pastor of St. Mary's Parish in New Bedford.

A Revival of Catholic Schools

Catholic Schools continued to be of extraordinary importance in spite of the expense involved for the church and for families. Bishop Cronin was able to direct the income received from the sale of the former St. Mary's Home in New Bedford to a fund from which financial assistance could be given to students attending Catholic elementary schools. This became the St. Mary's Educational Fund, which now hosts two scholarship dinners a year. The first fall dinner was held in 1995, and a summer dinner on Cape Cod was initiated in 1998. From 1995 to 2002 these events have made it possible to distribute $2.6 million to 3,000 students. Bishop O'Malley judged the time was right to think of establishing new schools on the Cape and in other rapidly growing suburban areas. In September of 1994 two schools opened with grades K through 2 on Cape Cod. One was at Holy Trinity Parish in West Harwich where the Sisters of Mercy had previously staffed a school (1965-1971). The other was at St. Margaret's Parish in Buzzards Bay where the Trinitarian Sisters had once conducted a kindergarten. In September of 1996 St. Francis Xavier Preparatory School with grades 5 through 8 began in Hyannis. All three schools were able to make use of existing buildings. In September of 2002 St. Mary's School in Mansfield opened in the greatly expanded parish religious education center. A fourth new school for Cape Cod is scheduled to open in 2004 at St. Pius X Parish in South Yarmouth. In the spring of 2001 Bishop O'Malley announced the appointment of George A. Milot head of the Education Department and Superintendent of Schools. The first layman to hold the office, he had previously served as principal of both Bishop Stang and Bishop Feehan High Schools.

Bishop Sean with young students at the new St. Margaret's Regional School in Buzzards Bay

Parishioners in traditional Polish dress greet Bishop Sean at Holy Rosary parish in Taunton

The Great Jubilee

Faithful to the decree of the Holy Father that three years of spiritual preparation precede the Great Jubilee of 2000, the Diocesan family celebrated the year dedicated to Christ the Son on Ascension Day in 1997. Representatives from each parish came to the Cathedral to receive an icon of the Blessed Trinity to take back to their respective parishes. The principal observance of the year of the Holy Spirit took place on the Vigil of Pentecost in 1998, and the year of the Father was commemorated in 1999 on Friday of the First week of Lent, centering around the gospel of the day, the story of the return of the prodigal son to his merciful father. In November of 1999, Bishop O'Malley led over 60 people on a Jubilee pilgrimage to Rome. At Christmas Eve Mass at St. Mary's Cathedral, Bishop O'Malley ceremonially opened the Holy Door inaugurating the Jubilee Year, and he repeated the rite in Portuguese at the Midnight Mass at Our Lady of Mt. Carmel Church in New Bedford. At midnight on January 1, 2000, the Bishop celebrated the first Mass of the new millennium at St. Julie Billiart Church in North Dartmouth. In June the first Eucharistic Congress in the history of the Diocese was held. Beginning on Sunday, June 18, evenings of prayer and reflection were held in various areas. The Congress closed on Sunday, June 25, the Solemnity of Corpus Christi, with Mass celebrated at Kennedy Park followed by the procession with the Holy Eucharist with the traditional Benedictions being given before St. Anne's Church, Santo

St. Rose of Lima Church, Guaimaca, Honduras

Father Paul E. Canuel with his Honduran parishioners

Christo Church, and finally outside the Lady Chapel at St. Mary's Cathedral. Bishop Robert E. Mulvee of Providence and Bishop Aurelio Granada Escudeiro, retired Bishop of Angra, concelebrants at Mass, joined in the procession

Another very significant event of the Jubilee Year was the response of Bishop O'Malley and the Church of Fall River to the call of our Holy Father to see the Church of the Americas as one. On September 10, 2000 the Bishop commissioned a missionary team about to depart for Central America and the Archdiocese of Tegucigalpa in Honduras to staff the parish of Guaimaca which had no priest. The parish includes the Church of St Rose of Lima in Guaimaca and the Church of St. Francis of Assisi in the town of Orca. The two towns geographically about the size of Fall River and New Bedford are twenty-five miles apart in a mountainous area. Between them are 50 small Christian communities cared for by 60 dedicated lay leaders. The team was lead by Father Paul E. Canuel, pastor of Nuestra Senora de Guadalupe and St. Hedwig Parishes in New Bedford, Deacon James Marzelli of St. John the Evangelist Parish in Pocasset and his wife Joanne, a nurse, Presentation Dominican Sister Marie Ceballos, a nurse practitioner and Father Gustavo Dominguez, IVE of St. Kilian's Parish in New Bedford, to be succeeded by Father Joseph Blyskosz of Holy Trinity Parish in West Harwich in six months.

As the new century and millennium approached, Bishop O'Malley expressed his concerns for the future by establishing the Office of Pastoral Planning in 1998. For decades, as people moved from the cities to the surrounding towns, many of the older parishes had been struggling. The closing of parish schools and the reduction in the number of priests often provided a measure of relief, but it was really a matter of delaying the inevitable. Over the years, urban renewal, highway construction, and changes in the ethnic population of some neighborhoods had caused a few parishes to close. Now, the Bishop sought to consolidate parishes in order to create stronger and more effective parish communities. "Our task" the Bishop wrote "is to decide how best to put our human and material resources at the service of God's Kingdom" and to help parishes "move beyond their boundaries and cooperate with one another in order to further God's Kingdom." Through the leadership of the Bishop O'Malley the dedicated efforts of the priests involved, and the sacrifices of parishioners, parishes were closed and merged in Fall River, New Bedford, Taunton and Swansea permitting the Diocese between 1998 and 2001 to reduce by eleven the total number of parishes. In addition on the lower Cape in 1999, Sacred Heart Chapel in Truro was closed and North Truro and its mission church of Our Lady of Perpetual Help became part of St. Peter's Parish in Provincetown, while the mission Church of the Visitation and part of Eastham was separated from St. Joan of Arc Parish in Orleans and attached to Our Lady of Lourdes Parish in Wellfleet.

The beautifully refurbished church of the newly merged parish of The Holy Trinity, Fall River

Mother Teresa and Father Peyton

During the last decade of the twentieth century, the local church was touched by two religious figures widely venerated throughout the universal church. On June 14, 1995, Mother Teresa of Calcutta made a memorable visit to her Sisters in New Bedford. In the afternoon she attended a Mass celebrated at St. Lawrence Church and addressed the overflow congregation of clergy, religious, and laity. Mother Teresa's framed handwritten letter of thanks together with her photograph has an honored place in St. Lawrence Church, a gift from Bishop O'Malley on the occasion of the 175th anniversary of the parish celebrated in December of 1996. On June 3, 1992, Father Patrick Peyton, C.S.C. died in Los Angeles and was laid to rest in the Holy Cross Fathers Cemetery in North Easton on the grounds of Stonehill College. On June 1, 2001, the Bishop announced that the Congregation for the Causes of Saints had accepted the cause for Father Peyton's beatification presented by the Diocese of Fall River at the request of the Congregation of the Holy Cross. A few months later everyone in the Diocese joined the Holy Cross community in mourning the loss of Father Francis Grogan C.S.C., former assistant at Holy Cross Parish in Easton and more recently superior of the Mission House in North Dartmouth. Father Grogan en route to visit his sister in California was a passenger on one of the ill-fated planes that was crashed into the World Trade Center on September 11, 2001.

Looking forward to the 100th anniversary of the founding of the Diocese in 2004, Bishop O'Malley in June of 2000 set up an anniversary committee chaired by Monsignor Daniel F. Hoye, approved the date of March 14, 2004, for the celebration of the anniversary Mass, and encouraged the writing of this history. For the spiritual preparation of the faithful, the Bishop directed the parishes to become involved in RENEW 2000, but while the training was still in progress, the announcement came on September 2, 2002, that Bishop O'Malley had been named Bishop of Palm Beach by Pope John Paul II. Bishop's Sean's formal farewell took place at the annual candlelight procession and Mass for Peace on Columbus Day at St. Anne's Church. He concluded his homily with the words of the familiar hymn "All I ask of you is that you remember me as loving you." Bishop O'Malley was installed in Palm Beach on October 19, 2002, and on October 22, the Diocesan Consultors elected Monsignor Coleman Administrator of the Diocese of Fall River.

In succeeding months the day-to-day life of the church continued. On March 14, 2003, the Diocese bade farewell to the Carmelite Sisters for the Aged and Infirm who felt it necessary, because of the decreasing number of Sisters, to end their 63 years of service at the Catholic Memorial Home. The previous August, the Dominican Sisters of Hawthorne had closed the Rose Hawthorne Lathrop Home where they had cared for those suffering with incurable cancer since 1932. The reason was not so much the scarcity of religious, but the small number of patients

Blessed Teresa of Calcutta speaking at St. Lawrence Church in New Bedford when she visited the Diocese in 1995

Servant of God Patrick Peyton, C. S. C. for whose beatification we pray

due in part to the increasing number of health care facilities and the availability of Hospice care. The need for updating the home was also a factor in the decision. Both these communities have been a great blessing in the history of our Diocese. Bishop O'Malley was invited to return for the ordination of two deacons on March 29, and on Tuesday of Holy Week the Retired Bishop of Springfield, Joseph F. Maguire, consecrated the Sacred Chrism and blessed the Holy Oils.

7. We Are The Lord's: Giving Thanks For A Hundred Years

In the second week of the Easter season, on April 30, the Apostolic Nuncio in Washington, Archbishop Gabriel Montalvo, announced that our Holy Father had appointed a member of our own body of priests, Monsignor George W. Coleman, the Administrator of the Diocese, seventh Bishop of Fall River. The new Bishop, was born on February 1, 1939, the son of George W. and Beatrice (Shea) Coleman. He grew up in St. Patrick's Parish in Somerset, together with his sister Eileen, now the wife of Thomas C. Keegan and mother of their son, Christopher. Bishop Coleman attended Somerset schools and Monsignor Coyle High School in Taunton, Holy Cross College, St. John's Seminary, and made his theological studies in Rome at the North American College, and the Gregorian University where he received a graduate degree in Sacred Theology. His ordination to the priesthood took place on December 16, 1964, at the altar of the Chair in St. Peter's Basilica. He has served as assistant at the parishes of St. Kilian in New Bedford, St. Louis in Fall River, and at Our Lady of Victory in Centerville. In 1977 Bishop Cronin appointed him Diocesan Director of Education, and in 1982, pastor of St. Patrick's Parish in Fall River. From 1985 until 1994, he served as pastor of Corpus Christi Parish in Sandwich, and while there, began the process of transferring the parish facilities to a new site in East Sandwich. In 1990 a parish center was completed including an attractive place for the celebration of the liturgy until a new church could be built, a church he would have the joy of dedicating as Bishop. On July 22, 2003, George W. Coleman was ordained seventh Bishop of Fall River by Archbishop Gabriel Montalvo appropriately assisted by the fifth and sixth Bishops of Fall River, Daniel A. Cronin, Archbishop of Hartford and Sean O' Malley named Archbishop of Boston on July 1. The Church of Fall River now has a new shepherd to lead it into its second century. He will build on the scholarship of Stang, the bene-volence of Feehan, the boldness of Cassidy, the honesty of Connolly, the diligence of Cronin and the patience of O'Malley.

Bishop George W. Coleman

Through his motto, *Super Rivos Aquarum Fructificate,* Bishop Stang counseled our forebears, *Bear Fruit by Streams of Waters.* Now Bishop Coleman through his motto, *Domini Sumus,* encourages all in the Church of Fall River to give thanks to God for the blessings of a hundred years of diocesan life and to continue to bear fruit faithfully, remembering *We are the Lord's.*

The Most Reverend George W. Coleman is ordained seventh Bishop of Fall River by Archbishop Gabriel Montalvo, assisted by the fifth and sixth Bishops of Fall River, Archbishops Daniel A. Cronin and Sean O'Malley, O.F.M. Cap.

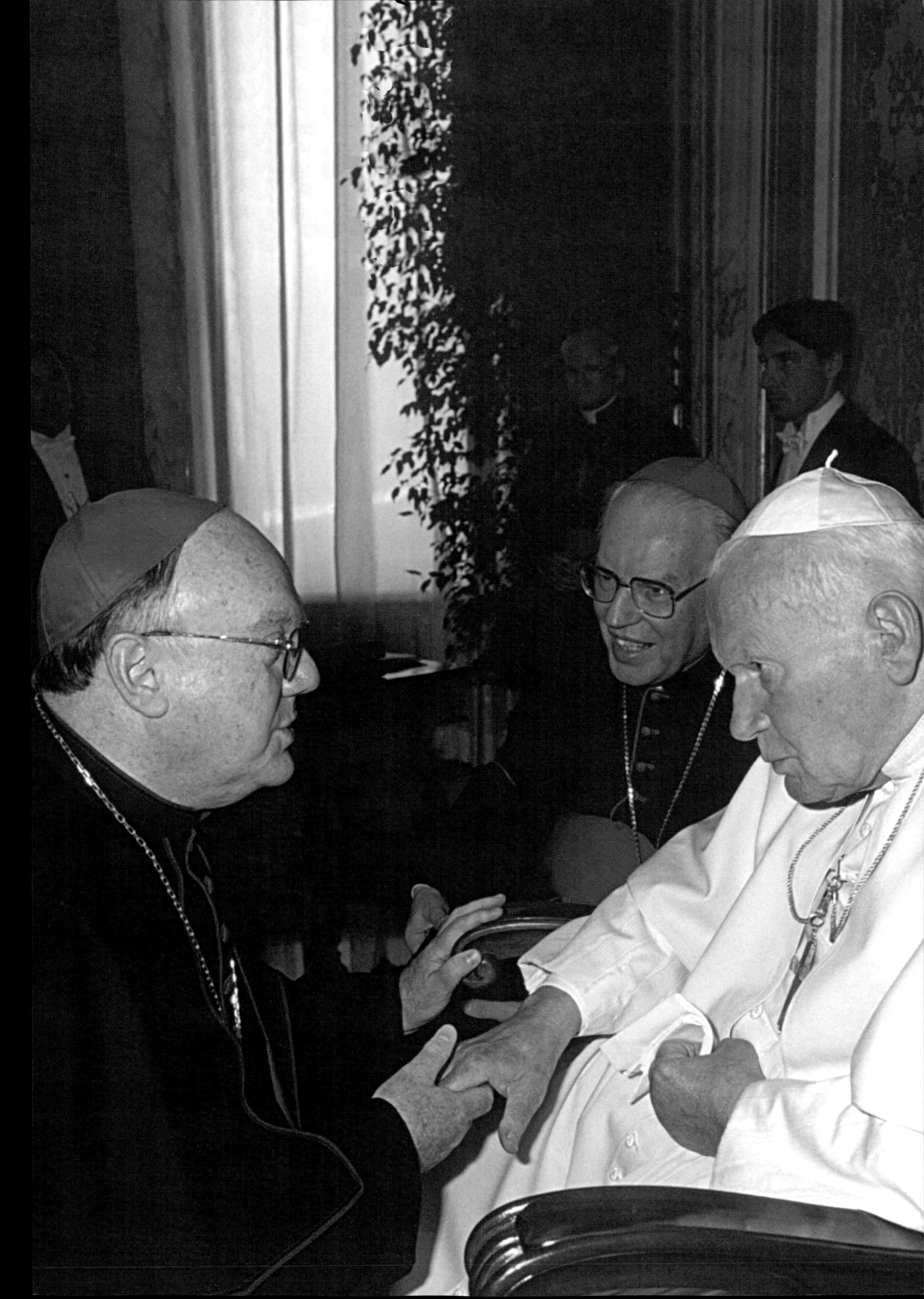

Parishes in the Diocese of Fall River

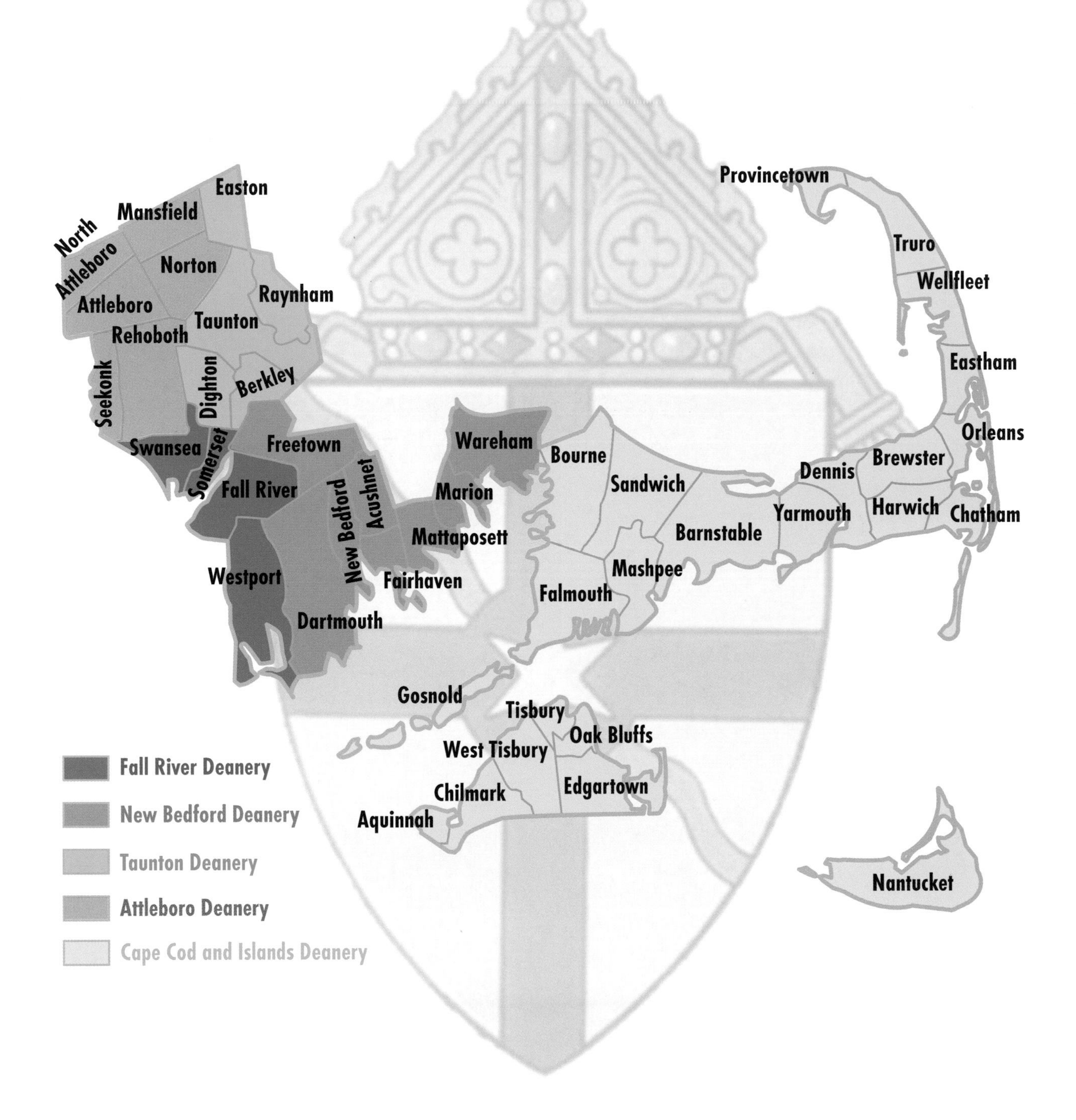

The towns of Freetown, Rehoboth,Wareham and Westport are in more than one deanery

The Parishes of
the Fall River Deanery

Cathedral Church of St. Mary of the Assumption

St. Mary's Cathedral

In 1836 a small wooden church named for St. John the Baptist was constructed on Spring Street in Fall River by Father John Corry, pastor in Taunton. The sacramental records date from 1838. The present church of native granite, designed by Patrick C. Keely, was dedicated on December 16, 1855, under the title of St. Mary of the Assumption during the pastorate of Father Edward Murphy (1840-1887). With the founding of the Diocese of Fall River St. Mary's became the Cathedral. In 2000 the St. Louis Parish community was merged with St. Mary's. St. Louis Church was dedicated in 1887 two years after the founding of the parish.

St. Anne Parish

Father Paul Adrien Montaubricq purchased land at Hunter and Williams Streets and a substantial wooden church was constructed and dedicated on November 13, 1870. From 1887 to 1978 the pastoral care of the parish was in the hands of Dominican Friars who built a new church and friary on South Main Street. The Church containing the shrine of St Anne, revered throughout the city and beyond, was dedicated on July 4, 1906. At various times, the Sisters of Mercy, Holy Cross Sisters, the Presentation Dominicans, and the Brothers of the Christian Schools have served in the parish where the school continues in the charge of lay educators. When Saint Mathieu Parish, founded in 1887, closed in 1988 many parishioners elected to join St. Anne's Parish.

Sacred Heart Parish

In 1872 Father Murphy of St. Mary's began construction of a church at Linden and Pine Streets and, after Christmas Father Francis J. Quinn became the pastor of the new parish of the Sacred Heart. The church was not ready for dedication until October 7, 1883. The Sisters of the Holy Union of the Sacred Hearts established their first foundation in the United States here in 1886.

St. Joseph Parish

Established for the diverse Irish and Canadian population of the north end of the city in 1873, the present St. Joseph's Church was dedicated on May 30, 1885. For several decades the parish school was staffed by the Sisters of Mercy and the parish is noted for numerous vocations to the priesthood and religious life.

Notre Dame de Lourdes Parish

Notre Dame parish was established in 1874 for the French-speaking Canadians of the East end of Fall River. The original church was replaced by a magnificent church in Baroque style, dedicated in 1906. The church known for its stained-glass and painted ceiling was destroyed by fire in 1982. The Religious of Jesus and Mary came in 1877 and many years later were joined by the Brothers of Christian Instruction in the teaching apostolate. For many years the Sisters of Charity of Quebec conducted Mt. St. Joseph Orphanage.

The school, now the oldest in the diocese, continues under lay administration. When St. Rock's Parish, which was founded in 1899 closed in 1982, the records were transferred to Notre Dame. The Sisters of St. Joseph came first to St. Rock's in 1902.

Immaculate Conception Parish

This parish was formed for the Irish parishioners of Notre Dame Parish in 1882. A large wooden church served the parish until the present beautiful Romanesque church was dedicated in 1929.

Santo Christo Parish

The first parish in the city for Portuguese parishioners was founded in 1892. The completion of the superstructure of the church did not take place until after the Second World War. The parish is the focus of the annual Santo Christo Feast on the last Sunday in June.

Saints Peter and Paul Parish at Holy Cross Church

Saints Peter and Paul Parish was established in 1882 for the people of the Niagara section of the city. In 1973 the beautiful Spanish baroque church, designed by Ralph Adams Cram, was destroyed by fire and a new church was created on the first floor of the school. In 1998 when the Franciscan Conventual Friars withdrew from Holy Cross Parish, founded in 1917 for Polish parishioners, Holy Cross Church became the parish church for the two merged communities.

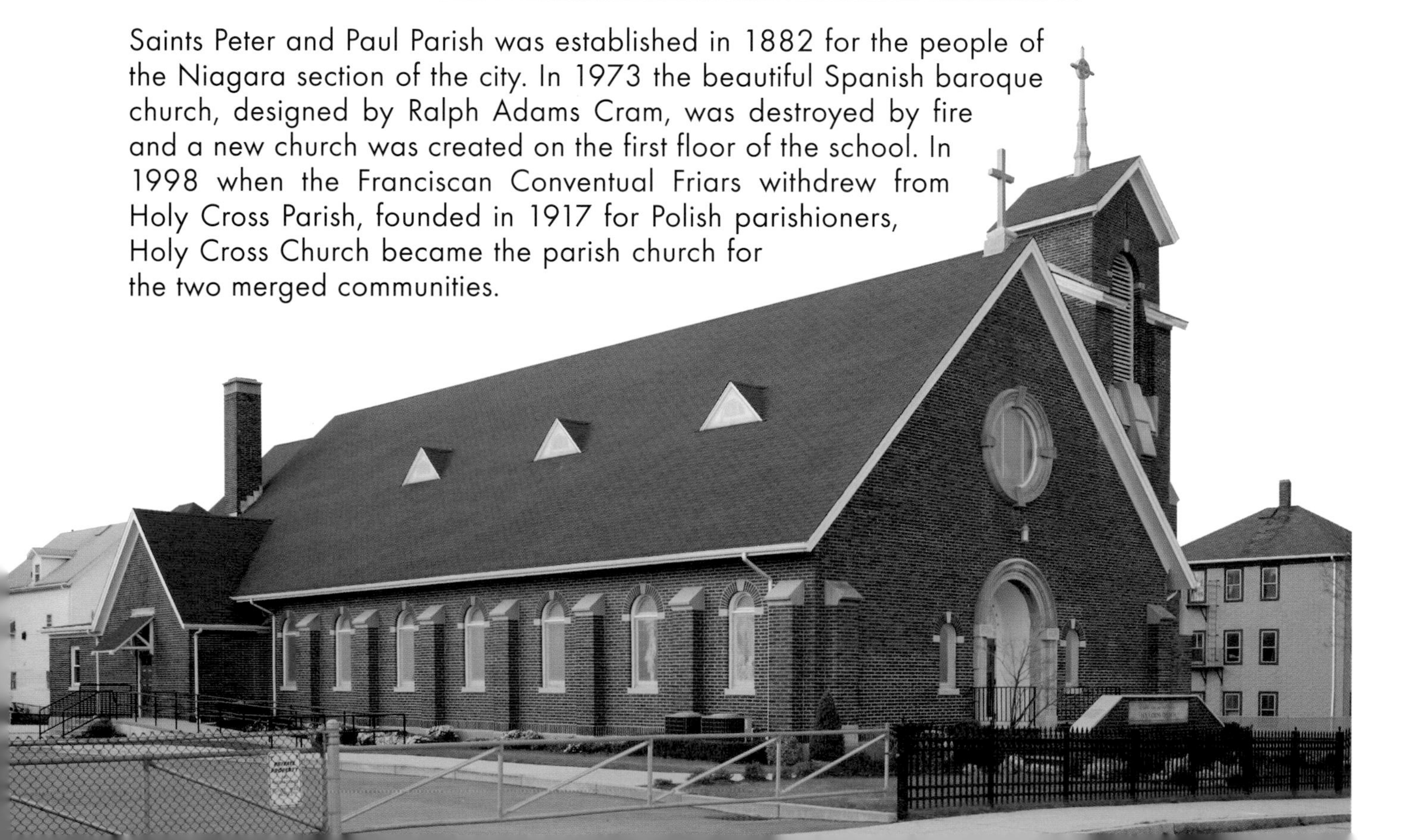

St. Stanislaus Parish

Fall River's first Polish parish was established in 1898. When the parish church tragically burned in 1991, a beautiful new church was provided by a creative renovation of the school. The school, the first for Polish Catholic children in Massachusetts, was founded in 1906 and was staffed for many years by the Felician Sisters.

Our Lady of the Holy Rosary Parish

Late in 1902 a priest came from Providence and ministered to the Italian Catholics of Fall River at St. Rock's Church until 1904 when Holy Rosary Church was dedicated. The superstructure was completed and dedicated in 1915.

St. Michael Parish

The parish was founded in 1902 for the Portuguese-speaking people of the north end of the city. The red brick gothic Church was dedicated in 1922. The future Cardinal, Humberto S. Medeiros, served as pastor from 1960 -1966. The Sisters of the Holy Union together with lay teachers staff the school.

Espirito Santo Parish

This was the first parish established in the new Diocese of Fall River in 1904 and the first Luzo-American parish school opened here in 1910, staffed by the Franciscan Missionaries of Mary. The present church was dedicated in 1963.

St. Anthony of Padua Parish

Begun as a mission of Santo Christo Parish in 1908, with Masses being celebrated in the basement of St. Rock's Church, St. Anthony's became a parish in 1911. The original church, dedicated in 1913, was replaced by a striking modern church in 1969.

Holy Name Parish

The parish was established in 1923 and the first services were held in a tent. The original church was built on Read Street and replaced by the present Georgian colonial church in 1941. Holy Name School opened in 1960 under the direction of the Holy Union Sisters.

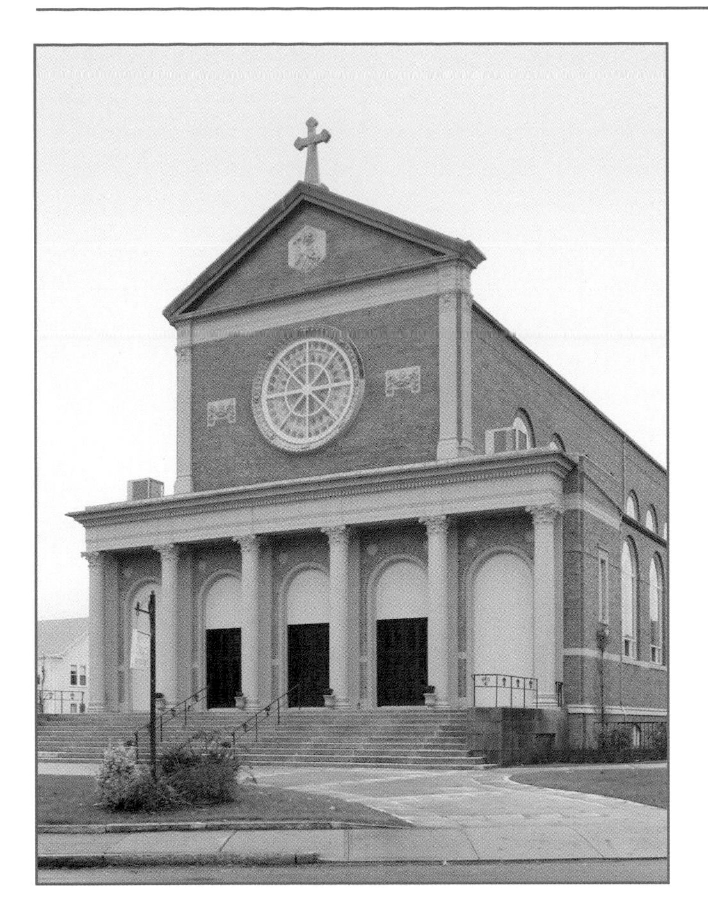

The parish was formed in 2000 through the merger of three parishes in the Maplewood section of the city. St. William's Parish was founded in 1905 to serve the English-speaking of the area and the granite basement church was replaced by a church of modern Georgian design in 1961. St. Elizabeth's Parish was established in 1915, having been a mission of Espirito Santo Parish, St. Jean Baptiste Parish was founded in 1901. The Roman basilica style church was dedicated in 1926 and now extensively refurbished, serves as the church for the new parish. The parish school staffed, for many years by the Sisters of St. Joseph, continues under dedicated lay leadership.

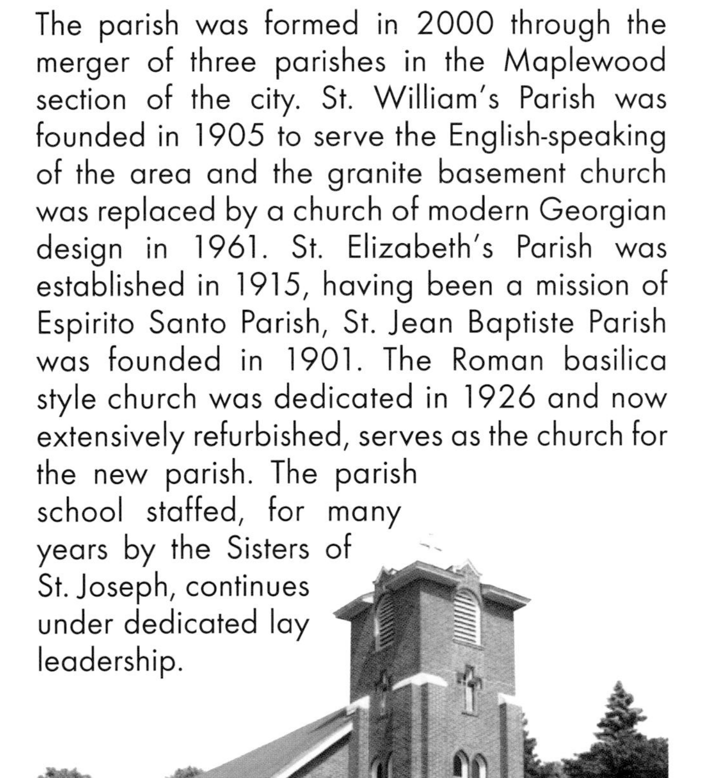

OUR LADY OF HEALTH PARISH

While still a mission of Espirito Santo Parish, the first Mass was celebrated in the church on Christmas 1923. The parish was established in 1924 and the church dedicated in November of that year.

Good Shepherd Parish

In 2002 the parish was created by the merger of three south end parishes: Blessed Sacrament Parish was founded in 1892; the first church was called St. Dominic's. Our Lady of Angels Parish was founded in 1915 for Portuguese-speaking parishioners and the church was dedicated two years later. St. Patrick's Parish was established in 1873. The Keely designed church of native granite was dedicated in 1888, and now beautifully renovated, serves the new parish. The Sisters of Mercy taught generations of parishioners in the former parish school.

St. Patrick Parish, Somerset

The Catholics of Somerset were placed under the care of the pastor of St. Joseph's Parish in Fall River when that parish was founded. St. Patrick's Church was dedicated on November 2, 1873. The parish was established in 1883 and remained for three decades the only parish west of Fall River.

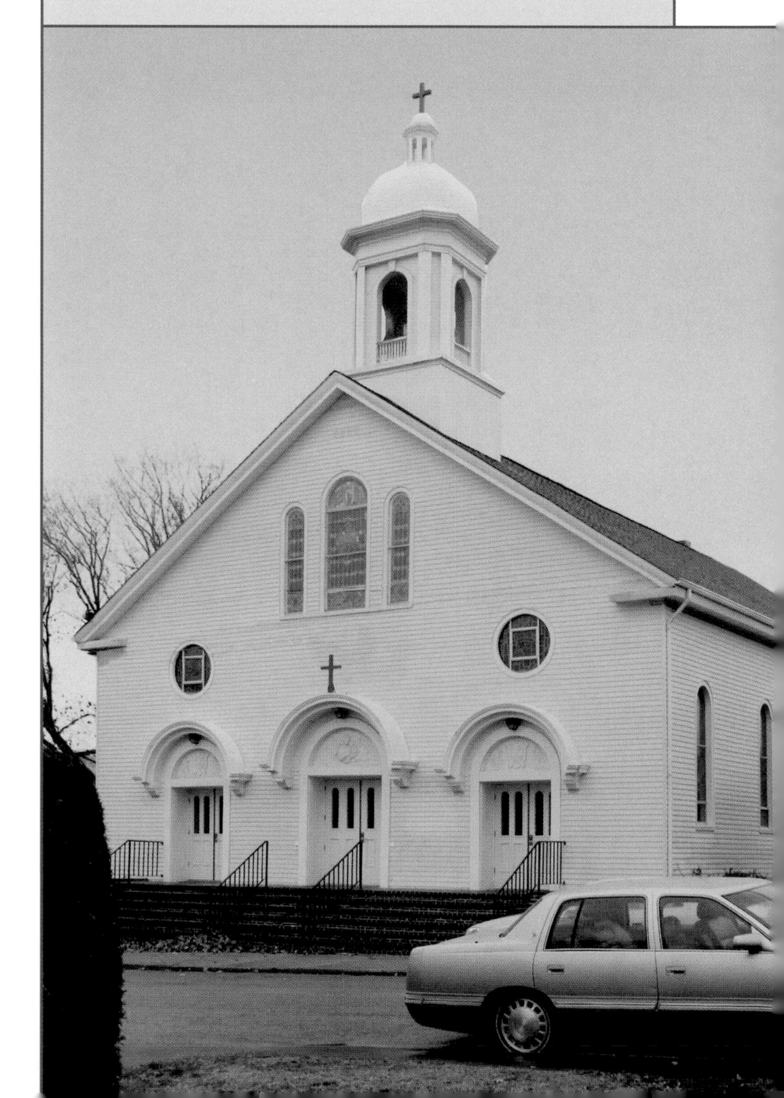

St. Thomas More Parish, Somerset

Built as a mission of St Patrick's Parish, the original church was dedicated in 1938. St. Thomas More Parish was established in 1949 and the present church was dedicated on November 6, 1966.

St. John of God Parish, Somerset

The parish was founded in 1928 for Portuguese-speaking people in Somerset. The first church was dedicated in 1930. The present church with its distinctive bell tower, suggesting the mast of a tall ship, was dedicated in 1978.

St. Dominic Parish, Swansea

In the fall of 1911 the Dominicans from St. Anne's Shrine in Fall River were asked to staff a parish in Swansea. Early in 1912 St Dominic's Church was dedicated. Meanwhile an unused Protestant chapel in North Swansea was presented to the Bishop by a concerned employer of many Catholic farm workers. Dedicated in honor of St. Francis Xavier, the chapel served as a mission until it was torn down after sustaining serious damage in the 1938 hurricane.

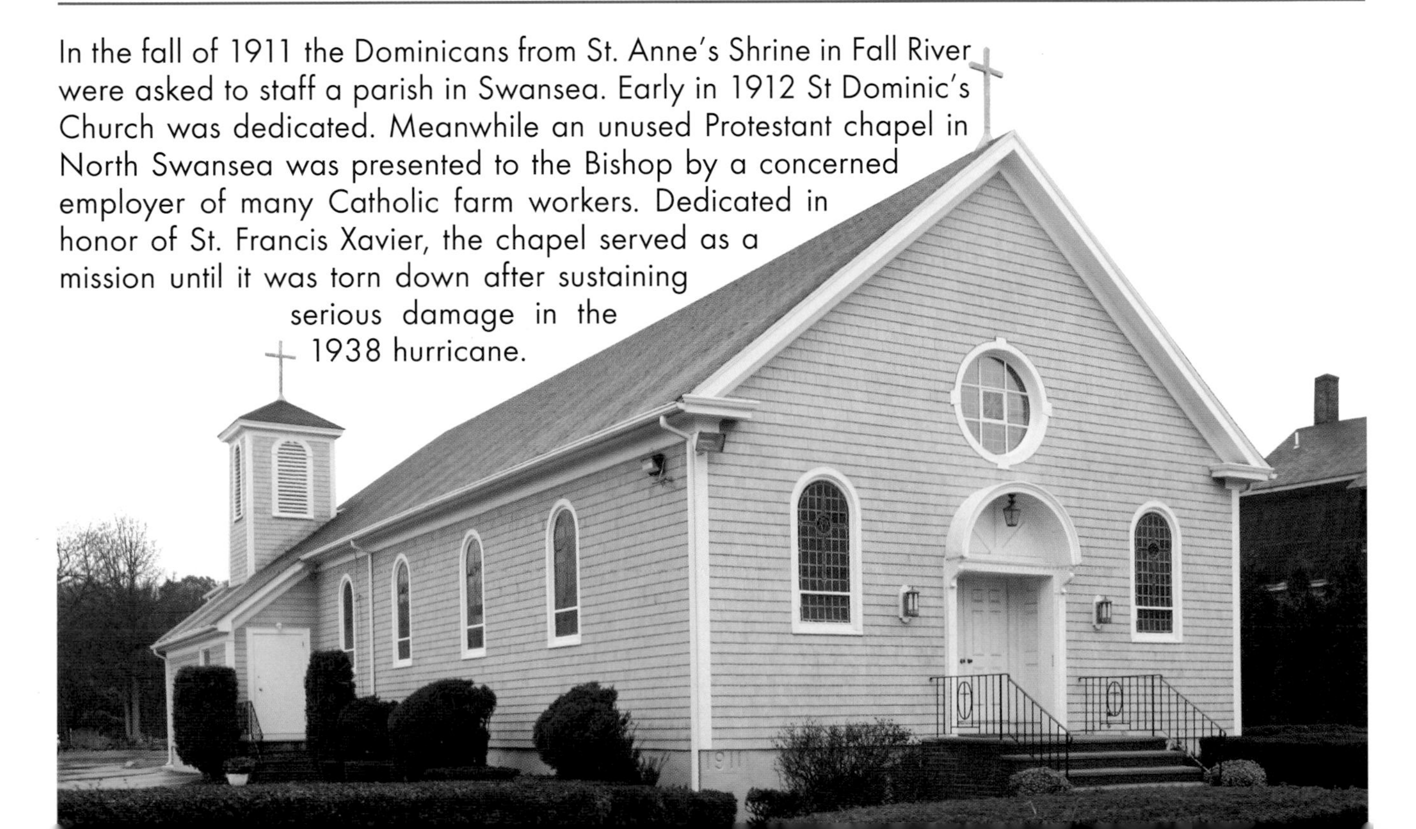

St. Michael Parish, Swansea

By 1922 the growing French Canadian population justified the creation of a parish in the Ocean Grove section of Swansea. A school was opened in 1931 and the church was extensively renovated in 1963. A portion of the parish became part of Our Lady of Fatima Parish when it was established in1958. In June of 2001 Our Lady of Fatima ceased to be a parish, but the clergy of St. Michael's continues to serve the faithful at both churches.

St. Louis de France Parish, Swansea

This parish was established in 1928 to care for French Canadian parishioners living in the eastern part of Swansea and Somerset. In 1931 the Sisters of St. Joseph opened a convent where they began a small parish school. The original church was replaced by the present colonial style church in 1951.

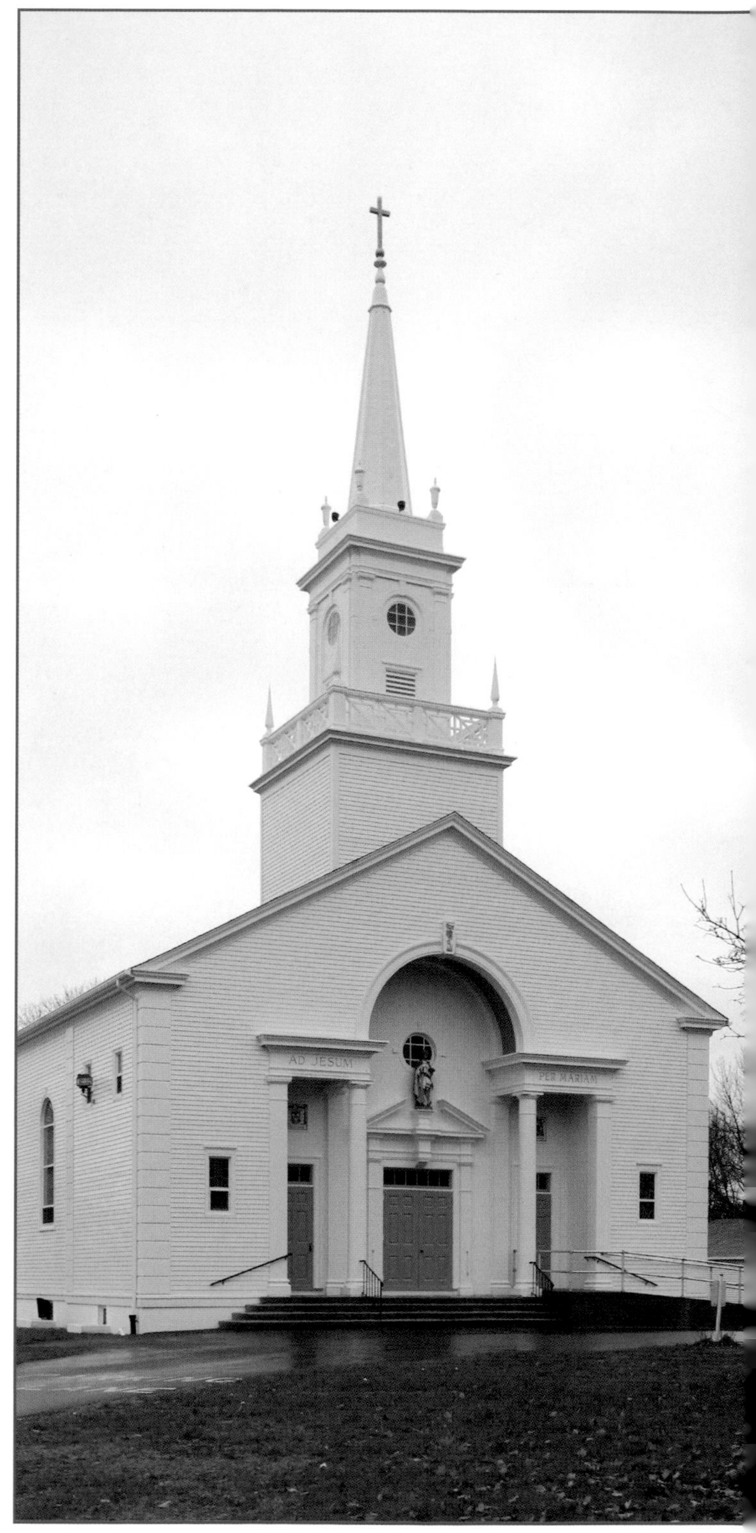

St. John the Baptist Parish, Westport

The original St. John the Baptist Church at Central Village was built in 1912. It was a mission of Espirito Santo Parish, and after 1915 of Saint Anthony of Padua Parish, both in Fall River. St. John's became a parish in 1930, and in 1932 St. Rose of Lima Chapel, a summer mission at Horseneck Beach, was dedicated. The chapel was completely destroyed in the 1938 hurricane. The present church with a parish center on the lower level was dedicated on July 13, 1980.

St. Bernard Parish, Assonet

Catholics in this part of Freetown were cared for by the priests of St. Joseph's and St. Michael's Parishes in Fall River until 1927, when the chaplain of St. Vincent's Home was placed in charge of the mission. Although this arrangement continued until 1977, there is good reason to believe St. Bernard's has had parochial status since 1962. An attractive small church was built in 1938 replacing the house chapel where people had gathered to worship for twenty years. In 1981 the parish was able to enhance its facilities by purchasing the former First Christian Church and parsonage. The church, built in 1832, is the oldest church building in the diocese.

Our Lady of Grace Parish, Westport

Formed in the fall of 1954 the parish embraces 10 square miles and was the 100th parish in the Diocese. A year later the present colonial church was dedicated on October 5, 1955. The parish center was completed in 1977. For many years the parish provided bus transportation, often with one of the priests at the wheel, for children attending Catholic schools in Fall River.

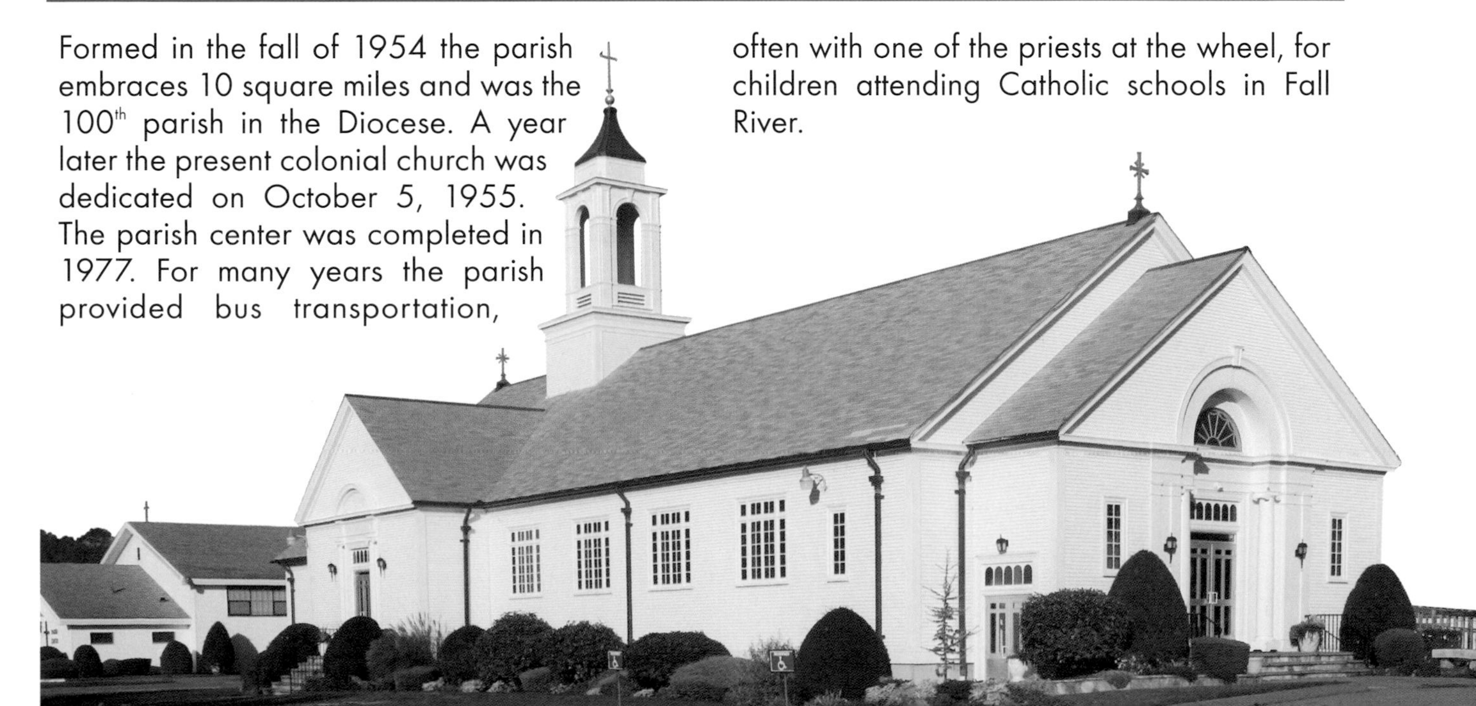

THE PARISHES OF

the New Bedford Deanery

A winter scene at Cathedral Camp, East Freetown

Annunciation Chapel, Bishop Stang High School

St. Lawrence Parish

The parish traces its origin from the first church built within the present Diocese in 1821. A monument marks the site at Allen and Orchard Streets. The present Keely Gothic church was dedicated in 1871. The Sisters of Mercy opened the first convent here in 1873. The parish maintained Holy Family High School and its predecessor St. Joseph's High School for a hundred years, closing in 1985. The elementary school, merged with Holy Name School, remains under lay direction. The parish has had only six pastors since the Civil War.

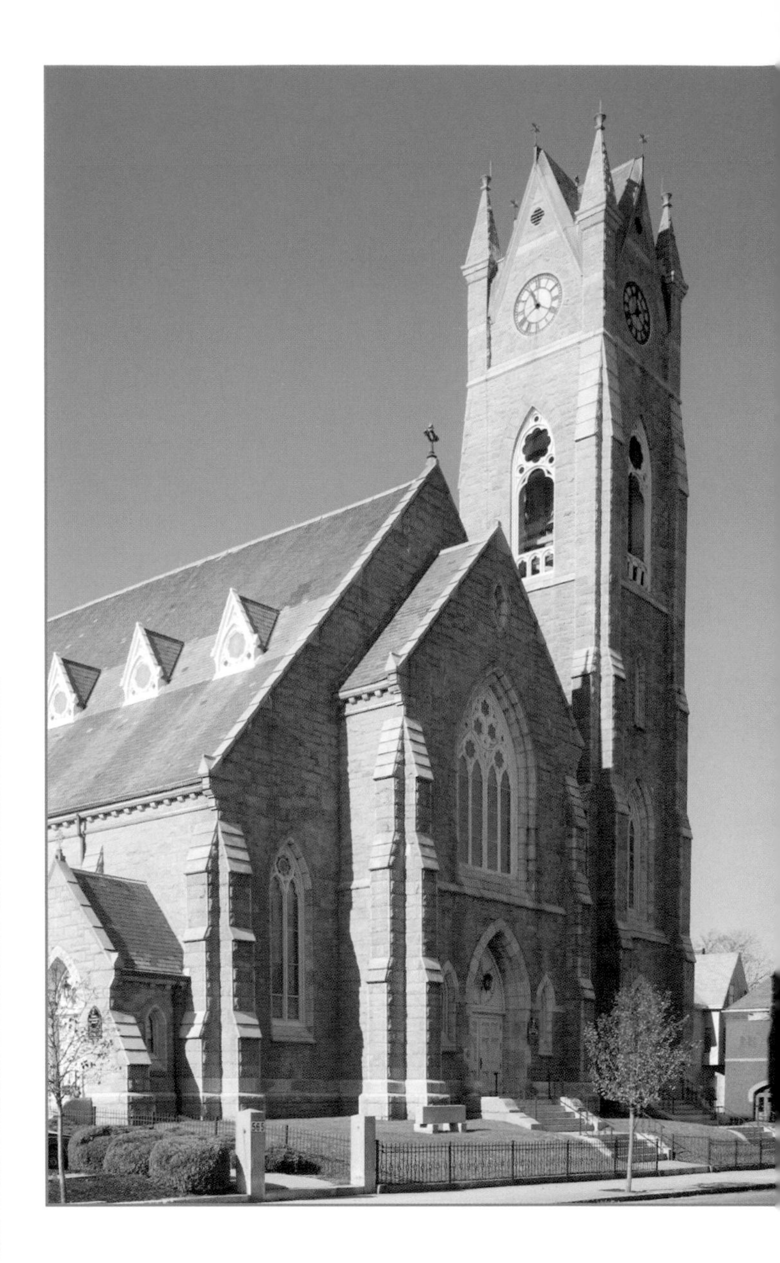

St. John the Baptist Parish

The first Portuguese congregation was formed in 1869 and the parish, the first for Portuguese-speaking parishioners in America, was formally established in 1871. The original church, dedicated in 1875, was destroyed by fire, and the present Romanesque church was dedicated in 1913. The Franciscan Missionaries of Mary and the Sisters of Mercy have engaged in the catechetical and teaching apostolates here. The parish school is now merged with St. James School.

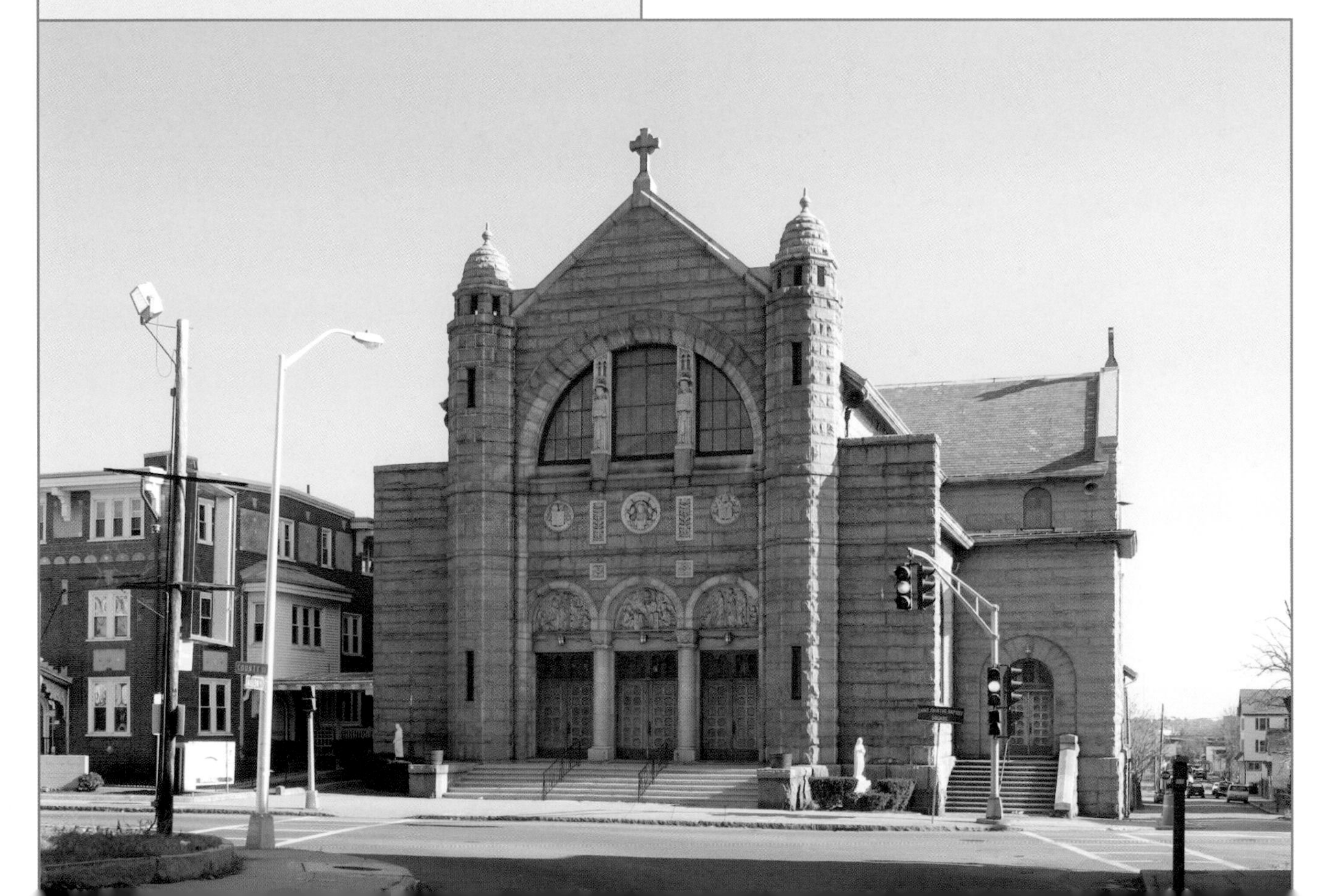

St. James Parish

Set off from St. Lawrence Parish in 1888 to provide for the people of the south end of the city, the parish began with a school already established and staffed by the Sisters of Mercy. The lower church was completed in 1892 and the superstructure of the graceful gothic church was dedicated in 1907. When neighboring St. Hyacinth's Parish, founded in 1890 for French Canadian Parishioners closed in 1977, the church became the Regina Pacis Center for the Hispanic community and the parish records were transferred to St. James Parish.

St. Kilian Parish

Established in 1896, the superstructure of granite Romanesque church was not dedicated until 1927. The former parish school was staffed by the Sisters of Mercy. The Franciscan Friars administered the parish from 1974 to 1996 when they were succeeded by the Incarnate Word Fathers.

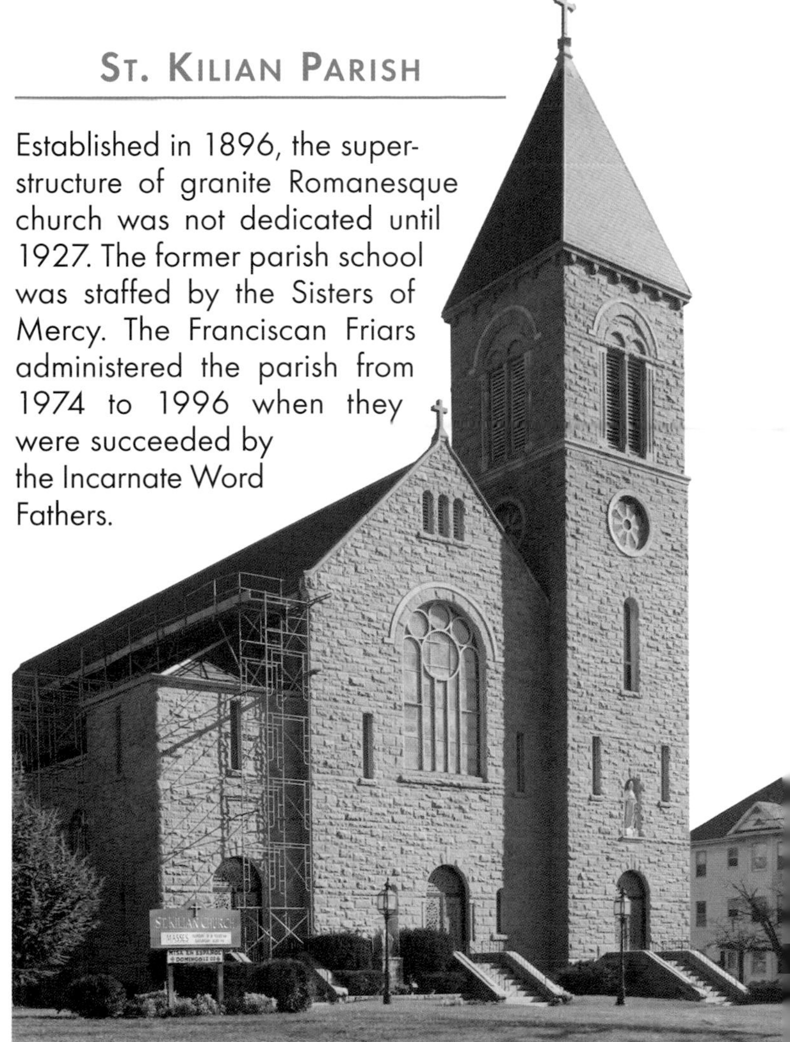

Saint Anthony Parish

The parish was founded in 1895 for French Canadians. The present church, which dominates the skyline of the north end of New Bedford, was completed in 1912. The striking interior is decorated in ornate baroque style. The elementary school was formerly staffed by the Holy Cross Sisters. The High School was discontinued in 1978. When Holy Rosary Parish, founded in 1908, closed in 1966, the parish records were transferred to St. Anthony's Parish. The Holy Rosary Church was built in 1896 as the Guardian Angels Chapel and Day Nursery by the pastor of Sacred Heart Parish.

Our Lady of Perpetual Help Parish

While different dates are sometimes given for the foundation of the parish, a rectory was acquired late in 1903, and the church was dedicated on the last day of 1905. A parish school was opened in 1927 under the direction of the Bernadine Sisters. In 1933 the Conventual Franciscan Friars were given charge of the parish, and when St. Casimir's Parish, established in 1926, closed in 2000 the church became a mission of Our Lady of Perpetual Help Parish.

Our Lady of Mt. Carmel Parish

This second parish for Portuguese parishioners in New Bedford was established in 1902. The lower church was dedicated in 1904 and the upper church in 1913. The Sisters of St. Dorothy came to teach in the parish school when it opened in 1941. Monsignor Antonio P. Vieira served as pastor for 56 years, dying at age 98 in 1964.

Our Lady of The Assumption Parish

Established in 1905 for Cape Verdian people, the parish has been staffed from the beginning by the Sacred Hearts Community. A new brick church replaced the original small frame church in 1957.

St. Anne Parish

The parish was established for French Canadians in the extreme southern portion of New Bedford in 1908. A school had already been established by the pastor of St. Hyacinth Parish with the Holy Cross Sisters as teachers. The present Federal style church was dedicated 1948.

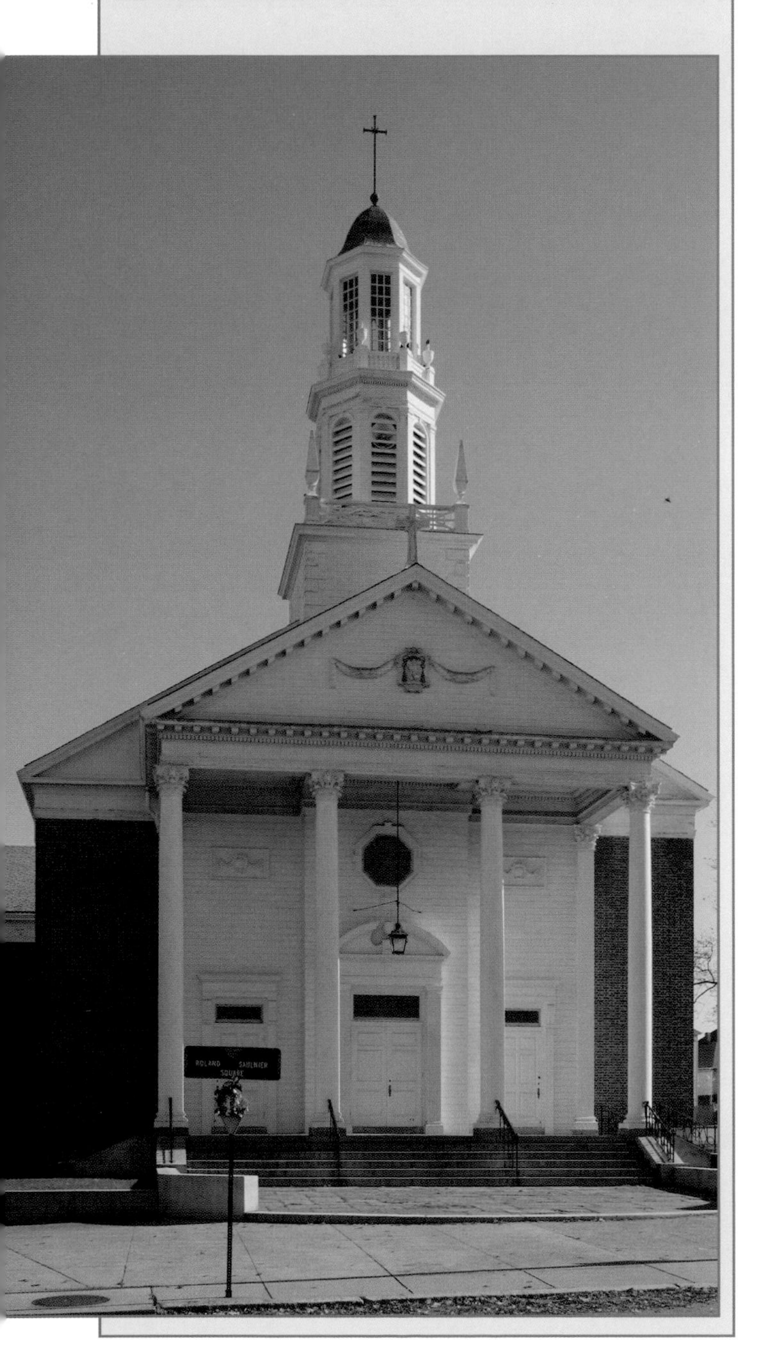

St. Hedwig Parish

Founded for Polish-speaking parishioners of the south end of the city in 1908, the Franciscan Conventual Friars took charge of the parish in 1951. In 1961 a new church and rectory were built. The Franciscans were succeeded in 1993 by the pastor of Nuestra Senora de Guadalupe Parish.

Nuestra Senora de Guadalupe Parish

The first parish for Hispanic parishioners was formally established in 1993 although Hispanic ministry was begun in 1961 with the founding of the Regina Pacis Center. The Guadalupanos Missionary Sisters of the Holy Spirit have been an important part of this apostolate since 1975. The pastor serves also as pastor of St Hedwig's Church where both communites worship.

Immaculate Conception Parish

Founded for the Portuguese-speaking people of the north end of the city in 1909, the church was dedicated in 1913.

A parish school staffed by the Sisters of the Holy Names of Jesus and Mary was maintained from 1958 to 1970.

St. Mary Parish

Established for English-speaking Catholics in the far north end of the city in 1927, the small church was destroyed in the 1938 hurricane and the parish was discontinued. It was reopened in 1951 and a basement church was built, which has been incorporated into a new church, dedicated in 1988. The school opened in 1966 staffed by the Sisters of Mercy, continues under lay leadership.

St. Francis of Assisi Parish

The Italian community in New Bedford was placed in the care of the pastor of Holy Rosary Parish in Fall River in 1914. In 1928 a former Protestant church was acquired and a year later a parish was established. The church was substantially enlarged and rededicated in 1971.

Our Lady of Fatima Parish

The parish was established in 1966 by a division of St. Mary's Parish. The chapel formerly attached to St. Therese Parish became the parish church.

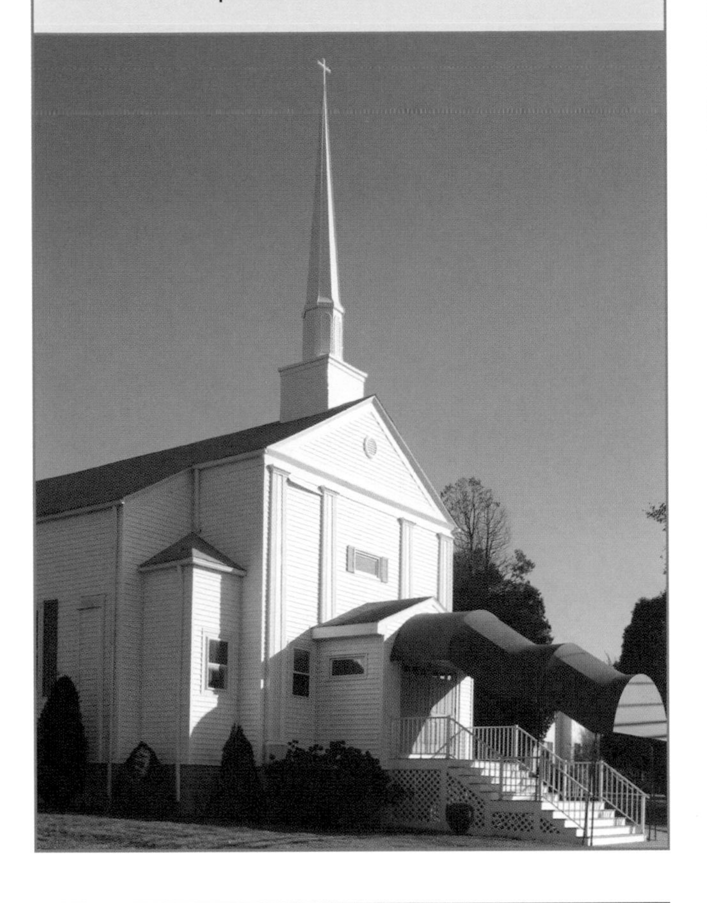

Holy Name of the Sacred Heart of Jesus Parish

The present parish was formed in 1999 by the merger of two parishes. Sacred Heart Parish, the first for French Canadians in New Bedford was founded in 1876. The wooden Gothic church was dedicated in 1877. The parish school opened in 1886 with the Sisters of the Holy Cross in charge. Holy Name Parish was established in 1909. The new parish received from St. Lawrence Parish St. Joseph's School and St. Mary's Church on County Street built as a mission chapel. A new church was dedicated on April 19, 1941, and now serves the merged parish. When St. Boniface Parish closed in 1987 the parish registers were transferred to Holy Name Parish. The former parish had been established in 1906 for people of German and Austrian background and was in the care of the Sacred Hearts Community from the beginning.

St. Joseph - St Therese Parish

The present parish came into being in 1999 through the merger of two French Canadian parishes in the north end of New Bedford. St. Joseph's Parish founded in 1910 was at first served by a combination church and school building. In due course, an impressive parish plant evolved consisting of a parish school still maintained, a convent for the Sisters of St. Joseph, a rectory and a magnificent Romanesque church. Dedicated on September 29, 1940, it is now the church of the combined parish.

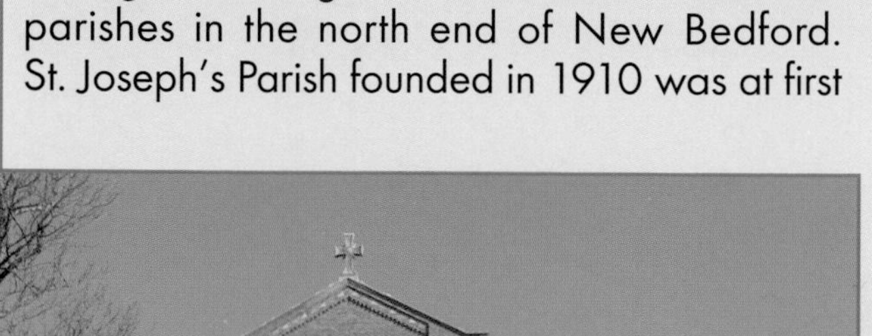

St. Therese Parish was established by a division of St Joseph's Parish in 1926. The plans of the church built in 1929, provided for school classrooms on the first floor. A replica of the shrine of St. Therese at the Lisieux Carmel became a place of devotion.

St. Mary Parish, Dartmouth

A country parish when it was founded in 1930. The needs of a growing suburban parish required the replacement of the original church in Padanaram Village with the present colonial style church, dedicated in 1956. A parish center was added to the complex in 1968.

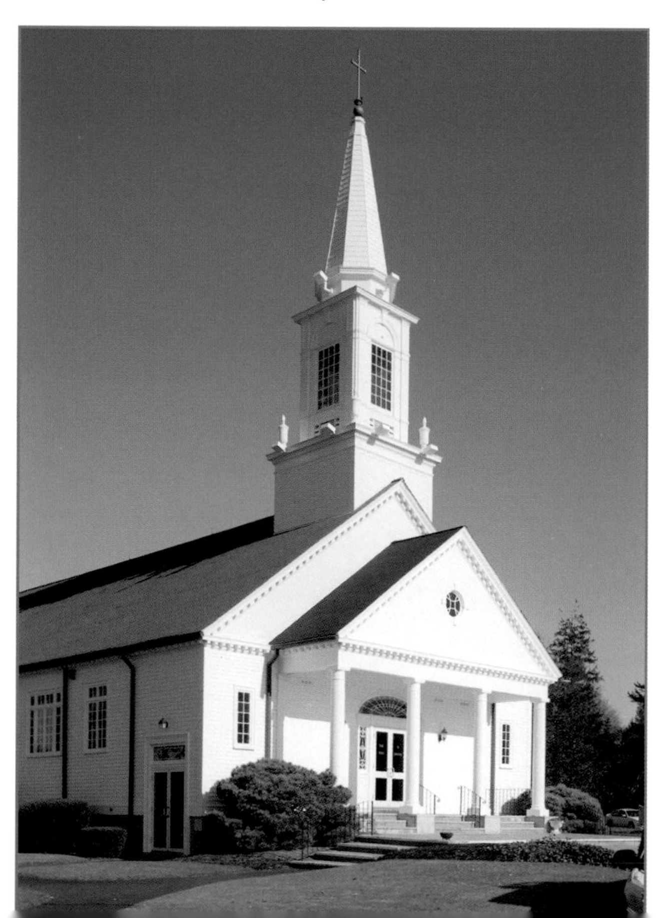

St. Julie Billiart Parish, Dartmouth

Established in 1969, the parish was named for the foundress of the Sister of Notre Dame de Namur serving on the faculty of the adjacent Bishop Stang High School. The church was dedicated in 1971 and skillfully enlarged and refurbished in 1993.

St. John Neumann Parish, East Freetown

The parish founded in 1984 was first centered at the Chapel of the Assumption at Cathedral Camp. The lakeside church was completed and dedicated in 1988.

St. George Parish, Westport

When founded in 1914 the parish covered large portions of the towns of Dartmouth and Westport. The church was dedicated in 1924, and in 1956 a parish school was opened with the Sisters of the Holy Cross serving as teachers.

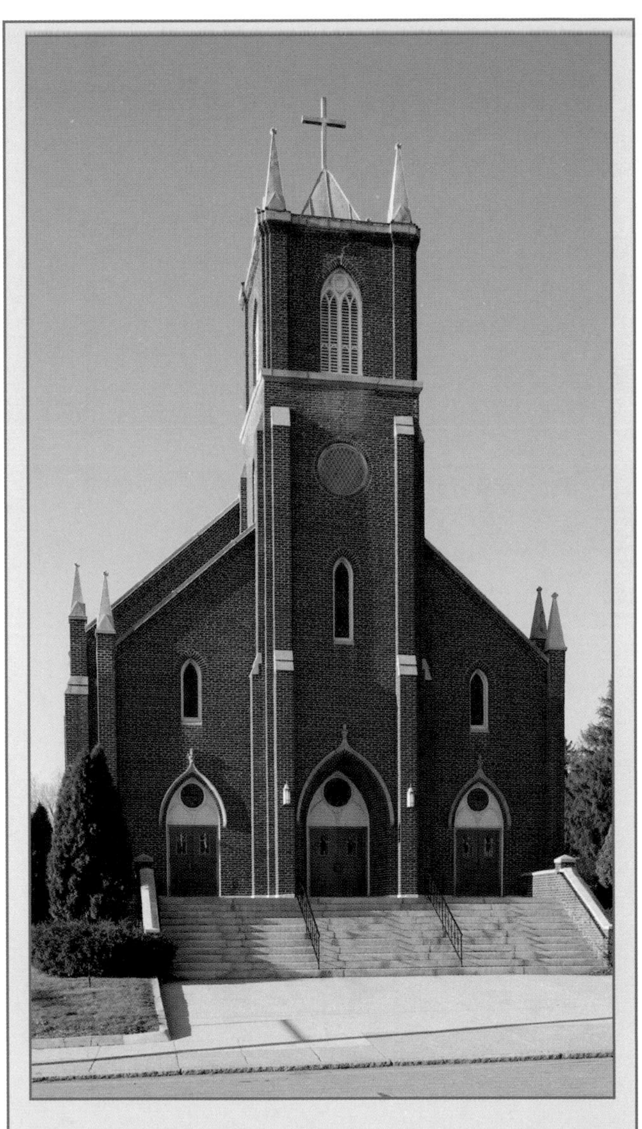

St. Joseph Parish, Fairhaven

The parish was established upon the arrival of three priests and two brothers of the Sacred Hearts Community in May of 1905. When the present church was dedicated in 1925 the former combination church and school building could be used exclusively as a school. The school staffed by the Sisters of the Sacred Hearts of Jesus and Mary moved into a completely new facility in 1964.

St. Mary's Parish, Fairhaven

A mission of St. Joseph's Parish, St. Mary's has enjoyed parochial status since 1927. a basement church was built in 1925 and replaced by the present church in 1966. For many years the pastor resided at the rectory of neighboring Sacred Hearts Parish, which was founded for French Canadians in 1908 and closed in 1987.

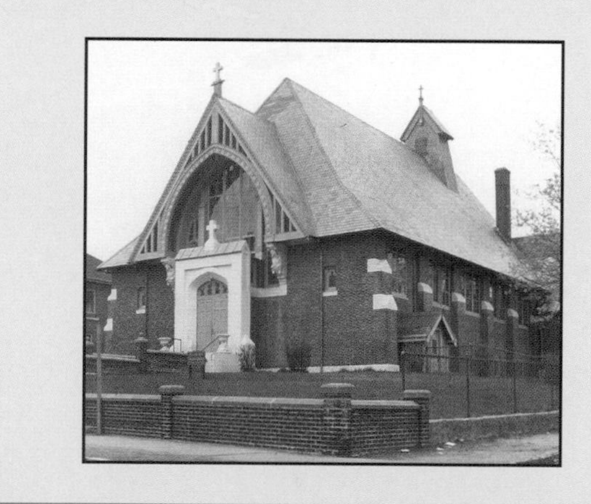

St. Francis Xavier Parish, Acushnet

The parish was established in 1915. The present church was dedicated in 1916, replacing the former church destroyed by fire. In 1965 a new building was completed for the parish school, which opened in 1922 in the care of Fall River's Dominican Sisters of St. Catherine.

St. Anthony's Parish, Mattapoisett

Established as a mission of St. Joseph's Parish in Fairhaven in 1906, the congregation converted the former Advent chapel into a place of worship in 1908. A new church was built in 1911 and later enlarged. In 1954 the mission became a parish with a resident pastor. The present church was dedicated in 1974 and in 1988 the care of the parish passed from the Sacred Hearts Community to the diocesan clergy.

St. Rita Parish, Marion

The parish, established in 1972, had long been a mission of St. Patrick's Parish in Wareham. The church was dedicated in 1916.

St. Patrick Parish, Wareham

A mission of Sandwich for 80 years, the first church was a former Baptist chapel purchased in 1865. St. Patrick's became a parish in 1911, and the beautiful colonial church was dedicated in 1940. The Missionary Servants of the Blessed Trinity opened a cenacle here the same year. Mass has been offered regularly in West Wareham since 1928 and St. Anthony's Church was dedicated in 1935.

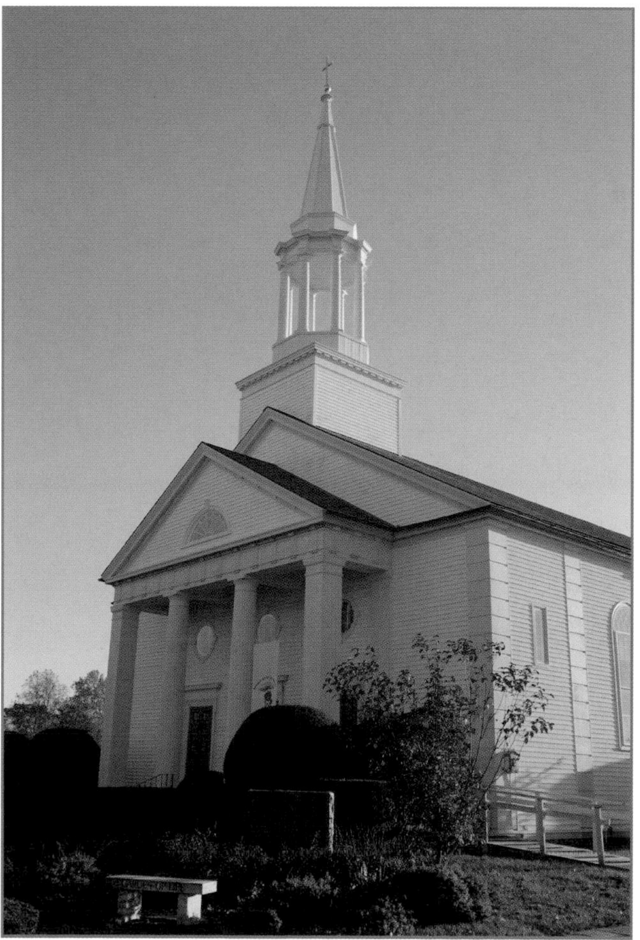

STONEHILL
STONEHILL

The Parishes of

the Taunton Deanery

Immaculate Conception Parish

Established in the Whittenton section of Taunton in 1882, the congregation was a mix of French Canadians and Irish. A large wooden church, dedicated in 1885, was replaced by the present church in 1954. Taunton's first Catholic school opened here in 1891 with the Holy Union Sisters in charge.

St. Mary Parish

The first Mass was celebrated in Taunton in 1828. In November of 1830 the first resident pastor arrived and a church was built and dedicated in 1832. The present St. Mary's Church, a Taunton landmark for generations, took about a decade to build and was dedicated in 1872. The parish school opened in 1908 and St. Mary's High School in 1911, both staffed by the Holy Union Sisters. The parish has been in the care of the Holy Cross Fathers since 1999.

St. Joseph Parish

The parish was formed from the western portion of St. Mary's Parish in 1896. St. Joseph's Church dedicated on January 1, 1911, was built in English gothic style. For many years the Holy Union Sisters staffed the former school opened in 1954.

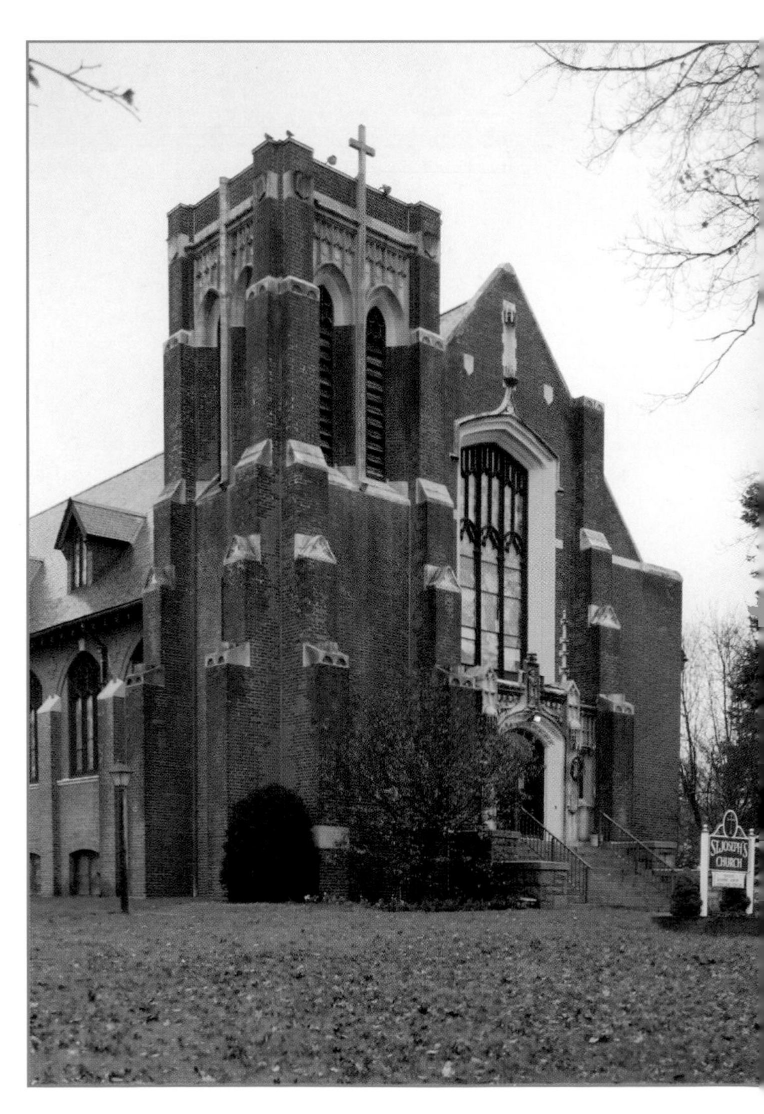

Holy Family Parish

Established as a parish in 1900, the first Holy Family Church in East Taunton was built as mission of St. Mary's Parish in 1858 and was later served by priests from Sacred Heart Parish .The present church was completed in 1909.

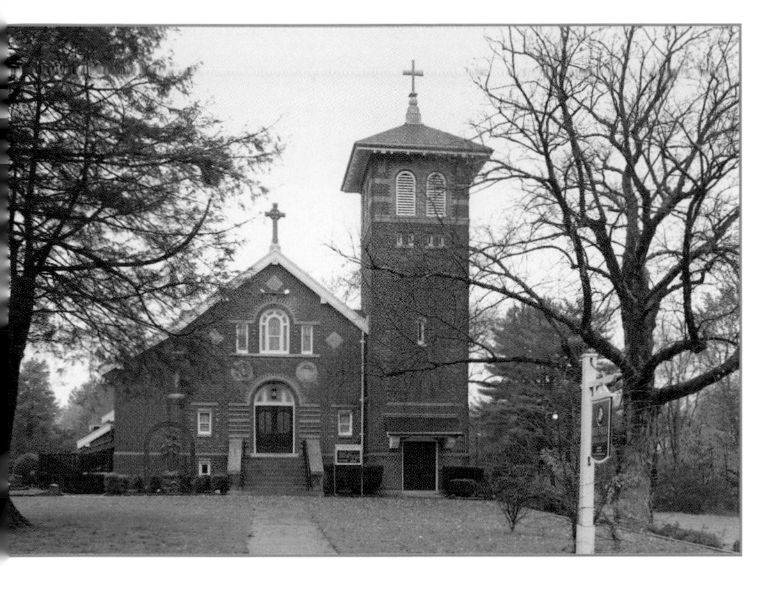

St. Anthony Parish

The first parish in Taunton for the Portuguese-speaking community was established in 1903. When the present church was dedicated in the summer of 1951 the classrooms for a new parish school were built above the former basement church. After this building was damaged by fire in 1990 a new parish center was constructed.

St. Paul Parish

The parish today includes the Oakland section of Taunton and a portion of Rehoboth and when it was founded in 1904, the town of Norton as well. The original church dedicated in 1905 was substantially enlarged and renovated in 1965.

St. Jacques Parish

The parish was established for French Canadians in Taunton in 1904. A basement church, built in 1906, served the parish for many years. The superstructure was completed and dedicated on the feast of St. James in 1953. The former parish school staffed by the Holy Union Sisters opened in 1913.

Our Lady of The Holy Rosary Parish

Taunton's only Polish Parish was founded in 1907. The church was dedicated in 1909. In 1923 the parish passed to the care of the Franciscan Conventual Friars. In 1984 the parish center was completed.

Annunciation of The Lord Parish

The parish was formed in 2000 by the merger of Our Lady of Lourdes Parish, Taunton's second parish for Portuguese-speaking parishioners, established in 1905, and Sacred Heart Parish, founded in 1873. The church, dedicated in 1912 now serves the merged parish as does Our Lady of Lourdes School opened in 1963, staffed by the Sisters of Mercy.

Immaculate Conception Parish, North Easton

One of the oldest centers of Catholic life in the Diocese the parish was formally established in 1871. The congregation has worshiped in three churches, the first built in 1851, the second in 1865, and the present church dedicated on April 19, 1904. The parish center, built in 1962, was greatly renovated and improved in 1994.

Holy Cross Parish, South Easton

The parish, established in 1966, has been in the care of the Holy Cross Fathers since its foundation. The church was dedicated in 1967 and the parish center in 2001.

St. Joseph Parish, North Dighton

Begun as a mission of Sacred Heart Parish in Taunton in 1887, St. Joseph's became a parish in 1913. The original church was replaced in 1935 by the present church. The parish center was built and dedicated in 1984 after the old parish hall was destroyed by fire.

St. Peter Parish, Dighton

The pastor of Sacred Heart Parish in Taunton built St. Peter's Church in 1901 and in 1903 the mission was attached to St. Anthony's Parish in Taunton. Established as a parish in 1925, the Monfort Fathers staffed the parish from 1967 to 1997. The parish center and hall was purchased from the Unitarian Society in 1993.

St. Ann Parish, Raynham

The parish was created by a division of St. Mary's Parish in Taunton in 1960 and the church was dedicated the next year. The Parish Center was completed in 1989.

THE PARISHES OF

the Attleboro Deanery

LaSalette Shrine at Christmas

St. John the Evangelist Parish

Founded in 1883, having been briefly a mission of North Attleboro, a large wooden church was built in 1885. The present perpendicular gothic church, dedicated in 1932, has been complemented by the Hospitality and Administration Center of similar design opened in 1998. The parish school began in the fall of 1953.

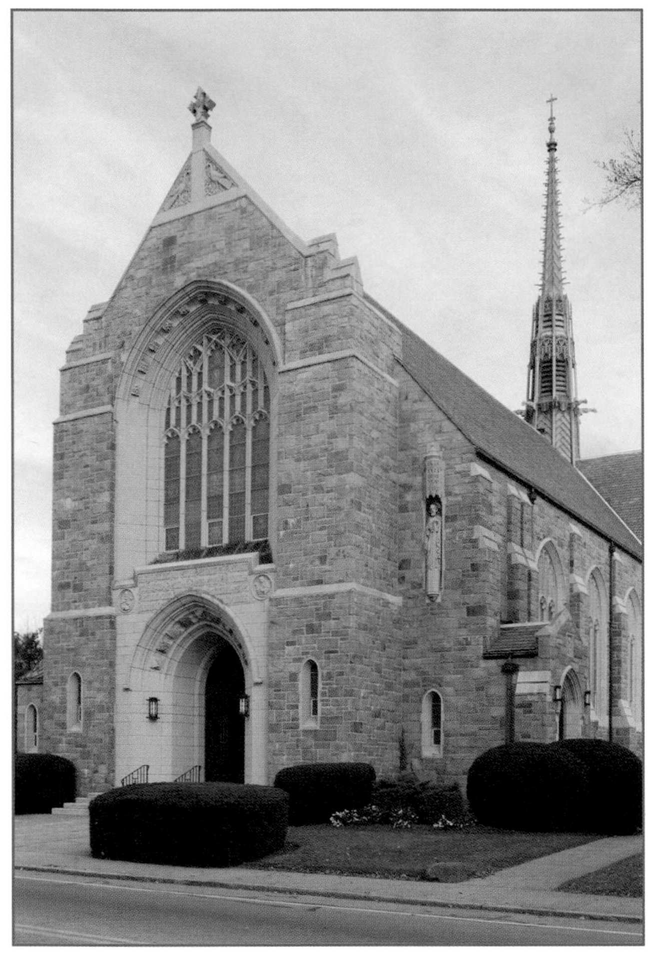

St. Stephen Parish

The church is the oldest in the area. Dedicated in 1875, it was a mission of St. Mary's in North Attleboro, and then of St. Joseph's in Pawtucket before becoming a parish in 1885. From 1905 to 1938 the parish served St. Rose of Lima mission in Hebronville. When this mission church was built it included classrooms, and for a time Attleboro's first Catholic school was conducted here.

St. Joseph Parish

The parish was established for French Canadians in 1904 and the Romanesque church was completed in 1929. The ministry to Spanish-speaking people of the area has been centered at St. Joseph's since 1970. The parish has been under the care of the priests of the Fraternity of St. Charles Borromeo since 2000.

St. Theresa of the Child Jesus Parish

In 1925 a parish was established for both the English and French-speaking Catholics of South Attleboro. A small wooden chapel, built as a temporary church in 1926, served the parish until the present church was completed and dedicated in 1957. The parish center was opened in 1970.

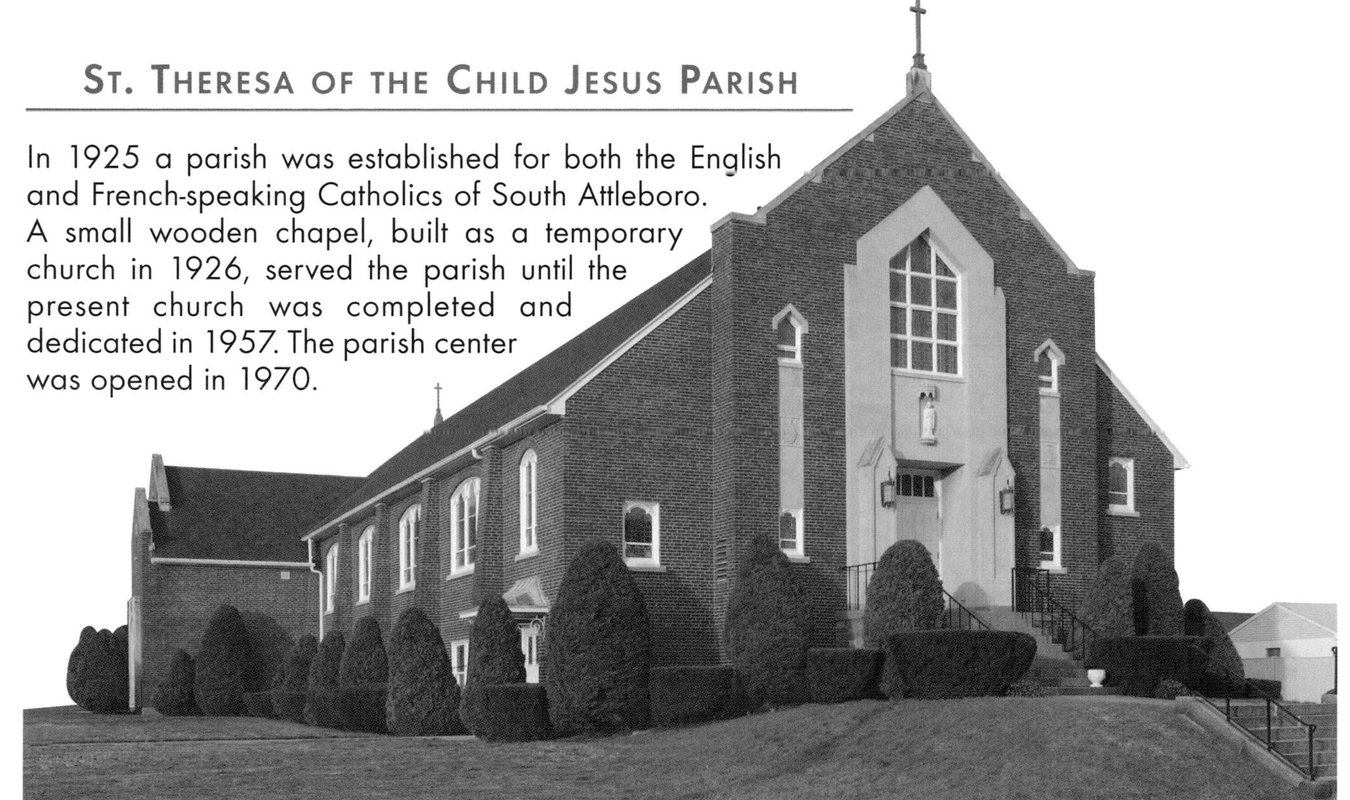

Holy Ghost Parish

The people of the Lonicut section of Attleboro were cared for by the pastor of Hebronville who built a church for them in 1921, and on the day it opened he spoke in English, Portuguese, French, and Italian. Later the same month a resident pastor was appointed. The Trinitarian Sisters arrived in 1939 and conducted a kindergarten and served as catechists in the parish for many years. The present brick colonial church was dedicated in 1964.

St. Mary Parish, North Attleboro

The oldest parish in the area, the first church was built in 1859 at Attleboro Falls. In 1877 the present site in North Attleboro was acquired. An octagonal stone building on the property served as a church until the basement of the present church was ready. The completed church was dedicated on the patronal feast of the Immaculate Conception in 1901. A school and a convent for the Sisters of Mercy opened in 1924.

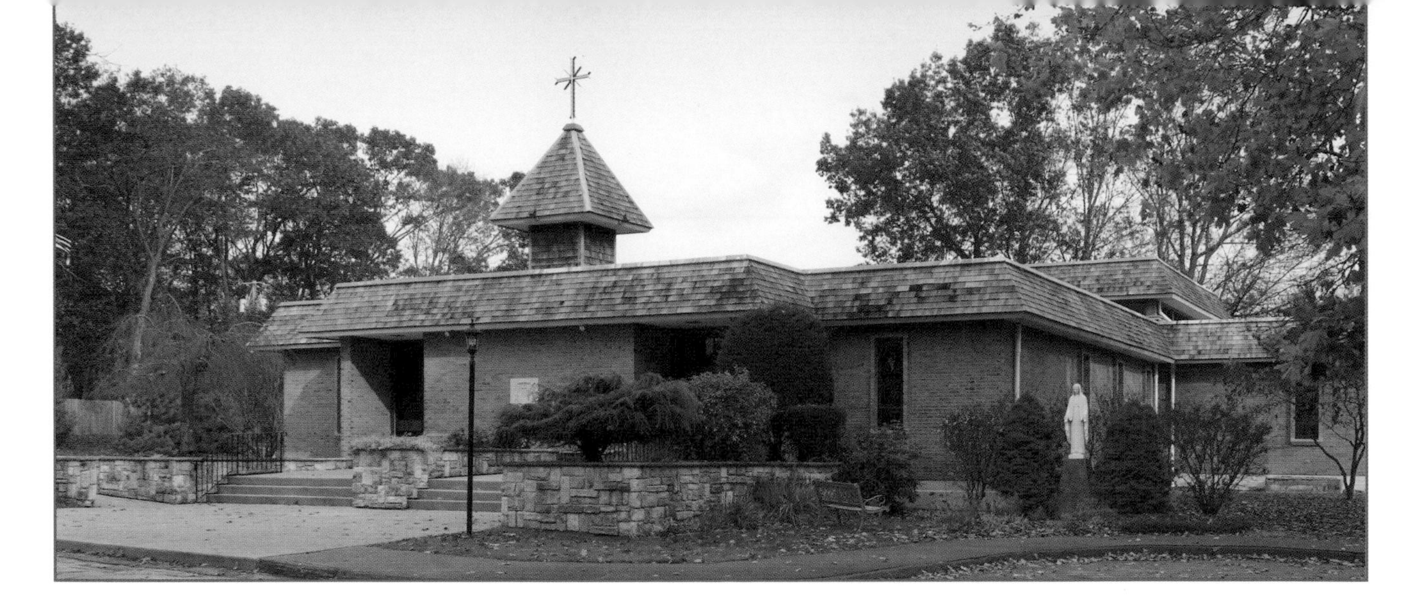

St. Mark Parish, Attleboro Falls

The youngest parish in the area was founded in 1967. The new parish community worshiped at Bishop Feehan High School until the new church was completed in 1971.

Sacred Heart Parish, North Attleboro

The parish, long desired by the town's French Canadian population, was established in 1904. The school, staffed by the Holy Union Sisters, opened in 1923, has been merged with St. Mary's School. The upper church was completed in 1929.

St. Mary Parish, North Seekonk

The parish was established in 1906 and a church was built in the Attleboro village of Hebronville for the English-speaking Catholics. St. Stephen's Parish, which formerly served a mixed congregation, became the French-Canadian parish for the area. In 1957 the new St. Mary's Church, built over the town line in North Seekonk, was dedicated. In 1970 a parish center was opened and in 1987 a new rectory replaced the original one in Hebronville.

Our Lady of Mt. Carmel Parish, Seekonk

The original Mt. Carmel Chapel was built in 1908, and was successively served by priests from Sacred Heart and Our Lady of Lourdes Parishes in Taunton and Holy Ghost Parish in Attleboro until a parish was established in 1922. The parish also includes a large portion of the town of Rehoboth. A parish center, built in 1965, provided much needed space for the increasing numbers attending Sunday Mass. The present church was dedicated in 1982.

St. Mary Parish, Mansfield

The parish was established in 1894. The first church was built in 1871 as a mission of St. Mary's in North Attleboro. It was replaced in 1915 by a brick church of Gothic design. In 1965 the present church was built on a new site. The parish center was dedicated in 1987 and recently expanded to accommodate the new parish school, which opened in 2002.

St. Mary's Parish, Norton

The first church was built in 1868 as a mission of St. Mary's in Taunton, and it was later served from St. John's in Attleboro and St. Paul's in Taunton. The present church was built in 1924 and the mission was raised to parochial status in 1925. The parish center was completed in 1961.

The Parishes of

the Cape Cod and Islands Deanery

St. Joseph Bell Tower, Woods Hole

Window of Our Lady of the Isle ,
St. Mary's Church, Nantucket

Corpus Christi Parish, Sandwich

The first church was dedicated in honor of St. Peter in 1830. When the third church was built in the center of town in 1901 it was dedicated under the title of Corpus Christi. In 1990 a parish center with a place for worship was built at an advantageous new site in East Sandwich. The new church was recently dedicated on August 31, 2003. The parish includes the mission chapel of St. Theresa at Sagamore, dedicated in 1926. Mass was first celebrated on a regular basis in 1918 for the Italian community in this village of the town of Bourne.

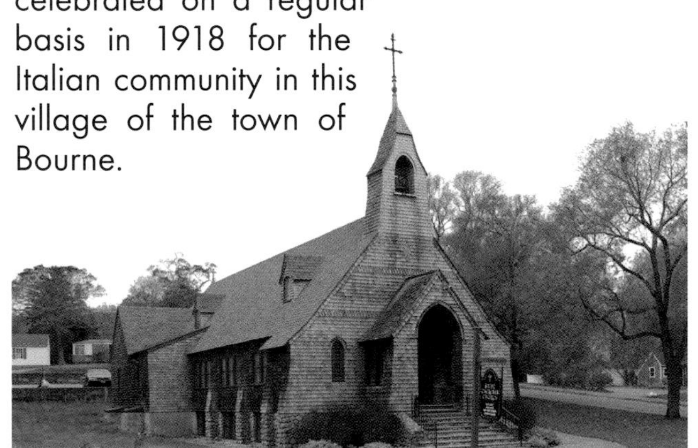

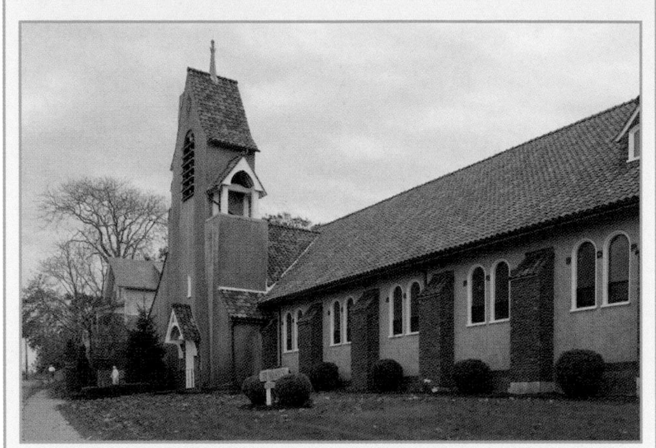

St. Margaret Parish, Buzzards Bay

Established as a parish in 1946, St. Margaret's Church was built as a mission of Corpus Christi Parish in 1915 to serve that part of the town of Bourne on the north side of the Cape Cod Canal. Also included in the parish is the Onset section of Wareham, St. Mary Star of the Sea Church, dedicated in 1924, was then a mission of St. Patrick's Parish in Wareham. St. Margaret's Regional School opened in1994 in the facility built as a parish center in 1969.

St John the Evangelist Parish, Pocasset

Mass was first offered here by the pastor of Corpus Christi for summer vacationers in a barn in 1912 . By 1924 land had been purchased and a building moved to the site, which was converted into St. John's Chapel. The present church was dedicated in 1931. Established as a parish for the Monument Beach, Pocasset and Cataumet sections of Bourne in 1969, the parish center was completed in 1980 and the church refurbished and enlarged in 1983.

St. Francis Xavier Parish, Hyannis

The parish established in 1902 traces its origin to the small St. Patrick's Chapel built in the Catholic Cemetery in 1874 by the pastor from Sandwich. The present church, completed in 1904, has been enlarged over the years. A new altar, given in memory of Lt. Joseph P. Kennedy, Jr., USN was dedicated by Bishop James E. Cassidy in 1946. The parish center built in 1969 was transformed into St. Francis Xavier Preparatory School in 1996. The Trinitarian Sisters carried on a catechetical and social apostolate for many years beginning in 1944. The parish serves Sacred Heart chapel in Yarmouthport, built as a mission of Woods Hole in 1899.

St. Pius X, South Yarmouth

The parish was established in 1954 and a shingled church of colonial design was built. The present spacious church was dedicated in 1969. A new parish center was added to the complex in 1990 and presently a school is under construction. The parish includes Our Lady of the Highway Chapel at Bass River, built as a mission of Hyannis in 1949.

Our Lady of The Assumption Parish, Osterville

The church greatly remodeled over the years was built as a mission of Hyannis in 1905. The parish, established in 1928, included the villages of Santuit, Cotuit, Centerville, West Barnstable, and Marstons Mills in the town of Barnstable, and after 1960 the town of Mashpee, previously part of the Sandwich parish. At the same time Our Lady of Hope Chapel in West Barnstable became the responsibility of the Centerville Parish. St Jude's Chapel in Santuit was dedicated in 1940 and Queen of All Saints Chapel was dedicated in 1968 to serve the people of Popponesset Beach and New Seabury in Mashpee.

Our Lady of Victory Parish, Centerville

A few months after construction of the church was begun the parish was established on July 1, 1957. In 1960 the parish boundaries were expanded to include Our Lady of Hope Chapel in West Barnstable. The distinctive chapel with Spanish / Moorish accents was dedicated in 1915 as mission of Hyannis. The parish center was built in 1983.

Christ The King Parish, Mashpee

Formed from two missions of the Osterville Parish, St. Jude's Chapel at Santuit and Queen of All Saints Chapel at Popponesset Beach, the parish was formally established in 1984, encompassing the town of Mashpee and the villages of Santuit, Cotuit and Marstons Mills in the town of Barnstable. A large church of Georgian colonial design, incorporating St. Jude's Chapel, which was dramatically moved to the site, together with a Parish Hall and Center, was dedicated on the feast of Christ the King in 1989. The Dominican Sisters of Hope direct the catechetical program.

Holy Trinity Parish, West Harwich

The first Holy Trinity was built at Harwich Center in 1866. The people were served over the years by resident pastors or by priests from other Cape parishes. In 1927 the church, then a mission of Wellfleet, was destroyed by fire. A new church was built in 1930 at West Harwich and the following year parochial status was granted. This church also burned in 1963. The present church was dedicated in 1965. Meanwhile the mission church of the Annunciation in Dennisport was built in 1953. The same year the Victoryknoll Sisters began their catechetical apostolate. They were succeeded by the Sisters of Mercy who conducted a parish school from 1965 to 1971. The parish passed from the care of the Sacred Hearts Community to the diocesan clergy in 1991. Recent accomplishments include the opening of Holy Trinity Regional School in 1994 and the dedication of Our Lady of Life Chapel, devoted to perpetual adoration of The Eucharist, in 2002.

St. Peter the Apostle Parish, Provincetown

The first church in Provincetown was a school building purchased in 1853 and converted into a chapel with quarters for a visiting priest. The first resident priest came in 1873 and St. Peter the Apostle Church was built and dedicated in 1874. The annual Blessing of the Fishing Fleet on the last Sunday in June began in 1948. From 1965 to 1971 a parish school functioned under the direction of the Religious of the Love of God, exiles from Cuba, who had come to St. Peter's in 1961. In 1999 the congregation of Our Lady of Perpetual Help Church in North Truro, built in 1915 as mission of Wellfleet, was transferred to the care of the pastor of Provincetown.

Our Lady of Lourdes Parish, Wellfleet and North Eastham

The first church was small chapel built as mission of Provincetown. In 1911 a parish was established and Our Lady of Lourdes Church was dedicated in 1912. The parish, served by the Sacred Hearts Community until 1987, was for many years the center of pastoral ministry for at least six towns on the lower Cape. With the hope of providing a new church, Our Lady of Lourdes Church and Sacred Heart Church in Truro, built as a mission of Provincetown in 1895, have been closed. Parish life is now centered at the Church of The Visitation in North Eastham. Built in 1952 as a mission of Orleans, it became part of the Wellfleet parish in 1999.

St. Joan of Arc Parish, Orleans

Established in 1947, the parish included not only Orleans, but also Eastham and Brewster. The original St. Joan of Arc Church was dedicated on August 15, 1947. From 1953 to 1969 the parish maintained a school staffed by the Sisters of Divine Providence. In 1984 the present church was completed and dedicated on August 12.

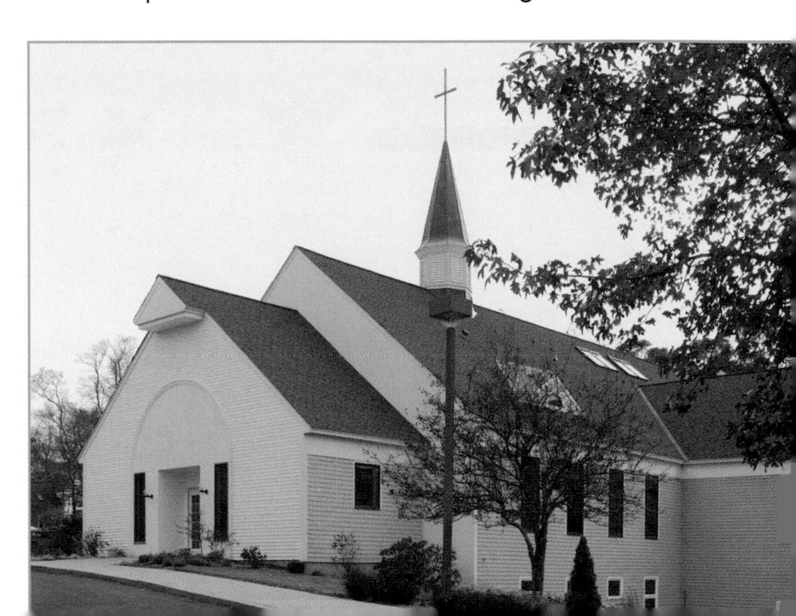

Our Lady of the Cape Parish, Brewster

Established in 1961, and placed in the care of the Missionaries of Our Lady of LaSalette, the parish had its beginning at the Immaculate Conception Chapel in East Brewster. This small church, built in 1907, has successively been a mission of Harwich, Wellfleet, Orleans and Brewster. A year later Our Lady of the Cape Church was dedicated and it is now in the process of being enlarged and virtually rebuilt.

Holy Redeemer Parish, Chatham

The church was built in 1916 as a mission of Wellfleet, and in 1931 Holy Redeemer became a mission of West Harwich. The church has undergone many improvements over the years, and in 1955 the mission became a parish. In 1963 the mission church of Our Lady of Grace was opened in South Chatham. The Sacred Hearts Community handed over pastoral responsibilities to the diocesan clergy in 1988.

St. Joseph Parish, Woods Hole

The church was built by the pastor of Sandwich to provide for the growing number of Catholics especially in the summer. It was dedicated in 1882. In July of the following year the first pastor was appointed. The pastor also had the care of Nantucket. In 1929 the wife of Dr. Frank R. Lillie, director of the Marine Biological Laboratory, the former Frances Crane, a physician and a convert to Catholicism, gave the now familiar stone bell tower. Its two bells were cast in England and named for the Catholic scientists Mendel and Pasteur.

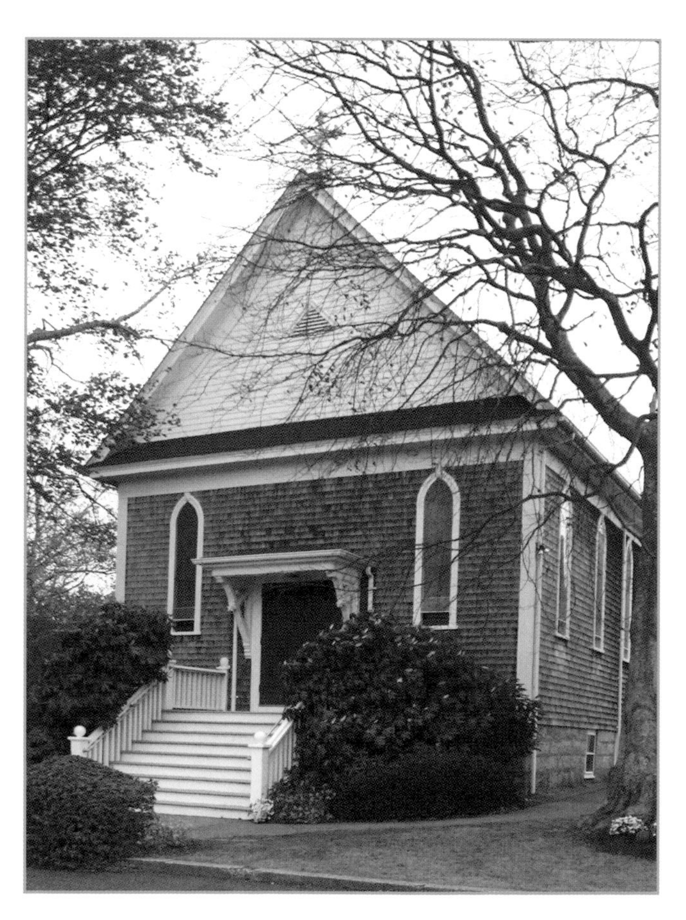

St. Patrick Parish, Falmouth

The parish was established in June of 1928 with St. Thomas the Apostle Chapel at Falmouth Heights as the parish church. The building, a ball room where Mass was first celebrated in the summer of 1918, was purchased in 1921 by the pastor of St. Joseph's in Woods Hole. Another of Woods Hole's missions, Immaculate Conception at Megansett in North Falmouth, was assigned to the new parish. Mass had been offered there first in a summer casino in 1915, and the hall was purchased in 1920. In March of 1931 St. Patrick's Church in Falmouth, built in 1899 and up to now a mission of Woods Hole, became the Falmouth parish church, and St. Thomas Chapel the mission. The Megansett chapel was then returned to the care of Woods Hole Parish.

St. Elizabeth Seton Parish, North Falmouth

In 1977 a parish was established in North Falmouth and the Immaculate Conception mission closed. A rectory and a shingled church of colonial design were built on land bought twenty year previously.

St. Anthony Parish, East Falmouth

In 1921 when parishioners from the Azores and Cape Verde requested a Portuguese-speaking priest, a parish was established and St. Anthony's Church was dedicated the next year. In 1977 the boundaries of the Falmouth parishes were adjusted, and St. Anthony's became the territorial parish for the East Falmouth area.

Since 1996 the three parishes on the island of Martha's Vineyard have been in the care of a single pastor and parochial vicar. Sacred Heart Parish in Oak Bluffs was established in 1903. The original church was built in 1880 by the pastor of St. Lawrence Parish, and later served by St John the Baptist Parish in New Bedford. In 1965 it was converted into a parish hall. The property was recently sold, since the parish has acquired a new facility for a center. The Star of

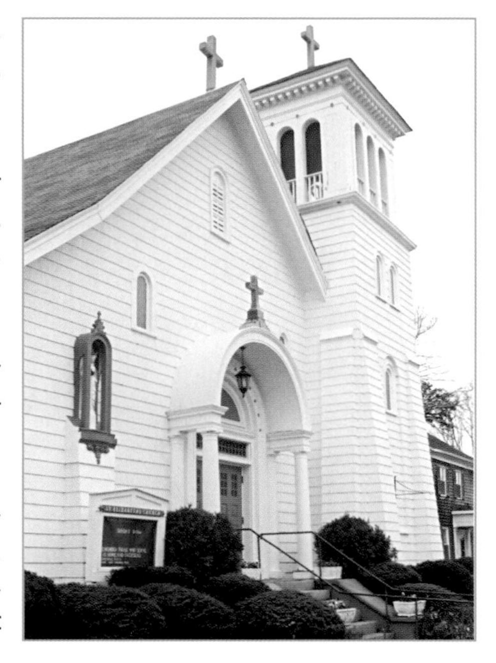

the Sea Church, built in 1920 to accommodate summer residents, serves as the parish church. St. Elizabeth Parish in Edgartown was established in1969, having been a mission of Oak Bluffs almost from the beginning of the parish. The present church was dedicated in 1925. St. Augustine's Parish in Vineyard Haven, was established in 1957 comprising the towns of Tisbury, West Tisbury, Aquinnah and Chilmark. The original church, built a mission in 1911, was replaced by the present church in 1962.

ST. MARY, OUR LADY OF THE ISLE PARISH, NANTUCKET

The church was built in 1897 by the pastor Woods Hole. It replaced the original church building acquired in 1856. The parish was established and a resident pastor appointed in 1903. The present rectory was purchased in 1928. For many years Mass has been offered at Siaconset during the summer season.

Schools in the Diocese of Fall River

	Schools in the Diocese of Fall River	Founding Religious Communities
1874	The Academy Fall River	Sisters of Mercy
1875	St. Mary Fall River	Sisters of Mercy
1876	Notre Dame* # Fall River	Religious of Jesus and Mary 1877 Brothers of Christian Schools 1893
1877	Jesus-Mary Academy Fall River	Religious of Jesus and Mary
1879	St. Anne* Fall River	Sisters of Mercy Sisters of the Holy Cross 1883 Dominicans of St. Catherine 1895 Brothers of Christian Schools 1895
1883	St. Joseph (Holy Name)+ New Bedford	Sisters of Mercy
	St. Joseph High (Holy Family) New Bedford	Sisters of Mercy
1885	St. Mary (St. James)+ New Bedford	Sisters of Mercy
1885	St. Mathieu**# Fall River	Sisters of Charity (Grey Nuns) 1896 Sisters of St. Joseph 1905
1886	Sacred Heart New Bedford	Sisters of the Holy Cross
1886	St. Patrick Fall River	Sisters of Mercy
1886	Sacred Heart Fall River	Sisters of The Holy Union of The Sacred Hearts
1886	Sacred Hearts Academy Fall River	Sisters of The Holy Union of The Sacred Hearts
1891	St. Dominic (Blessed Sacrament) Fall River	Dominicans of St. Catherine Sisters of Charity (Grey Nuns) 1893 Sisters of St. Joseph 1905
1891	Immaculate Conception Taunton	Sisters of the Holy Union of The Sacred Hearts
1892	St. Hyacinth New Bedford	Sisters of The Holy Cross
1895	Dominican Academy Fall River	Dominican Sisters of St. Catherine
1897	St. Anne Commercial College Fall River	Brothers of Christian Schools
1898	St. Jean Baptiste (Holy Trinity)+ # Fall River	Sisters of St. Joseph 1903
1902	St. Rock Fall River	Sisters of St. Joseph
1902	Holy Family+ New Bedford	Sisters of Mercy
1905	St. Jacques Taunton	Sisters of The Holy Union of The Sacred Hearts
1905	St. Stanislaus* Fall River	Felician Sisters
1905	St. Jean B. de LaSalle (St. Anne) New Bedford	Holy Cross Sisters
1906	St. Louis Fall River	Sisters of Mercy
1907	St. Joseph Fall River	Sisters of Mercy
1908	Fairhaven College (Academy) Fairhaven	Congregation of The Sacred Hearts
1908	Sacred Hearts Fairhaven	Sisters of The Sacred Hearts
1908	Holy Rosary New Bedford	Sisters of The Holy Cross
1908	St. Mary* Taunton	Sisters of The Holy Union of The Sacred Hearts
1908	St. Joseph* Fairhaven	Sisters of The Sacred Hearts
1909	St. Joseph Attleboro	Sisters of Christian Education Sisters of The Holy Cross 1913
1910	St. Kilian New Bedford	Sisters of Mercy
1910	Espirito Santo* Fall River	Franciscan Missionaries of Mary
1911	St. Mary High School Taunton	Sisters of The Holy Union of The Sacred Hearts
1911	Sacred Hearts Academy Fairhaven	Sisters of The Sacred Hearts
1913	St. Joseph* New Bedford	Sisters of St. Joseph
1922	Holy Cross Fall River	Franciscan Sisters of St. Joseph
1922	St. Francis Xavier* Acushnet	Dominican Sisters of Saint Catherine
1923	SS Peter and Paul* Fall River	Sisters of Mercy
1924	St. Mary + North Attleboro	Sisters of Mercy
1924	Sacred Heart+ North Attleboro	Sisters of The Holy Union of The Sacred Hearts
1927	Our Lady of Perpetual Help New Bedford	Bernardine Franciscan Sisters

	Schools in the Diocese of Fall River	Founding Religious Communities
1927	Msgr. Prevost Fall River	Brothers of Christian Instruction
1929	St. Theresa New Bedford	Sisters of St. Joseph
1931	St. Louis de France Swansea	Sisters of St. Joseph
1931	St. Michael* Fall River	Sisters of The Holy Union of The Sacred Hearts
1931	St. Michael Swansea	Sisters of Saint Joseph
1933	Msgr. Coyle High School+ Taunton	Brothers of The Holy Cross
1934	Msgr. Prevost High School+ Fall River	Brother of Christian Instruction
1940	Our Lady of Mount Carmel* New Bedford	Sisters of St. Dorothy
1940	St. Anthony High School New Bedford	Sisters of The Holy Cross
1941	St. John Academy+ New Bedford	Sisters of Mercy
1946	Mt. St. Mary Academy Fall River	Sisters of Mercy
1952	St. Anthony Taunton	Sisters of The Holy Union of The Sacred Hearts
1953	Sacred Heart Taunton	Sisters of The Holy Union of the Sacred Hearts
1953	St. Joan of Arc Orleans	Sisters of Divine Providence
1954	St. Joseph Taunton	Sisters of The Holy Union of The Sacred Hearts
1955	St. John Evangelist* Attleboro	Sisters of Mercy
1956	St. George Westport	Sisters of The Holy Cross
1957	Immaculate Conception New Bedford	Sisters of The Holy Names
1957	Nazareth Hall Fall River	Sisters of Mercy
1960	Holy Name* Fall River	Sisters of The Holy Union of The Sacred Hearts
1960	Nazareth Hyannis	Sisters of Mercy
1961	Bishop Feehan High School* Attleboro	Sisters of Mercy
1962	Our Lady of Lourdes* Taunton	Sisters of Mercy

	Schools in the Diocese of Fall River	Founding Religious Communities
1963	Bishop Cassidy High School+ Taunton	Sisters of The Holy Union of The Sacred Hearts
1964	St. Peter Provincetown	Sisters of The Love of God
1965	Holy Trinity West Harwich	Sisters of Mercy
1966	Bishop Connolly High School* Fall River	Society of Jesus
1966	St. Mary* New Bedford	Sisters of Mercy
1969	Nazareth Attleboro	Sisters of Mercy
1971	Bishop Gerrard High School Fall River	Sisters of Mercy Religious of Jesus and Mary Dominican Sisters of St. Catherine
1971	Taunton Catholic Middle* Taunton	Sisters of The Holy Union of The Sacred Hearts
1994	St. Margaret Regional* Buzzards Bay	
1994	Holy Trinity Regional* West Harwich	
1996	St. Francis Xavier Preparatory* Hyannis	
2002	St. Mary* Mansfield	
2004	St. Pius X South Yarmouth	

The Brothers of Christian Instruction with Bishop O'Malley

* Remains Open
+ Merged with another School
# Began with lay teachers
**Pre-dated the parish